India's Global Wealth Club

The Stunning Rise of Its Billionaires and the Secrets of Their Success

India's Global Wealth Club

The Stunning Rise of Its Billionaires and the Secrets of Their Success

Geoff Hiscock

WILEY

John Wiley & Sons (Asia) Pte Ltd

This publication is designed to provide accurate and authoritative information in
regard to the subject matter covered. It is sold with the understanding that the publisher is not engaged in rendering professional services. If professional advice or other
expert assistance is required, the services of a competent professional person should
be sought.

Other Wiley Editorial Offices

John Wiley & Sons, Inc., 111 River Street, Hoboken, NJ 07030, USA

John Wiley & Sons Ltd, The Atrium Southern Gate, Chichester P019 8SQ, England

John Wiley & Sons (Canada) Ltd, 5353 Dundas Street West, Suite 400, Toronto,
Ontario, M9B 6HB, Canada

John Wiley & Sons Australia Ltd, 42 McDougall Street, Milton, Queensland 4064, Australia

Wiley-VCH, Boschstrasse 12, D-69469 Weinheim, Germany

Library of Congress Cataloging-in-Publication Data
ISBN: 978-0470-82238-8

Typeset in 11 on 13 points, Times by SNP Best-set Typesetter Ltd., Hong Kong
Printed in Singapore by Saik Wah Pte Ltd
10 9 8 7 6 5 4 3 2 1

Contents

Part Two
THE PROFILES

Acknowledgments

This book draws on numerous primary sources, including a number of working visits I have made to India for CNN and *The Australian* newspaper, and interviews with business people, academics, economists, commentators, and observers with an interest in India. Among secondary sources, I have turned time and again to India's pre-eminent business historian Dr. Gita Piramal, whose own books, *Business Maharajas* and *Business Legends*, along with her articles in *The Smart Manager*, have provided an invaluable trove of reference material. Dr. Piramal has been generous with her friendship and counsel.

The following business people granted me interviews, or responded to my questions and follow-up inquiries: N.R. Narayana Murthy, Infosys; Adi Godrej, Godrej Group; Anand Mahindra, Mahindra & Mahindra; Uday Kotak, Kotak Mahindra Bank; Grandhi M. Rao and Srinivas Bommidala, GMR Group; Kiran Mazumdar-Shaw, Biocon; Bharat Desai, Syntel; Rahul Bajaj, Bajaj Auto; Rajendra Pawar, NIIT; K. Ram Shriram, Sherpalo Ventures; Dr. K. Anji Reddy, Dr. Reddy's Laboratories; Rana Kapoor, YES Bank; Raghav Bahl, TV 18 Group; R. (Gopal) Gopalakrishnan, Tata Sons; S. Ramadorai, Tata Consultancy Services; N. Soonawalla, Tata Group; Arvind Singhal, Technopak Advisors.

I had the opportunity to listen to, and question, a number of other business identities at press conferences, launches, seminars, and similar events. They included: Mukesh Ambani, Reliance Industries; Ratan Tata, Tata Group; Ravi Kant, Tata Motors; Rajiv Dube, Tata Motors; Shiv Khemka, SUN Group; Captain G.R. Gopinath, Air Deccan; Rakesh Gangwal, IndiGo; Urvi Piramal, Ashok Piramal Group; Rahul Patwardhan, IndiaCo Ventures; Harish Manwani, Hindustan Unilever; Manmohan Shetty, Adlabs Films; O.P. Bhatt, State Bank of India; Gunit Chadha, Deutsche Bank, India; Dr. Anil Khandelwal, Bank of Baroda; Haseeb Drabu, Jammu and Kashmir Bank;

Rakesh Jhunjhunwala, Rare Enterprises; Naresh Goyal, Jet Airways; Kartar Singh Thakral, Thakral Group; Rajat Gupta, McKinsey & Co.; Shashi Tharoor, author and former UN Under-Secretary General; Rohit Khosla, Taj President, Mumbai; Larry D'Souza, executive director, Bombay Chamber of Commerce & Industry; Russell Farmery, former South Asia managing director, ACNielsen, Mumbai; Chetan Ahya, chief economist, JM Morgan Stanley, Mumbai.

I benefited greatly from visits to the campuses of Infosys and Wipro in Bangalore, and also to the Azim H. Premji Foundation, next-door to the Wipro headquarters, where Anina Chacko gave me a briefing. Others who gave of their time and knowledge include economist Adit Jain of IMA India and his colleague Richard Martin of IMA Sydney; S.K. Kulkarni, general manager, GMR Infrastructure and Vijay Vancheswar, head of corporate communications, GMR Group; Roma Balwani, Nikita Singh, and Jatin Aggarwal, corporate communications, Mahindra & Mahindra; Shivanjali Singh, NIIT; Mark Mendelson, Basell Polyolefins; Biswadeep Gupta, Genesis Burson Marsteller; Suresh Rangarajan, Vaishnavi Corporate Communications; Helen Chang, media relations manager, and Sarah Jones, office of executive education, Stanford Graduate School of Business; Jayant V. Pendharkar, head, global marketing, Tata Consultancy Services; Shamala Padmanabhan, corporate communications, Tata Consultancy Services; Debais Ray, corporate communications, Tata Motors; Yogesh Desai, formerly of Reliance Industries; Anis Saif, Wharton School of Business MBA class of 2007; Archana Pradhan, Source Strategic Communication; Ranjani S. Roy, Gutenberg Communications; Kaavya Kasturirangan, Infosys; Nikita Suratwala, YES Bank; Sunayna Malik, general manager, corporate communications, HCL Technologies; Abha Neghi, general manager, corporate communications, Jindal SAW; Ashim Gupta, Max India; Vandana Dhir, Jubilant Organosys; Srirupa Sen, Jet Airways; Oves Cassubhoy, Wockhardt; Uday Baldota, Sun Pharmaceutical.

A book of this nature draws on the work of many previously published accounts; a full list of sources appears in the Bibliography and the chapter endnotes, but I would like to acknowledge my debt in particular to a number of other writers and publications. Again, first to Gita Piramal; second, to CNN's New Delhi correspondent Satinder Bindra for his outstanding coverage of Indian business identities in programs such *as Talk Asia*; next, to the many contributors to other CNN programs such as *Eye on India*; and finally, to the journalists, producers, researchers, and other staff working on the array of Indian newspapers, business magazines, websites, and television programs that provide such comprehensive coverage of the Indian economic and business scene. The ones I turn to most frequently are *The Economic Times, The Financial Express, Mint, The Times of India, The Hindu, Hindustan Times, The Deccan Chronicle, The Telegraph, Business India, Business Today, Business Standard, Business World, Outlook Business*, and the websites moneycontrol.com, domain-b.com, myiris.com, rediff.com, timesnow.tv, ndtvprofit.com, ibnlive.com, and zeenews.com. Directorsdatabase.com was a useful cross-checker. Internationally, the coverage of India by the *Financial Times, The Asian Wall Street Journal, BusinessWeek, Fortune,* and Bruce Loudon of *The Australian* has been invaluable for me, as have the annual *Forbes* and *Sunday Times* rich lists. Investment bank Goldman Sachs provides long-range forecasting on the outlook for India through its series of BRICs (Brazil, Russia, India, China) reports. For global and regional economic data, the most useful sources for me have been the annual outlooks released by the International Monetary Fund, the World Bank, the Reserve Bank of India, the Asian Development Bank, the UN Human Development Program, and Morgan Stanley and HSBC's more frequent Asian reports. Various bodies such as the World Economic Forum, the Heritage Foundation, Mercer Consulting, and Transparency International publish useful rankings on global competitiveness, economic freedom, city living costs, corruption, ease of doing business, and so on.

Former CNN colleagues Ian Macintosh, Satinder Bindra, and Ram Ramgopal helped me with access and feedback, as did my former colleagues at *The Australian* newspaper, online managing editor Grant Holloway and business editor Andrew White. A number of other journalists and business people who helped me would prefer to remain anonymous.

At John Wiley & Sons, publisher Nick Wallwork was enthusiastic about this project from the outset and gave me a very speedy go-ahead, for which I am grateful. Editorial executive Fiona Wong looked after the business side with a minimum of fuss, and managing editor Janis Soo delighted me with her encouragement, instant feedback, and general good cheer in getting this manuscript into print. Robyn Flemming was a meticulous copy editor with a wonderful eye for consistency.

Geoff Hiscock
September 2007

Introduction

I like to write about people, and so the focus of this book is on some of the personalities who enliven Indian business and what they have to say about their own companies, various parts of the economy, making money, and Indian society in general. Along with business people based in India, I have included others of Indian origin living and working around the world, primarily in North America, the Middle East, Europe, Africa, and other parts of Asia. I hope readers will share my interest in their observations and insights, which I think help shape the global Indian entrepreneurial spirit and contain the essential "seven secrets of success." While there is broad agreement on what India needs to do to make the most of the economic opportunities available in the first decade of the 21st century – a list that usually includes fixing education, infrastructure, employment, environmental degradation, communal tensions, rural and urban poverty, corruption, red tape, and social injustices such as child labor and general abuse of the underprivileged – there is a wide range of opinions on what should take priority. Each of these men and women offers a unique perspective, and their advice may spur action and success. My list of the Top 100 and the accompanying profiles are designed to whet a reader's appetite to look further at a particular individual, company, or industry sector.

During the course of the book, I canvass the multitude of serious obstacles that might derail India's progress in the years ahead, but for now I will focus on the positive, and simply mention some of the companies that might be termed its business advance guard. The Indian success story in information technology and pharmaceuticals is already well known, driven by the creators of companies such as Wipro, Infosys, TCS, HCL, Satyam, Sun Pharma, Ranbaxy, Dr. Reddy's, and Cipla. But some of the people behind other companies in these sectors are relatively new names on the global business scene – the Saldanhas of Glenmark Pharma, for example, or Cyrus

Poonawalla of Serum Institute of India. The same applies in other sectors such as automotive, where Mahindra, Tata, Bajaj, Hero, and TVS are building cars and two-wheelers that have an eye to emerging markets beyond India. In real estate, DLF, Unitech, Parsvnath, and Sobha are just some of the names riding the housing boom. In retailing, market leaders Pantaloon and RPG must do battle with a whole host of new contenders that include domestic giants such as Reliance, Birla, Godrej, and Bharti. Some of those names occur again in telecommunications, where Bharti leads a pack that includes Vodafone Essar, state-owned BSNL, Birla, Reliance, and Tata. India's financial services sector is another huge growth story, where Uday Kotak and newcomers such as Rana Kapoor's YES Bank and Jignesh Shah's Financial Technologies are challenging for a piece of the pie. In media, Kalanithi Maran's Sun TV and Subhash Chandra's restructured Zee TV are the heavyweights of the small screen, but face a diverse array of competitors offering news and entertainment in multiple languages. Aviation has seen the emergence of new carriers Kingfisher, Air Deccan, SpiceJet, IndiGo, and GoAir, the takeover of Air Sahara by Jet, and the consolidation of state carriers Air India and Indian. In manufacturing, Bharat Forge and integrated wind turbine maker Suzlon are setting world benchmarks; in metals and mining, groups such as Tata, Essar, Jindal, and Sterlite are making the most of opportunities within and without India; and in infrastructure development the GMR and GVK groups are helping create new airports, roads, and power stations. With an economy that has grown in recent years at better than 8–9% per annum, there are tremendous changes taking place all the time in India. Because of the breadth and pace of that change, all I can claim for this book is that it is a snapshot of parts of the Indian business scene, circa mid-2007. However, it does draw on my reporting of India over the past 25 years, including my most recent assignments as Asia business editor of CNN.com from 2001 to 2006, and as international business editor of *The Australian* newspaper from 1995 to 2000.

Compiling the Global Wealth Club or Top 100 "rich list" has been an intriguing exercise for me, and one that I hope readers will find equally revealing. There isn't much doubt about the names who should be in an Indian Top 20 or even Top 50, but after that – and particularly when the net is expanded to include non-resident Indians – the potential for divergence can be very wide. As with most lists of this nature, the end result is a "best guess" of estimated net worth for the families and individuals involved. I have used publicly available information on shareholdings in listed companies as the basis for my calculations, and where private companies are involved, I have used the average earnings multiple that applies to the industry sector. The market capitalizations are at June 1, 2007, and the exchange rate I have used is 40.5 rupees to the US dollar, the rate prevailing on the same day. But readers should bear in mind that a year earlier the rupee was about 45 to US$1. The rupee hit a nine-year high of 40.28 at the end of May 2007, and volatility is possible in the months ahead.

I was fortunate enough to interview some of the people on the Top 100 list, and to elicit comments from others at press conferences, seminars, and other events. Some of the people I approached declined to cooperate, as is absolutely their prerogative, and others simply ignored my requests for information. To help offset those rejections, I have dipped deeply into the well of Indian corporate information, particularly the material that is available from the Securities and Exchange Board of India. The draft and final prospectuses of companies looking to list are excellent sources for working out ownership and the background of company promoters. So, too, are the statements that companies regularly post with the exchanges where they are listed, covering everything from quarterly results to shareholding patterns, to significant new investments or restructurings.

The challenge in dealing with the huge amount of information available on India is to separate fact from fiction. That has been my goal with this book, but if any errors of fact have occurred, they are mine alone.

PART ONE

The India Story

CHAPTER ONE

India as No. 1?

Good economics works for everyone, but not for everyone at the same time.
—India's Finance Minister, P. Chidambaram[1]

Midnight in Mumbai, the sprawling mega-city that sees itself as India's Manhattan. At this time of night, the drive from the airport to the symbolic Gateway to India monument on the harborfront takes less than an hour, compared with two hours or more during the day. We trundle out of the airport and swing south toward the city on a wet and windy August night. As the southwest monsoon rain picks up intensity, the driver of the battered blue and white Premier taxi pulls over and fishes in the glove compartment for a single wiper blade. Once attached to the wiper arm, the blade delivers us a meager arc of vision. For the next 50 minutes, we will need every bit of illumination we can muster to avoid the massive potholes that are a legacy of the driving rain and the city's abysmal road-mending skills.

India as No. 1? It hardly seems worth thinking about on this dark and treacherous night in a city of 15 million people, where thousands of homeless souls still sleep on the roadside and Asia's biggest slum, Dharavi, guards the northern entrance to the business districts. Three thousand miles (5,000 kilometers) to the east of Mumbai lies its archcompetitor – the giant Chinese megalopolis of Shanghai, where forests of skyscrapers underpin its own claim to Manhattan-esque destiny as Asia's financial capital (see Table 1.1). There can be no greater contrast in the way these two Asian cities allow visitors to make an entrance. Shanghai's 21st-century maglev train whisks travelers in whisper-soft comfort from the massive international airport to the city's Pudong area in eight minutes, covering the 18-mile (30-kilometer) distance at speeds of up to 270 miles (430 kilometers) per hour. Mumbai's cramped and decrepit airport sits cheek-by-jowl with thousands of low-slung houses; as jumbo jets move along the main

3

Table 1.1   Global Financial Capitals

Rank	Score
1. London	765
2. New York	760
3. Hong Kong	684
4. Singapore	660
5. Zurich	656
9. Tokyo	632
24. Shanghai	**576**
36. Beijing	513
39. Mumbai	**460**

Note: Score is out of 1,000 based on factors such as competitiveness, quality of lifestyle, and access to required skills and services.
Source: Global Financial Centers Index, March 2007

runway, the houses look so close to the wingtips it seems the jet blast and the noise must make life intolerable for their inhabitants.

The notion of India as No. 1 in Asia sounds preposterous in a country where a third of the population of 1.2 billion people live below the poverty line – that's 400 million people subsisting on US$1 a day.[2] Add a volatile mix of politics – Pakistan on one border, China on another, Bangladesh and Myanmar to the east, Sri Lanka in the south, and unstable mini-states such as Nepal to the north – and the geopolitical outlook is far from promising. Terrorism in the form of a Maoist-style Naxalite insurgency, along with assorted banditry and domestic issues of caste, religion, race, the rural–urban divide, corruption, and power-sharing tensions between states and the central government in New Delhi, all weigh heavily on the country. India's infrastructure is underfunded and hugely inadequate for a potential superpower. Its agricultural sector has pockets of modernity, but much of the farming community remains locked in a feudal mode, robbed blind by too many middlemen and with a woeful supply chain that spoils food. For many farmers, suicide seems the only escape. The country's social and health problems are legion, from AIDS to cholera to virtual slavery for whole subsets of the population. Female infanticide robs the country of a precious resource, and India remains the world capital of child labor: too many children still don't go to school because they are toiling in the fields or selling food from roadside stalls. Those that do make it to school must cope with a dysfunctional

education system where teachers are often poorly trained and a quarter
of whom simply don't show up for work. Even 40 or 50 years from
now, will India really have solved its problems to the extent where it
can draw level with or surpass the economic, political, and scientific
power of China, the United States, Western Europe, and Japan?

CREATING WEALTH

For a growing number of influential Indians, the answer is "Yes, India
can become a superpower." India's richest resident businessman,
Mukesh Ambani, says it is possible for India to go from a 2006 gross
domestic product (GDP) of US$800 billion to US$7.5 trillion in the
next 25 years. Early in 2007, Ambani, head of the country's most
valuable company, Reliance Industries, told a gathering in Mumbai:
"We led the world in the past – in medicine, science, surgery, naviga-
tion. We were an economic superpower in the 18th century, when we
contributed a quarter of global output." To reach those lofty heights
again, one of the biggest challenges, Ambani says, is to take corporate
India to the country's rural heartland, where 650 million people live
and where a family's fortune can turn on the fickle favor of the
monsoon rain. At a Mumbai conference on innovation run by his alma
mater, Stanford University, Ambani told his attentive audience: "In
the 1980s, India's slogan was 'remove poverty.' Now the time has
come to think about creating wealth."[3]

With a net worth of about US$30.5 billion, Ambani is one of the
pre-eminent members of India's global wealth club, the 100-plus men
and women around the globe who have built billion-dollar fortunes
– some in decades, some in just a few short years – in textiles, steel,
petrochemicals, soap, spices, pharmaceuticals, energy, heavy industry,
agriculture, autos, information technology (IT), and telecommunications. Names such as Birla, Tata, Godrej, Hinduja, Mahindra, Wadia,
and Mittal have been joined by the technology pioneers Murthy,
Premji, Nadar, Nilekani, Pawar, and Raju; while Reddy, Ranbaxy's
Singh brothers, Cipla's Hamied, Sun's Shanghvi, and Biocon's Mazumdar-Shaw patrol the frontiers of pharma and biotech. Now, new fortunes beckon in banking, tourism, retailing, and real estate. With the
growth of these sectors, a different set of names is emerging: Tanti
in wind energy, K.P. Singh and Chandra in housing and construction, Kotak and Kapoor in finance, Biyani in retail, and Rao in infrastructure. In the skies, Mallya, Goyal, and Gopinath are three who
have transformed India's aviation sector in just a couple of years,

bringing low-cost travel to hundreds of thousands of people for whom the notion of an affordable air ticket was incomprehensible a decade ago.

Ambani's father, the late Dhirubhai Ambani, would have heartily approved of his elder son's wealth-creation focus. Ambani senior, a self-confessed "riff-raff boy" who began his business career pumping petrol in Aden, returned to Mumbai in 1960 with US$100 in his pocket, determined to build a company based on two principles: invest in businesses of the future, and invest in talent. His creation, Reliance Industries, prospered mightily in the late 20th century – despite furious clashes with competitors and officials alike – to deliver wealth to thousands of small shareholders for whom Ambani senior was an investment guru. When Ambani died in 2002, Mukesh and his marathon-running younger brother Anil took the company reins. But there was no happy ending for the Reliance fairytale: after an acrimonious 39 months of power-sharing that kept the Indian corporate world agog, the brothers split the empire in January 2006 and went their separate ways, carving out dominant stakes in sectors such as heavy industry, energy, telecommunications, and retailing. Largely on the strength of a buoyant Reliance Communications, Anil Ambani now ranks third in India's global wealth club on US$21 billion, behind London-based steel tycoon Lakshmi N. Mittal (US$35 billion) and brother Mukesh.

FAME AND FORTUNE

On the same day Mukesh Ambani was laying out his blueprint for India's global "top three" status by 2025, the country's movie-going masses were delivering their first verdict on *Guru*, Bollywood's colorful rendition of the Dhirubhai Ambani story. Seen initially as a niche film at best – ambitious, charismatic Indian businessman rises from humble origins, battles bureaucracy, treachery, and ill health to emerge triumphant, supported by beautiful, loyal spouse – the response in domestic and international cinemas was electrifying, drawing urgent requests for more prints from big markets such as North America, the United Kingdom, and the Gulf. The story struck a chord with India's aspirational masses. Nor did it hurt that the movie starred India's showbiz power couple, Aishwarya Rai and Abishek Bachchan, respectively the world's most beautiful woman and the country's most eligible male. The announcement of their engagement straight after *Guru*'s international première in North America kept the media in a frenzy. Predictably, it was "Guru gets the girl" as 38 Indian TV news channels vied to tell the same breathless story. It was an illuminating demonstration of brand power in India, with the focus on Abishek's father, Amitabh Bachchan, the "Big B" of Bollywood.

Fame, fortune, and inclusive growth that reaches the rural masses is a recurring theme. Mumbai-based billionaire industrialist Adi Godrej says: "We have created and perfected the concept of the micro-sale. It is a model we can use not just in India – where rural people buy their needs on a daily basis – but we can take it to the rest of the developing world. And that is a much bigger market than the developed world."[4] India's "Scooter King," Rahul Bajaj, chairman of Bajaj Auto, is another industrialist who sees no limit to the country's potential: "There is now an unstoppable momentum taking India forward," he told an Indian economic summit.[5] Or the IT pioneer Azim Premji: "We can be number one." These billionaires represent old money and new; what they share is a fervent conviction that the country which was so often derided in the postwar era for its "Hindu rate of growth" has thrown off those shackles and is making its own great leap forward to regional, and perhaps global, pre-eminence. Since 2005, India's growth rate has ticked above 8%, sometimes edging past 9%. London-based Srichand P. Hinduja, head of the global Hinduja Group, thinks the rate could hit 11% if the full potential of India's 25 million NRIs (non-resident Indians – or, as he prefers to call them, "national resources of India") is tapped.[6]

THE VIEW TO 2020

The views of these business leaders won a global imprimatur of sorts with a January 2007 update by US investment bank Goldman Sachs of its landmark October 2003 research on the BRIC (Brazil, Russia, India, and China) economies. In its original report, Goldman Sachs saw China as the world's fastest mover, eclipsing US economic output (but not per capita income) by 2041 and everybody else well before that, by 2016. That remains the likely scenario, but India is now seen as capable of making the sustained run that its supporters have always envisioned for it, to the point where it will overtake the UK economy before 2015, then Germany, Japan, and finally the US economy before 2050. "We project India's potential or sustainable growth rate at about 8 percent until 2020. The implication is that India's contribution to world growth will be even greater and faster than implied in our previous BRICs research," say Tushard Poddar and Eva Yi, the authors of the 2007 paper.[7] India's per capita GDP will quadruple between 2007 and 2020, and the projected potential growth rate is an average of 6.9% out to 2050. That level of growth, allied to a population expected to reach 1.63 billion by 2050 (overtaking China's 1.44 billion in the process), has massive implications for India's energy demands and its consumption of steel, plastics, and other commodities, as the country's consuming class expands by hundreds of millions of people. Concomitant with that is the impact such a level of consumption will have on the environment, short of a technological green revolution. Air and water pollution are already past dangerous levels in parts of Mumbai and other big Indian cities, though they are not yet at the death-dealing heights found in the inland China mega-city of Chongqing and a dozen other suffocating, suppurating Chinese urban sprawls.

But growth projections are only that; India's prosperity could be put at risk by any number of factors. The one most often identified by experts is not a natural disaster or a catastrophic 9/11-type terrorist attack, but a more fundamental and fixable problem: the diabolical state of India's primary and secondary education system. Goldman Sachs warns: "To embark upon its growth story, India will have to educate its children and its young people (especially its women) and it must do so in a hurry." It describes lack of education as a "critical constraint" on the growth of knowledge-based sectors such as information technology, as well as in the move to mass employment in manufacturing. "The demographic dividend may not materialize if India fails to educate its people," the researchers conclude.[8]

It is a refrain taken up by business and political leaders, numerous social and economic commentators, and conspicuously by Azim Premji, the Wipro technology tycoon who quit Stanford University without finishing his course so that he could take up the reins of the family business after his father's sudden death. Premji, who has already committed a significant part of his US$15 billion fortune to education initiatives that focus on quality, decries "autocratic classrooms, mechanical teaching, negligible intrinsic motivation and learning that is estranged from reality."[9] He says the choices India makes in education will determine if its economic development will be for the greater good of 1.2 billion people. "Education offers the possibility of lifting our entire country from its mire of poverty and inequity," he says.

For the immaculately attired Mumbai industrialist Anand Mahindra, whose trucks, SUVs, and Mahindra tractors are the choice of farmers from Kansas to Korea, agriculture is India's other big challenge after education. "What's missing, is that we can't get to high growth above 8% or 9% without growth in agriculture. . . . This is where India's retail revolution is important, because the mega-businesses [such as US retailer Wal-Mart] entering the sector will transform the rural supply chain," he observed early in 2007.[10] Mahindra points to the lack of a cold chain (a system for storing and distributing perishable food) for farmers as one of the biggest burdens for agriculture, which supports about 60% of the population but accounts for just 26% of national output. If new players such as Bharti, Wal-Mart, and Reliance develop efficient logistics systems that will stop fresh food spoiling on its journey from farmgate to the consumer, agricultural growth will soar, he believes. "Getting the agricultural sector moving will help stave off social pressures. This is something China has now recognized. Initially it put a lot of emphasis on manufacturing, but now China is radically revising its approach," he notes.[11]

In Manindra's view, another key management problem today is managing growth efficiently. "Here's the difference between India and China. Since the mid-1980s, when China's economic growth really started to take off, the Chinese managers have never experienced a recession. Since I came back from Wharton [Business School] in 1981, I've been through three recessions. That can make you risk-averse, but it also teaches you how to cope. So we can say to investors, we know how to cope with a downturn. In fact, at Mahindra our 'margin of safety' target is that we can still break even at 50% of output." Mahindra's point is that every Indian company has been through hard times. "That is our real strength," he says.[12]

MORE THAN ONE WINNER

Will it be enough? Or does it really matter if India fails to match China in the great economic growth race? IT pioneer N.R. Narayana Murthy, whose Infosys Technologies is a byword for proficiency, consistency, quality, and integrity in the IT services sector, believes there is room for more than one winner. "Frankly, I'm not given to rhetoric on the India–China rivalry thing. My principle is that performance brings recognition; recognition brings respect; respect brings power. These things will happen naturally."[13] But like Mahindra, Murthy sees a pressing need to focus on agriculture's supply chain, along with low-tech manufacturing to boost job availability, and underpinned by better education to make young people employable. "Supply chain management is crucial. The government must fix this area. India needs much better infrastructure, including customs, transport efficiency, port clearance," Murthy says. Nor has India done enough in education and healthcare, he believes. "To secure our future 10 to 15 years from now, we have to do the following: The present literacy rate of 65% must grow to 95%. The quality of primary and secondary education must improve. Without this, most people will not be employable."[14] Murthy notes that poor kids are hungry kids, which makes it hard for them to study. He believes India should embark on a massive drive to provide breakfast, lunch, and, if possible, dinner for children at school. "If I were in charge, I would increase taxes on corporates and spend it all on better nutrition for poor children. They are so vulnerable to disease. Giving them three meals a day would ease this vulnerability."[15]

So, these are some of the difficulties. Yet, the optimism in the face of adversity is palpable in India's great centers of commerce, technology, and government. "India poised to be No. 2 economy," reads the headline atop the front page of *The Times of India* after the Goldman Sachs report.[16] "Poised" may seem a little premature for an event unlikely to happen until 2042 at the earliest, but it reflects a bright outlook that flows on from earlier slogans such as "India Shining" (2003/04), "India Everywhere" (Davos, 2006), and the newspaper's own 2007 "India Poised" campaign.

In a powerful speech to the Wharton Business School's annual India forum held in Philadelphia in November 2006, Rahul Bajaj said it was not important whether India became a "so-called superpower" over the next two decades. "My dream for India, 20 years from today, is a country where poverty has been banished. Where parental income is not a barrier to good health and education, where talent is encouraged, achievement celebrated and the weak can also live with dignity. A country retaining its age-old humanism, tolerant of differences and with a world view that is a cross between that of a yogi and an entrepreneur. A country that retains its soft power in offering an alternative, attractive way of life, that celebrates life, to the world."[17]

SEVEN SECRETS

If India is to achieve the heady economic and social development goals that business thinks it capable of, it will be helped by what might be called the seven secrets of its recent remarkable resurgence. In a nutshell, those secrets are India's size, its science, its diaspora, its

cultural history, its English literacy, its strategic weight, and its switch
to a globalization mindset. India's domestic market is big enough to
be both a home base and low-cost testing ground for any Indian corporate looking for multinational glory; in its science, pharma, and
biotech labs, "imitate" has long given way to "innovate"; its 25 million-
strong diaspora is a source of commercial energy, capital, and advocacy around the world; its creative culture – be it literature, art, film,
fashion, music, or a dozen other manifestations – finds a ready international audience; its widespread use of English gives it a huge head
start in global business, far beyond the initial outsourcing rationale;
its growing strategic importance as the South Asian anchor means
that the United States, China, Europe, Russia, and Japan are obliged
to treat it with respect and equality; and its switch from suspicion of
outside investors to a mindset that sees the world as a source of customers, talent, ideas, finance, and mutually beneficial relationships
has brought India to the point where, as Infosys's Murthy puts it,
business is "comfortable in interacting with people from multiple
cultures."

A further key element – a product of the liberalization that began
in the early 1990s – is the democratization of capital. Economic
observer D.N. Mukerjea says the process of capital creation in India
today "cuts across class, caste, clans and creed."[18] No longer is it the
sole prerogative of the traditional moneymakers – the Marwari, Parsi,
Chetty, and Gujarati communities – to create fortunes from business.
Today, entrepreneurship in India is open to anyone with a bright idea,
a little money, and the willingness to give it a go. Finance is trickling
ever deeper down to what US-based academic C.K. Prahalad calls the
bottom of the pyramid – that economic space occupied by the poorest
consumers, but consumers nonetheless. The stereotype of the Indian
call center, with a roomful of young people in Bangalore adopting
Mid-Western accents as they handle customer requests from North
America, has broadened into something much more rounded. There
are plenty of people with a concept, a vision, and a passion to succeed,
in sectors that extend beyond IT to embrace agriculture, entertainment, education, finance, fashion, pharmaceuticals, real estate, retail,
services, tourism, aviation, automotive, and heavy industry. One of the
pioneers of India's information technology industry, Rajendra Pawar,
chairman of the IT services giant NIIT, calls it a "triad of democracy,
liberty, and wealth," India may indeed have hundreds of millions
of people at the bottom of the pyramid, but according to Cap
Gemini's annual wealth report, in 2006 it also had 100,000 high net

worth individuals – defined as people with financial assets of at least US$1 million, excluding real estate. About 8,000 of these are "ultra high net worth individuals" (above US$30 million in assets), and a hundred or more are in the billionaire class.[19] In the pages that follow, we will meet some of those billionaires as they share the secrets of their success, and their hopes and aspirations not just for themselves, but for the 1.2 billion people with whom they share a country.

ENDNOTES

1. In P. Chidambaram, *A View From the Outside: Why Good Economics Works for Everyone* (Penguin Books India, 2007).
2. "Economic Growth in South Asia," report by the World Bank, June 25, 2006.
3. Speech by Mukesh Ambani to "Stanford in India" innovation conference, Mumbai, January 16, 2007.
4. Interview with Adi Godrej, Mumbai, August 28, 2004.
5. Speech by Rahul Bajaj to Wharton India Economic Forum, Philadelphia, November 11, 2006.
6. S.P. Hinduja, quoted in "Redefining NRIs," *The Economic Times*, January 22, 2007.
7. Tushard Poddar and Eva Yi, *Global Economics Paper No. 152: India's Rising Growth Potential*, Goldman Sachs Global Research, January 22, 2007.
8. ibid.
9. Azim H. Premji, "The Significance of Education," in newsletter of Azim Premji Foundation, November 2006.
10. Interview with Anand Mahindra, Mumbai, January 18, 2007.
11. ibid.
12. ibid.
13. Interview with N.R. Narayana Murthy, Mumbai, January 15, 2007.
14. ibid.
15. ibid.
16. "Indian poised to be No. 2 economy," in *The Times of India*, January 24, 2007.
17. Bajaj, op. cit.
18. D.N. Mukerjea, "Commons Rising," in *BusinessWorld* magazine, January 3, 2000.
19. *11th World Wealth Report*, Merrill Lynch and Cap Gemini, New York, June 27, 2007.

CHAPTER TWO

The Role of the Non-resident Indians

If those who are better off do not act in a more socially responsible manner, our growth process may be at risk, our polity may become anarchic and our society may get further divided.
        —India's Prime Minister, Manmohan Singh[1]

The story of the Indian diaspora could start anywhere: 25 million non-resident Indians (NRIs) or persons of Indian origin (PIOs) make a powerful contribution to the Indian global wealth story, whether it is Narain Karthikeyan driving for the Indian A1 race team in New Zealand, a Gujarati construction worker toiling in the desert heat of a Dubai high-rise hotel, a student pouring one of Karan Bilimoria's "less gassy" Cobra beers in a London curry-house, or the next Sabheer Bhatia (the man who sold Hotmail to Bill Gates) delivering a two-minute pitch to a group of venture capitalists in California's Menlo Park.

The diaspora stretches across the globe, from North America to Southeast Asia, Africa, the Middle East, and the United Kingdom/Europe, creating a potent economic force with an annual income of US$300 billion, second in influence only to that of the Overseas Chinese. Every year, about 10 million workers, including about three million in the Gulf states alone, send money back to their families in India. The flow has grown rapidly over the past 15 years, up from US$2.1 billion in 1990/91 to US$27 billion in 2006/07, making India the world's largest recipient of overseas remittances. North America, home to 1.7 million Indians, is the most important source, accounting for about 44% of total remittances. The Gulf and East Asia between them contribute about 32% – though this figure undoubtedly understates the importance of the Gulf's financial remittances, since much of the money sent home from Dubai is by the unregulated *hawala* system.[2] There are big communities, too, in the United Kingdom (1.2 million), South Africa (1 million), Myanmar, Malaysia, and on the South Pacific island nation of Fiji, where the relative economic strength of 336,000 people of Indian origin creates a sometimes resentful relationship among the native Fijians that has manifested in political coups.[3]

Among the diaspora's most high-profile members are such business superstars as UK-based steel tycoon Lakshmi Mittal; the multi-locational Hinduja brothers of London, Geneva, and Mumbai; California venture capitalist Vinod Khosla and early Google investor Ram Shriram; PartyGaming whiz kids Anurag Dikshit and Vikrant Bhargava of Gibraltar; Vancouver-based developers the Lalji brothers; consumer goods specialist Mike Jatania in London; Singapore trader Murli Kewalram Chanrai; the effervescent Hari Harilela and his brothers in Hong Kong; and the guru of angel investors, Kanwal Rekhi, whose early funding efforts in the United States led to the creation of the global self-help organization now known as TIE (The Indus Entrepreneurs). And while each member of the Indian diaspora has a tale to tell, nowhere has its story been more gripping than in East Africa, where the post-colonial excesses of military despots such as Idi Amin drove thousands of Indian-origin families to quit the countries where they had chosen to put down roots.

REFUGEE CHILD

Mombasa-born Bharat Desai is one such member of the diaspora who knows what it's like to be poor and outcast. As a boy of 11, he fled Kenya on a refugee boat back to India, and watched his parents struggle with the loss of their worldly possessions on arrival in Mumbai. His father had only a seventh-grade education and started work when he was 12, but Desai vividly recalls his father's prescience as the British handed Kenya over to its new African rulers in December 1963. "He told me we would have to leave Kenya soon," Desai says. Within six months, the family was in Ahmedabad, a city about 370 miles (600 kilometers) north of Mumbai. "But my mother never spoke of those hardships. She looked only forward. . . . It was a remarkable lesson for me. . . . It left me with a huge desire to help my family, and secondly, to accept failure and move on, as my mother did."[4]

Today, failure seems a far cry from the world of Desai, who is one of the richest Indians in North America and a passionate entrepreneur and philanthropist. After graduating in electrical engineering from the Indian Institute of Technology (IIT) in Mumbai in 1975, he joined the pioneering IT company Tata Consultancy Services (TCS), and was sent to work on a project in the United States. He left TCS to stay on in the US, opting for part-time work and a place in the University of Michigan's MBA program. The MBA was put on temporary hold in 1980, when Desai and his wife Neerja Sethi, a fellow student at Michigan who had kept her job at TCS, decided to go into business together. They founded their company Systems International (now known as Syntel) with US$2,000 and have seen it grow since to a company with annual revenues of US$180 million and a market capitalization of about US$1.45 billion in June 2007. In the hunt for customers, Desai recalls, there was a lot of banging on doors in the first few years. Today, Syntel is ranked among the best 200 small companies in the US. While its head office remains in Troy, Michigan, the main focus of operations has shifted to Pune, Chennai (formerly Madras), and Mumbai. A decade ago, the company had 1,500 people in the US and just 100 in India. In 2006 the figures were 500 in the US and 7,000 in India, growing to about 10,000 by the end of 2007. Desai, who now lives in Miami with occasional trips to Michigan, remembers Kenya and sees in it a lesson for India.

"India is still a young nation that has made remarkable progress. International success so far has come largely in services. Now there needs to be a cultural change in business. The next step is to create a culture that accepts both success AND failure," he says. The reason? In Desai's view, India needs significant investment in fundamental research. "And there's a high failure rate in this area," he warns. Still, Desai says he is excited and bullish about the future for India, particularly in terms of its ability to make the most of the globalization of services.[5]

"The key is global demographics. The US, Japan, and Western Europe all have aging workforces. So, that means there is a huge workforce shortage coming up, as the baby boomers retire. The generation behind them is much smaller." He sees the globalization of services as an ideal solution that will lead to "multiple social phenomena." And for budding entrepreneurs, Desai's message is simple: "They have to believe in and love their cause. And they have to be ready for a long, hard road."[6]

NORTH AMERICAN HOME

North America clearly is home to the greatest concentration of over-seas Indian wealth, from men like Desai to Wall Street bankers to motel-chain owners, from software programmers to professors in the top B-schools and medical colleges. Indian migrants have been behind 28% of all startups in the United States – notably in the information technology area, to the extent that the early joke in Silicon Valley was that "IT" really stood for "Indians and Taiwanese." In the heady days of the dotcom boom before the April 2000 meltdown, fortunes were accumulated by a host of high-flyers: men like the Ravi brothers of SonicWALL, Sanjiv Sidhu of i2 Technologies, Gururaj "Desh" Deshpande of Sycamore, Pradeep Sindhu of Juniper Networks, Rakesh Mathur, founder of Junglee, Romesh Wadhwani of Aspect, K.B. Chandrasekhar of Exodus Communications, and Naveen Jain of InfoSpace. Some have moved on to other hi-tech pastures, but remain significant players in the Indian investment arena.

In the US hospitality services sector, there is proportionately an even stronger presence. Of the 53,000 motels and hotels in the United States, more than 20,000 are Indian-owned, with total assets estimated at US$40 billion, according to the Asian American Hotel Owners Association. Many of these NRIs came from East Africa in the 1960s, and have the popular Gujarati name "Patel," prompting the "motel, hotel, Patel" line that symbolizes the mid-size hospitality industry in the United States. One of the most high-profile hoteliers is Mukesh "Mike" Patel, a soccer-playing Gujarati from Uganda (via London) who, with his brother R.C. Patel, set up the Diplomat Hotel Corp. in Atlanta, Georgia, in 1981. Patel's Diplomat Group has 18 properties in four states, with a total of about 2,500 rooms. Another Atlanta-based duo, Bharat Shah and son Mitesh, own 25 properties through their Noble Investments. On the US West Coast, B.U. Patel, founder of California-based Tarsadia Hotels, controls 16 properties; while the South Carolina-based Rama brothers of JHM Hotels have about 3,800 rooms in their care.

In the petroleum sector, Sikh businessman Darshan Singh Dhaliwal of Bulk Petroleum Co. runs more than 400 petrol stations across eight US states from his base in Wisconsin. He is known as one of the most generous NRI donors to universities in the United States. As Prime Minister Manmohan Singh said at the 2007 Pravasi Bharatiya Diwas (gathering of NRIs) in New Delhi, India is the home of the ancient universities of Takshasila, Nagarjuna, and Nalanda, to which students came from afar.[7] Nowadays, apart from the handful of elite institutes of technology or management, Indian students prefer to study in the top US universities, where they can interact with such Indian academic luminaries as Nobel Prize winner Amartya Sen at Harvard; C.K. Prahalad, author of *The Fortune at the Bottom of the Pyramid* and *Competing for the Future* at Michigan; Jagdish Bhagwati at Columbia; Pradeep Khosla at Carnegie Institute of Technology; and Homi K. Bhaba, director of Harvard's Humanities Center. All told, Indian Americans are the country's super-achievers, mainly well-educated professionals with a median income 50% higher than that of the American population as a whole.

ACTIVITY IN THE GULF

The Arabian Gulf is another focus of NRI activity. It is the starting point, for example, of the story of the Ambani family, the richest in India. Oil, textiles, spices, gold from Switzerland – all of it can be traded along Dubai Creek, where hundreds upon hundreds of wooden dhows stand ready to transport all manner of goods – food, consumer electronics, car parts – to Iran, East Africa, Pakistan, or ports in India 1,200 miles (2,000 kilometers) to the east. But for the great majority of the Indians in the Gulf, finding a fortune here starts with back-breaking work in the burning heat and stinging sand of United Arab Emirates (UAE) boom towns such as Dubai and Abu Dhabi. Construction, known as a "3D industry" for its reputation of being dirty, dangerous, and dusty, runs in the Gulf on the sweat of workers from India, Pakistan, Bangladesh, Sri Lanka, Indonesia, and the Philippines. About 1.5 million of the NRIs in the Gulf countries can be found in Saudi Arabia, with almost another million in the UAE. About 70% of them are semi-skilled and unskilled workers – mostly single young males with little formal education, who labor in brutally hot conditions on construction projects alongside similar young men from Bangladesh and Pakistan. According to a landmark report on the Indian diaspora, life for most NRIs in the Gulf is hard and unforgiving. "They are usually fed and housed in barrack-like tenements," the report notes.[8] Among the hardships they face is that "several months of work may have to be devoted initially to the settlement of debts incurred in meeting the fee extorted from them by their recruiting agents in India." Of course, it is not all slave labor. White-collar workers make up about 20% of the total, and professionals are another 10%. The Gulf has been good to a great many Indian businesses, including the Chhabria family's diversified Jumbo Group and the UK-headquartered Jatanias of Lornamead. Property developers such as Micky Jagtiani's Landmark Group in Dubai and P.N.C. Menon's Sobha Developers in Oman are making real estate forays back into India from their Gulf bases.

EXPENSIVE ADDRESS

The United States may have more NRI millionaires, but it is in the United Kingdom where the man who heads India's global wealth club, Lakshmi Niwas Mittal, resides in his US$120 million Kensington Palace Gardens mansion, the most expensive private home in Britain. It is a far cry from his home-town of Sadulphur in Rajasthan, a dusty outpost where electricity and running water were luxuries initially unknown to the Mittal family. Mittal, known for his epic struggle to secure a US$34 billion merger with European steel major Arcelor in 2006, now stands firmly atop the world's steelmakers. His combined Arcelor–Mittal Group produces 110 million tonnes a year, well ahead of second-placed Nippon Steel on 35 million tonnes. Only the 2007 Tata Steel takeover of Corus (the former British Steel and Hoogovens of the Netherlands) has produced more business triumphalism in the Indian media.

Until the early 1990s, Mittal was barely known outside the steel industry. He had made a tenuous start in 1976 with a steel mill in Indonesia, but it was hard going. Keen to make bigger strides, he split from his family's Ispat steel business in 1994. (His entrepreneurial father had gone beyond Rajasthan to rejuvenate a steel mill in Kolkata (formerly Calcutta), then set up greenfield plants across India.) Mittal took over the international operations of Ispat, using Ispat International NV as his main vehicle. He began acquiring a string of underperforming steel mills in places such as Trinidad, South Africa, and Kazakhstan, then added Inland Steel of the United States in 1998 and Usinor's Unimental Group in 1999. In 2000, when his LNM Group was producing a combined 17 million tonnes a year, he believed he could be steel's No. 1 "within a decade." He achieved that goal with four years to spare, helped by a 2005 takeover of International Steel Group (ISG) in the United States that gave him 23 million tonnes of extra capacity, and then the herculean Arcelor deal a year later. Early in 2007, Mittal and his family made a pilgrimage back to Sadulphur to inaugurate a US$1 million community center built in memory of his mother, Geeta Devi.

It has not all been plain sailing for Mittal, both in business and politics. He was at the receiving end of European hauteur during the takeover duel with the Arcelor board, with Arcelor chief executive officer Guy Dolle pointedly claiming that Arcelor made steel at the "perfume" level, while Mittal was only making substandard "eau de cologne" steel. Mittal kept his cool, and ultimately prevailed with a bid of such proportions (more than 40% higher than the original proposal) that not even Dolle and chairman Joseph Kinsch could resist the value available to shareholders. Mittal emerged with a 43% stake and Dolle was out of the picture. A new CEO, Roland Junck, lasted just three months before he, too, was out and Mittal took over as CEO of the merged entity. Son Aditya Mittal is chief financial officer. The younger Mittal said in February 2007 that a successful integration was "absolutely our priority."[9] The focus was not just on integrating the operations of the two companies, he said, but on building a united culture. Despite the European sniping, the Arcelor victory won Lakshmi Mittal some establishment praise, with the *Financial Times* naming him its 2006 "Businessman of the Year." Earlier that year, he told CNN's Satinder Bindra about his approach to wealth: "When I earned my first million dollars, it mattered," he said. But after that, it didn't. "What matters is what you do in life. Are you happy, satisfied, successful? This has been my target, my vision: to create something unique and different in the business in which you are in."[10] Still, on the political front, Mittal's donations to the British Labour Party in recent years have brought him unwelcome publicity, particularly when the then UK Prime Minister Tony Blair allegedly intervened to help him buy a Romanian steelworks in 2001.

UNFRIENDLY HEADLINES

Like Mittal, another NRI family with UK ties has seen its share of unfriendly headlines. The Hindujas are four brothers based in three locations: Srichand and Gopichand in London; Prakash in Geneva; and the youngest, Ashok, in Mumbai. Between them, they run a vast US$15 billion global empire that encompasses everything from oil to heavy trucks, financial services, commodity trading, pharmaceuticals, project management, media, and information technology. The Hindujas operate in more than 20 countries and employ about 25,000 people. They are noted for their good works via their Hinduja Foundation, which has a focus on education. But for a family that cherishes austerity, piety, and philanthropy, the Hindujas have an unfortunate knack of attracting unfavorable attention. For years in India, they were dogged by a 1986 defense contract kickback scandal involving the Swedish arms firm Bofors, until the High Court cleared the brothers in May 2005. In the United Kingdom, brothers Srichand (who is the group's chairman) and Gopichand were refused British passports by the Conservative government in 1991, and in 2001, Peter Mandelson, a minister in Tony Blair's government, was forced to resign after admitting he made misleading statements about a 1998 British citizenship application by Srichand that was granted in March 1999.

The Hinduja story dates back to 1914, when the brothers' father, Parmanand Deepchand Hinduja, left his home in Shikarpur, Sindh (now part of Pakistan) for Mumbai, where he set up as a trader. By 1919 the group had its first overseas office, in Iran, and for the next 60 years, until the downfall of the Shah of Iran, the Hindujas' main operations were based there. From Iran they moved on to Europe, establishing offices in Geneva and London. They own a Swiss bank, Amas, but their most valuable global asset is the Gulf Oil brand, outside of the United States and Spain. In 1987, they returned to business in India by taking a controlling stake in the truck and busmaker Ashok Leyland, a company with a market capitalization now of about US$1.5 billion. They also own an Indian domestic bank, IndusInd Bank, and are backers of IndusInd International Federation, an organization set up to draw together the strength of NRIs from around the world. Hinduja Group chairman Srichand chairs the federation, and is an advisor to the Indian government on NRI matters. Srichand, who wants to see "NRI" stand for "national resource of India," has urged New Delhi to take courageous political action on the country's unregulated "parallel" or "black" economy. If the undeclared component of the economy could be regularized and put to productive use, it would speed up economic development, he argues.[11] According to the Hindujas, the group's business philosophy is built on service with devotion, active promotion of the interests of the collective, and respect for independent professional managers. They subscribe to their father's motto: "My duty is to work, so that I can give."

New Delhi-based Shiv Khemka of the SUN Group, a family-owned investment group with interests in Russia, Europe, the United States, and India, is another business leader who recognizes both the duty to give, and the depth of India's poverty problem. He worries that while India ranks eighth globally in the number of the world's millionaires created, it is only 127th on the United Nations Human

Development Index.[12] Khemka, who was born in New Delhi but grew up in England (where he attended Eton College), urges better education opportunities, religious tolerance, an emphasis on social stability, respect for the environment, and a greater focus on developing human capital. "We must look to the underprivileged," he told a gathering of business leaders at the Wharton economic forum in Philadelphia. "India will have greater problems if they are left out of growth over the next 30 to 40 years. So many people are still in the poverty trap and we've got a long way to go," he warns. "We've been lax in making our leaders accountable for the way they manage the country."[13]

Khemka's SUN Group has done well out of chaotic emerging markets such as Russia and the former Soviet Union states. Khemka led SUN's investment and entrepreneurial activities in Russia and Ukraine from 1990 to 2004, building the successful beverage company Sun Interbrew, and running one of the first private equity funds in Russia, Sun Capital Partners. So, it is with some authority that he says instability could be India's biggest calamity yet. Then he offers his audience of eager entrepreneurs what he says could be a suitable maxim: "Make as much, save as much and give as much as you can."[14] In the chapters that follow, we look at different industry sectors and the 100 members of India's global wealth club who have followed at least the first part of that advice: Make as much as you can.

ENDNOTES

1. Indian Prime Minister Manmohan Singh, address to Confederation of Indian Industry, New Delhi, May 24, 2007.
2. *Hawala* is a system of moving money internationally outside the regulated banking system. It is widely used between Dubai and India, and relies on trust between dealers operating in separate countries.
3. "Estimated Size of Overseas Indian Community," in *Report of the High Level Committee on the Indian Diaspora*, New Delhi, December 19, 2001.
4. Interview with Bharat Desai, Philadelphia, November 11, 2006.
5. ibid.
6. ibid.
7. Speech by Indian Prime Minister Manmohan Singh to the 2007 Pravasi Bharatiya Diwas, New Delhi, January 7, 2007.
8. *Report of the High Level Committee on the Indian Diaspora*, op. cit.
9. Aditya Mittal, in press release, "Arcelor Mittal launches ArcelorMittal TV," February 1, 2007.
10. Lakshmi Mittal, interviewed by Satinder Bindra on CNN's *Talk Asia* television program, September 30, 2006.

◆

CHAPTER THREE

The Global Top 10

*If I have to put my finger on one of the key drivers
of India's emergence as a global player, it would
undoubtedly be the entrepreneurship displayed by
Indian corporates.*
      —Aditya Birla Group Chairman, K.M. Birla[1]

In the ballroom of Mumbai's Taj Mahal Hotel, India's richest tycoon and Stanford old boy Mukesh Ambani is regaling his "Stanford in India" corporate audience with a tale about a boasting contest between an American, a European, and an Indian, all telecommunications experts. The American says: "A hundred years ago, if you dug a hundred meters into the ground in America, you'd find fiber optic cable." The European responds: "A thousand years ago, if you dug a thousand meters into the ground in Europe, you'd find copper cable." The Indian has the last word: "Ten thousand years ago, if you dug ten thousand meters into the ground in India, you'd find nothing. We were wireless even then."[2] Ambani's point is that India once led the world in scientific and economic achievement and could do so again. But there's a poignant twist to this telecom tale: as part of the 2005 carve-up of the Reliance Industries empire following an acrimonious family feud, Mukesh Ambani had to let his younger brother Anil take the telecoms business, Reliance Infocomm. Reconstituted as Reliance Communications, this has become the flagship of Anil Ambani's Reliance-ADA Group, with a market capitalization of almost US$27 billion. Still, Mukesh Ambani's Reliance Industries remains comfortably larger. It sits atop India's stock market as the country's most valuable company, with a market cap of more than US$60 billion in mid-2007.

Between them, the Ambani brothers preside over a swag of companies worth a total of US$100 billion. But "between them" is no longer the operative phrase. The brothers, who learnt business at the knee of their entrepreneurial father, the late Dhirubhai Ambani, made the dramatic split after Anil complained in July 2004 that he was being left out of the loop and raised corporate governance issues at Reliance Industries. Mukesh first acknowledged the tensions in November 2004, when he said there were "ownership issues" that were in the "private domain." But his words meant immediately that the issues were in the public realm. The separation was played out in the glare of constant headlines and TV grabs for six months until the deal was done on June 18, 2005. Despite the best efforts of their mother, Kokilaben Ambani, to patch over the brothers' differences, it was she who made the announcement that Mukesh would have "responsibility" for Reliance Industries and Indian Petrochemicals Ltd. (IPCL), while Anil would take responsibility for Reliance Infocomm, Reliance Energy, and Reliance Capital. "I have today amicably resolved the issues between my two sons, Mukesh and Anil, keeping in mind the proud legacy of my husband, Dhirubhai Ambani," she said.

Kokilaben Ambani, her two sons, with their wives and children, continued to live together in the same 18-story "Sea Wind" apartment tower on Mumbai's posh Cuffe Parade that has been their home for years, but Mukesh is building a bigger pile – 22 floors – in Altamount Road in the same area. Though he no longer controls Reliance Communications, it is obvious Mukesh Ambani has a passion for it: "It was my father's vision to roll out telecom services to the masses. In 2000, the cost of a phone call was $1 a minute. I thought that even getting down to 20 cents a minute would be good." But Ambani senior, who died on July 6, 2002, wanted to cut the cost of a call to lower than the cost of a postcard. "Well, we launched our telecom service on December 28, 2002 at 1 cent a minute," Mukesh Ambani tells his audience. "It shows what can be done."[3]

TANTALIZING MIX

The Ambani brothers rank No. 2 and 3 in India's global wealth club, with fortunes of US$30.5 billion (Mukesh) and US$21 billion (Anil), behind London-based steel tycoon Lakshmi Mittal ($35 billion). The makeup of the global top 10 is a tantalizing mix of diversity and concentration in the business sectors they occupy – the split comes in at five specialists, and five who favor diversity. The Ambanis, for example, are the masters of diversity – heavy industry, hi-tech, energy, finance, retail. But Lakshmi Mittal is a steel man through and through, known for his unrelenting focus on what he sees as the only game in town.

The key task for him and son Aditya over the next few years is to bed down their acquisition of Arcelor and unleash the synergistic value they believe is there. That may tax even Mittal senior's prodigious powers of energy and determination; the combined group has 320,000 workers in 60 countries and produces 10% of the world's steel, plus Mittal is keen to tackle the high-growth markets of China and India. Still, Mittal is more than optimistic. In March 2007, he declared the merger a success, saying it was underpinned by industrial logic that was "the foundation for the excellent results to date."[4]

THE SPECIALIST

Number 4 on the list is another specialist: Kushal Pal Singh (US$20.5 billion), founder of the housing and construction group DLF (formerly Delhi Land & Finance). Singh, who in June 2007 raised almost US$2.3 billion for DLF in India's largest initial public share offering (IPO), is both a precipitator and beneficiary of India's massive real estate boom. He notes that the building industry is India's second-biggest employer after agriculture, and argues that the government should focus its economic stimulus efforts on sectors with job-creating potential, such as the construction of infrastructure. The former army officer, who at one point served in the Deccan Horse cavalry regiment, had the vision and patience in the 1980s to buy a swathe of land at Gurgaon, on the southern outskirts of Delhi. Singh negotiated with scores of farmers to acquire the land in plots of four or five acres (about two hectares). He ended up with 3,500 acres (1,400 hectares) of land – more than half of it bought on credit from the farmers themselves. This is where DLF has developed DLF City – a massive 3,000-acre (1,200-hectare) complex of offices, shops, schools, hospitals, houses, apartments, and an Arnold Palmer golf course. Other developers have followed suit, establishing Gurgaon as a satellite city and home to most of India's hi-tech companies and multinationals. Singh has taken to the malling of India with a vengeance. Every second shopping center in Gurgaon bears the DLF name, and coming up is DLF's "Mall of India," a 400,000-square-meter giant that will eclipse North America's biggest malls in Minneapolis and Edmonton (but not a swag of super-malls in China and the Philippines).

With a pan-India land bank estimated at 4,200 acres (1,700 hectares) – much of it acquired at relatively low prices – Singh is well placed to meet India's burgeoning housing demand, even with a cool-off after interest rates rose again in 2007. A couple of years earlier, Singh outlined some of his business philosophy in a newspaper article: "It's essential to have big dreams and be a bit of a visionary. But it's equally necessary to be pragmatic and to acknowledge that things don't always work as planned," he wrote. "The key to success lies in being undaunted in the face of setbacks, and indeed, to learn from failure."[5] While some observers fret that the bursting of the property bubble will see a setback to DLF and India's high-priced listed real estate companies, there is no denying the size of the market opportunity. The value of commercial and residential construction is expected to grow from US$12 billion in 2005 to US$50 billion by 2010, according to a Merrill Lynch report, while the Asian Development Bank says India will need up to 10 million new houses a year by 2030.

ON THE WAVE

Number 5 on the list is Sunil Bharti Mittal (US$17.75 billion), *Fortune* magazine's 2006 "Asian Businessman of the Year" and recipient of a Padma Bhushan Award, one of India's highest civilian honors, in 2007 for his contribution to the development of the telecommunications sector. The latest moves for the wireless telecom czar include agribusiness, an insurance joint venture with France's AXA, and a retail venture with American behemoth Wal-Mart that could be the biggest success of them all. Mittal, who hails from the Punjab, started in business in 1976 selling bicycle parts, then moved into importing generator sets for Suzuki. Government regulations and hot competition soon left him looking for another business proposition. That turned out to be selling imported telephone equipment, which eventually morphed in the 1990s into Bharti Tele-Ventures (now Bharti Airtel), a cellular network that is the richest and most extensive in the country. Bharti's success in attracting 40 million mobile subscribers by mid-2007 has given it about 23% of the mobile phone market, ahead of state-run BSNL, Hutch Essar (bought by UK giant Vodafone in a US$13 billion deal in February 2007), and Reliance Communications.[6] The cash flow available from the market – Indians are avid mobile users – and extensive knowledge of the customer base made Bharti attractive to overseas investors; Singapore Telecom was an early partner, while Vodafone picked up a 5.6% direct interest for US$800 million in late 2005. It agreed to sell the stake back to Bharti for US$1.6 billion as part of the Hutch Essar takeover.

In late 2006, Indian Prime Minister Manmohan Singh was on hand with Mittal to open Bharti Enterprises' FieldFresh research and development (R&D) center at Ludhiana, in Punjab state. The center is designed to run crop trials and showcase best farming practices for growers supplying the FieldFresh Foods business. Mittal set up Field-Fresh as a joint venture with the Rothschild family's investment company ELRo Holdings to create a "farmgate to customer" food business. The goal is to have 20,000 acres (800 hectares) under cultivation, supported by modern pack houses and cold storage.

It's all part of being "on the wave," whether it's in mobile phones, insurance, fresh food, or organized retailing. Mittal is a master of seeing the opportunity and then moving quickly to take advantage of it, sometimes in partnership with an outsider providing specialist expertise or funding. And it works both ways. Wal-Mart opted for a tie-up with Bharti – despite the latter's lack of chainstore experience – because of its understanding of Indian consumers and its aggressive approach to new businesses. For both parties it's a big opportunity: India's retail market is expected to more than double by 2015 from US$300 billion in 2006. Large stores have just 3% of the market now, but should get to 18% by 2011/12, according to industry analyst Technopak Advisors.[7] While Mittal gets the Wal-Mart retail operation going to tap the rising middle-class thirst in India for air-conditioned shopping, he has to contend with some tough competition in his main business, now that Vodafone has Hutch Essar and Reliance Communications is stepping up its marketing efforts. Bharti Airtel and Vodafone have signed an agreement covering roaming, long distance, and infrastructure sharing, but the heat is on, nonetheless.

Away from business, Mittal has made a substantial commitment to improving education opportunities for mainly rural children, putting an initial US$45 million into his Bharti Foundation when it began in May 2006.

IT PIONEER

Number 6 on the global list, Wipro's Azim Premji ($15 billion), is known as one of India's IT pioneers, but he still keeps a toehold in other industries. After his father died suddenly at the age of 51 while Premji was studying at Stanford, he returned to take over a low-tech vegetable oil business. (Wipro's original name was Western India Vegetable Products.) Gradually he diversified into soap, cosmetics,

light bulbs, hydraulic cylinders, and construction equipment components. Globally, though, Wipro has made its name in information
technology. It started in IT in 1980 as a computer manufacturer (it
still makes PCs, laptops, and servers), but by the early 1990s Premji
realized the bigger opportunity was in services, selling technological
expertise to multinationals at a price that undercut Western competitors. As Premji once said: "They came for our cheap brainpower,
but they stayed for our quality." Despite the success of Wipro and
competitors such as Infosys and TCS, Premji and his peers recognize
that India cannot expect to ride this wave forever, without relentless
innovation and reskilling. Premji says it is critical that India constantly
upgrade the competencies of its people, not just in the latest technology but also in cross-cultural skills and the management of large,
complex projects. He has urged India's higher educational institutes
to gear up for a quantum leap if they are to have any chance of
meeting the projected demand for IT professionals worldwide. "In
the information age the critical resource is the power of the mind,"
he says.[8]

Premji is passionate about India's chances, and about what needs
to be done for the country to reach its full potential. For him, it starts
with education. In 2001, he used part of his fortune to set up the Azim
Premji Foundation, next-door to the Wipro headquarters on the outskirts of Bangalore. Its goal is to help more children in rural India –
particularly the underprivileged – get a high-quality primary education.
By early 2007, the foundation's programs, which operate in partnership with state governments, were reaching 18,250 schools, 56,000
teachers, and 2.5 million children across 18 Indian states. But the
educational needs of India are immense: there are 1.3 million elemen-
tary schools in India, 5.5 million teachers, and 200 million children in
the 6–14 age bracket. Sixty out of every 100 children who enter the
first grade will drop out by the eighth grade. Ridding India of class,
caste, and gender discrimination is another of the challenges Premji
has taken on. One solution he urges is more vocational training,
microfinancing, and access to technology to help poor people become
entrepreneurs.

Values are everything for the super-competitive Premji, including
in the way Wipro operates. Special commissions or kickbacks are not
tolerated; Premji says that integrity in business is actually a cost-saver,
reducing transaction costs. Wipro's values are summed up in three
phrases: intensity to win; act with sensitivity; unyielding integrity.[9]
Despite his wealth, Premji affects none of the trappings of the busi-

ness superstar: he drives a small car, flies economy within India (but business class overseas), and generally avoids what he calls a "five-star culture." That approach to fiscal rectitude applies throughout Wipro, giving it cost savings that are one more arrow in its quiver of competitiveness. In 2005, Premji was awarded the Padma Bhushan.

TRUE MULTINATIONAL

Seventh-placed Kumar Mangalam Birla (US$7 billion) heads the Aditya Birla Group (named after his late father), which claims to be India's first truly multinational corporation, with a workforce of 85,000 employees in 14 countries. Certainly, Birla is diversified and does things on a global scale. His latest acquisition is the world's biggest aluminum rolled products maker, Canada-based Novelis (spun off from Alcan in 2005), bought by the group's flagship Hindalco for US$6 billion. Birla said the deal "is consistent with our vision of taking India to the world."[10] Other key companies in the group are cement, iron, and fiber major Grasim; mobile telephony player Idea Cellular; UltraTech Cement; and the multi-industry conglomerate Aditya Birla Nuvo, which operates businesses in textiles, telecom, financial services, IT, branded garments, viscose filament yarn, carbon black, and insulators. The group made its first move into India's US$300 billion retail sector in early 2007, buying the supermarket and convenience chain Trinethra Superretail, which has 170 stores in the four southern states of Andhra Pradesh, Tamil Nadu, Karnataka, and Kerala.

Birla, like Premji, was thrust into a leadership role at an early age. He was just 28 when his father, Aditya V. Birla, died on October 1, 1995, struck down by prostate cancer at the age of 51. India's pre-eminent business historian, Dr. Gita Piramal, summed up Birla senior thus in her 1996 book *Business Maharajas*: "No other Indian businessman can claim to even remotely match Birla's ability to build factories from scratch."[11] Still, Birla junior has done a remarkable job of growing the family fortune. The group turns over US$20 billion a year, and the listed companies have a market capitalization of more than US$22 billion. Cement, aluminum, and copper are the biggest contributors to revenue, accounting for 47% of the total between them. But with India's burgeoning consumer class running into hundreds of millions, retail may yet prove the biggest money-spinner of them all. One thing is clear: Birla has inherited his father's passion for values. "The key to enduring leadership lies in knowing what we stand for and in living by that," he says. In an essay published early in 2007, he wrote how "wild west" business ethics in the housing sector until a decade ago had stunted its growth, despite the huge potential demand. He cited "unscrupulous builders, poor construction quality, unofficial payments and flimsy or non-existent consumer rights and questionable lending practices."[12] The introduction of order, transparency, and ethics by the Housing Development and Finance Corporation has helped the sector take off, with spectacular results in the quality of housing stock available to new buyers.

For eighth-placed Tulsi Tanti ($6.6 billion), "ride like the wind" might be the motto of the fast-moving founder of Suzlon Energy, the company responsible for some of the world's biggest wind farms. From nowhere a decade ago, Tanti has created an integrated wind energy company of massive proportions. No diversity here: the focus of this commerce graduate from Gujarat is wind energy, pure and simple. But it wasn't always like this. The Suzlon name was first used for Tanti's polyester business 25 years ago. In the early 1990s, rising power prices prompted him to look for alternative energy sources and, with government incentives on hand, he imported some windmills. That led to him setting up Suzlon Energy in 1995. He was able to convince Pune-based industrialists such as Rahul Bajaj to give wind energy a try, and as the electricity outgoings for Bajaj's plants fell, word spread that maybe this was an idea worth looking at. Like the wind, Suzlon's sales performance was variable in the early years, but a low-cost base and factories in China and the US have brought it to the point where it is the No. 5 wind turbine maker in the world and a real competitor for market leaders such as Vestas of Denmark and Germany's Enercon.

In March 2006, Suzlon bought Belgian wind turbine gearbox maker Hansen for US$565 million, giving it the full capability to design, make, and operate windmills. A year later, Suzlon made a successful US$1.6 billion bid for German wind turbine maker REpower Systems. Tanti says India's wind energy potential is 45,000 megawatts (MW), while Suzlon's annual manufacturing capacity is 4,200 MW. Tanti says the company's R&D focus is on getting the cost per kilowatt-hour down, so that Suzlon can reach out to smaller customers and harness wind power in hitherto unviable locations. But even Tanti's grand dreams for wind power won't be enough to keep India's economy charged up. India is the world's fifth-largest energy consumer, with an appetite that will almost double by 2015. It has about 135,000 MW of installed capacity (mostly coal-fired), but will likely need another 125,000 MW by then. To meet this staggering energy requirement, India needs every bit of generation capability it can get from oil, gas, coal, hydro, wind, and solar plants, plus – most controversially of all – nuclear power plants. US President George W. Bush's 2006 visit to India and his handshake with Prime Minister Manmohan Singh on a nuclear cooperation deal changed forever the relationship between Delhi and Washington. Under the *US–India Peaceful Atomic Energy Cooperation Act* signed into law by Bush in December 2006, India gets access to advanced civilian nuclear technology, and American business gets access to investing in India's civilian nuclear industry. Whatever the impact of the nuclear deal, Tanti knows that Suzlon's future rests with him making his turbines ever more efficient in order to reduce costs and become part of India's mainstream power supply. India produces about 55% of its electricity from coal, with a life-cycle production cost of about 6.5 cents per kilowatt-hour, according to the World Energy Council. The wind itself may come free, but wind power is more than twice as expensive as coal, at 14 cents per kilowatt-hour.[13]

THINK LOCAL

Sharing ninth place on India's global wealth club list are the four Hinduja brothers (US$6.5 billion), whose mantra is "think local but act global." They run a highly diversified conglomerate that operates in 50 countries from three key locations: London, Geneva, and Mumbai. The Hindujas' activities run the gamut of agribusiness, banking, real estate, chemicals, energy, manufacturing, automotive, healthcare, technology, and media. The trading business was once based in Iran, but the Hindujas relocated to Europe after the fall of the Shah of Iran in 1979. Among their most valuable assets is the non-US business of Gulf Oil, acquired in the 1980s. Srichand and Gopichand, the two eldest brothers, are notable figures on the London scene and have seen their share of controversy over their business dealings and their relations with the British government. Srichand heads a global federation representing non-resident Indians and strongly advocates a more integrated role for NRIs in the economic advancement of India. The Hindujas have a valuable banking license (Amas Bank) in Switzerland, where No. 3 brother Prakash is based. In India itself, domicile of No. 4 brother Ashok, the group's flagship is the truck and busmaker Ashok Leyland, in which they acquired a controlling interest in 1987. By sales volume, Ashok Leyland runs second in this sector to Tata and has a market capitalization of about US$1.5 billion. The company claims that 80% of metro state buses bear the Ashok Leyland name, and that they carry 70 million passengers a day, or more than the entire Indian rail network.

When the Hindujas bought out European major Iveco's stake in Ashok Leyland in 2006, company vice-chairman Dheeraj Hinduja (son of Gopichand Hinduja) said its ambitions went beyond vehicle manufacturing and marketing, with a talent pool deep enough to be a "significant global presence in the components business and in engineering design services."[14]

Like many other members of the global wealth club, the Hindujas' philanthropic activities embrace education. Their Hinduja Cambridge Trust in the United Kingdom promotes learning and research on South Asia.

Last on the global top 10 list is a specialist – relative newcomer Ramesh Chandra (US$6.4 billion), whose Unitech was the largest listed real estate company in India until DLF made its debut. Chandra, a structural engineer with qualifications from the Indian Institute of Technology, Kharagpur and the UK's University of Southampton, set up Unitech as a civil engineering company in 1974. Like DLF, Unitech is a major beneficiary of India's real estate boom of the past few years. While many observers expect this is a bubble born to be pricked, the share market valued Unitech at about US$11 billion by June 2007, compared with just US$14 million five years earlier. Unitech owns about 8,000 acres (3,200 hectares) of land across India, but much of it has been bought recently in a time of optimistic pricing. The company's big push came with top-range commercial and residential property in Gurgaon, and has since expanded to hotels in Gurgaon, Noida (on the outskirts of New Delhi), and Kolkata.[15] Its US$1.5 billion investment plan for 2006–10 includes the building of 15 hotels and seven IT parks in special economic zones. In December 2006, Unitech's overseas investment arm, Unitech Corporate Parks Plc, raised US$700 million from an IPO in London to invest in the Indian technology parks. The following month, US investment bank Goldman Sachs joined Unitech in a 33:67 venture, setting up a US$200 million fund to invest in Indian realty. The likely focus is around Delhi, Mumbai, and Bangalore's planned new airport. Chandra is close to Indonesia's Salim Group – it is a partner with Unitech in a Kolkata project – and a Salim associate, Prasoon Mukherjee, Indonesia-based chairman of Universal Success Enterprise, has taken a half-share in

Unitech Corporate Parks. For now, Chandra's corporate slogan for Unitech – "Dream. Believe. Create" – fits the mood of India's cashed-up house-hunters.

So, diversify or focus? Most investment experts will tell you that a diversified portfolio is the safest, steadiest path to wealth, along the lines of "don't put all your eggs in one basket." Following this route certainly has been good for the Ambani, Hinduja, Premji, and Birla families. But five of our top global wealth club members have played the game otherwise; determination and a focus on a single industry have brought them to the very pinnacle of business success. Ultimately, it comes down to what every smart business person instinctively knows: a good idea, good planning, good timing, good people, good finance, good luck, and absolute excellence in execution, most times will get you there. California-based mentor capitalist Ram Shriram, another member of India's global wealth club and the man who liked what he saw in the early days of Google so much that he ended up with more than five million shares after the search engine's 2004 IPO, says there is no doubt that a good idea must be backed up by good execution. "Otherwise, you are just another smart guy with a dream – and there are plenty of those."[16]

ENDNOTES

1. K.M. Birla, "Dare to Dream Big and Do It," *Business Today*, January 14, 2007.
2. Mukesh Ambani, address to the "Stanford in India" innovation conference, Mumbai, January 16, 2007.
3. ibid.
4. Statement by Lakshmi Mittal in press release, "Delivering the benefits of the merger," Brussels, March 28, 2007.
5. K.P. Singh, "Ear to the Ground," *The Economic Times*, March 4, 2005.
6. Figures released by the Cellular Operators Association of India, May 2007 and media release, "Bharti Airtel breaks into the 40 million mobile customer club," May 23, 2007.
7. Interview with Arvind Singhal, chairman, Technopak Advisors, March 15, 2007.
8. Azim H. Premji, emailed response to author's questions, May 19, 2000.
9. "The spirit of Wipro," on website www.wipro.com/aboutus/values.htm.
10. K.M. Birla in media release, "Hindalco Industries Ltd and Novelis Inc announce an agreement for Hindalco's acquisition of Novelis for nearly US$6 billion," February 11, 2007.
11. Gita Piramal, *Business Maharajas* (New Delhi: Viking Penguin Books India, 1996), p. 153.
12. K.M. Birla, "Values the Driving Force," *The Economic Times*, January 7, 2007.

13. "Survey of Energy Resources," on website of World Energy Council, www. worldenergy.org/wec-geis/publications/reports/ser04/countries.asp.

14. Dheeraj Hinduja, quoted in media release, "Hinduja Group acquires IVECO stake in Ashok Leyland," issued by Ashok Leyland, Mumbai, July 24, 2006.

15. Media release, "Unitech Ltd to build one of the largest group housing projects in Greater Noida," issued by Unitech, New Delhi, August 7, 2006.

16. Interview with K. Ram Shriram, February 15, 2007.

CHAPTER FOUR

The IT Scene: It's a Flattening World

If you want to empower people, give them the tools. There's enough entrepreneurship in this country to take care of the rest.

—HCL founder, Shiv Nadar[1]

There is no better example of how the information technology sector has broadened India's wealth club than to look at Infosys Technologies and the core group of young engineers who joined N.R. Narayana Murthy more than 25 years ago to build what is now one of the world's premier IT services brands. Even after share sell-offs (most recently, 13 million shares worth almost US$700 million into a US American Depositary Receipt raising in late 2006), the original Infosys team counts some of India's wealthiest people among its members. Chairman and chief mentor Narayana Murthy and family hold a stake of 5.12% worth about US$1.5 billion. Nandan Nilekani, the Infosys CEO until his elevation to co-chairman from June 2007, holds a stake with his family worth close to US$1 billion; CEO Senapathy "Kris" Gopalakrishnan and family are in a similar position, followed by K. Dinesh and family with 2.58% (about US$700 million) and new chief operating officer (COO) S.D. Shibulal and family with 2.26% (about US$600 million). The total stake for the original team is 16.94%, worth about US$4.6 billion at a market capitalization of US$27.2 billion for Infosys in June 2007. That stake is down from almost 29% in 2001. Jamuna Raghavan, wife of Infosys co-founder N.S. Raghavan (who retired as joint managing director in 2000), holds a share worth about US$320 million. Ashok Arora, also a co-founder, is no longer with the company. He quit in 1988, sold his shares back to the other six founders, and moved to the United States, where he works as an IT industry consultant.

The Infosys story has been told many times in business schools, but it remains a classic account of perseverance, intelligence, integrity, focus, and success. Using 10,000 rupees (then about US$1,250) in seed money borrowed from his wife Sudha, Murthy and six colleagues from Patni Computer Systems set out to create a new IT company. Despite early difficulties (no computers or phone lines, heavy-handed bureaucracy) and setbacks that included the collapse of a joint venture in the United States, the company gradually gathered momentum, writing code for US clients and getting a boost from the Y2K bug scare, all the time striving to crack into the market for more specialized talks. More than 25 years after the event, Murthy recalls how it was: "In January 1981, the seven founders of what was to become Infosys met in my small Bombay apartment. We discussed various goals as we tried to work out what we would be. I said: 'Why don't we say we will become the most respected company with all stakeholders. If we follow the principles of transparency, fairness, and goodwill, the rest will come naturally, including profits.'"[2]

Murthy, the socialist at heart with a capitalist head, is immensely proud of what Infosys has achieved: its innovation, the quality of the thousands of jobs it has created, the wealth it has spread, and the way it has raised India's image as a place where business can be conducted ethically and legally. He is passionate about its honesty, ethics, and strong stand on corporate governance as the foundation of its success. Plus, Infosys has set the benchmark for the way it trains and treats the people it hires. Its latest addition is the US$120 million Global Education Center at Mysore, one of the world's largest corporate training facilities, able to take 10,000 students a year. Competition for a seat at Mysore or any of the other Infosys campuses is tough: in the 2006/07 fiscal year, about 1.4 million people applied for jobs at the company; only 2% of them were accepted. But the rewards have been phenomenal, particularly since the 1990s. Murthy notes: "When the multinationals came into India, we used stock options to help retain our people. In the process we created 5,000 dollar-millionaires. No other Indian company has done this."[3]

Infosys sits at the top of the Indian IT services industry, along with its two great rivals, Tata Consultancy Services (market cap: US$29.4 billion) and Azim Premji's Wipro (US$19.6 billion). In fourth place is Ramalinga Raju's Satyam (US$7.8 billion), followed by Shiv Nadar's HCL Technologies (US$5.6 billion). Other top Indian companies include the Patni family's Patni Computer Systems and Rajendra Pawar's NIIT, which specializes in IT training (see Table 4.1). These

**Table 4.1   India's Leading IT Companies, by
Market Capitalization, June 2007**

1. Tata Consultancy Services	US$29.37 billion
2. Infosys Technologies	US$27.16 billion
3. Wipro Ltd.	US$19.6 billion
4. Satyam Computer Services	US$ 7.74 billion
5. HCL Technologies	US$ 5.64 billion
6. I-Flex Solutions	US$ 4.49 billion
7. Tech Mahindra	US$ 4.47 billion
8. Patni Computer Services	US$ 1.79 billion
9. Mphasis	US$ 1.24 billion
10. NIIT Technologies	US$ 576 million

are the names that have brought India to the frontline for global delivery of IT and IT-enabled services such as business process outsourcing (BPO) and knowledge process sourcing (KPO), helping to create an industry that is expected to grow export revenues by 33% during 2007 to more than US$31 billion. According to the industry association Nasscom, it is well on course to achieve a 2010 export target of US$60 billion for software and services (mainly to the United States and Europe), with the possibility that the total IT industry output could reach US$100 billion. On the jobs front, the number of people employed by the software and BPO sector has jumped from about 280,000 in 2000 to about 1.6 million in 2007. This has engendered a backlash from some Western labor unions and businesses who feel threatened by the Indian IT success story. But as McKinsey's Rajat Gupta noted at an Indian economic forum in 2006, when US politicians and commentators rail against jobs going overseas, more American CEOs ask themselves, "What am I missing out on?"[4]

NOT THE ANSWER

Murthy is the first to acknowledge that Infosys and similar companies are not the answer to all of India's myriad economic development problems. During an interview in his daughter Akshata's Mumbai apartment overlooking the Arabian Sea, Murthy says: "The IT sector has done well for a small group. IT and IT-enabled services have created jobs for several hundred thousand people. But it is not a solution. India has to become the factory of the world."[5] Murthy believes low-tech manufacturing is the only way to solve India's pressing need to create jobs, and there must be a better supply chain for farmers to help lift agricultural output and thereby boost rural incomes. He says the country must lift its exports significantly and should welcome foreign direct investment "in a big way." He says India needs to make quick decisions on investment, and stop sending confusing signals that sometimes suggest it is against multinationals.

As Murthy and other business leaders have noted, India ranks only 126th in the latest United Nations Human Development Index. Despite India's recent stellar growth rate and the global success of industry sectors such as IT, pharmaceuticals, and auto components, the UN report shows that hundreds of millions of India's poor are barely subsisting. According to Kevin Watkins, director of the UN Human Development Program's report office, about 300 million Indians survive on less than US$1 a day, almost half of India's children are underweight for their age, and 2.8 million children die each year from poor nutrition and preventable illnesses.[6] Fixing this shameful situation is an absolute priority, in Murthy's view: "There needs to be a massive drive to provide breakfast, lunch, and, if possible, dinner for children at school." Murthy says that if he were running India, he would raise corporate taxes and spend all the extra money on better nutrition for poor children. He also advocates education vouchers for children living below the poverty line as a way to get them a better education. "I understand it costs 16,000 rupees a year for a primary school student in Bangalore (the home town of Infosys). If this was in the form of a redeemable voucher, I believe we could create competition among schools in the private sector."[7]

Murthy says pressure must be brought to bear on India's leaders to come up with solutions that address poor education, poor nutrition, poor infrastructure, and poor job prospects in the rural community. "The Indian growth story depends on the ability of our leaders to straddle two worlds – the urban/rural and the rich/poor, the educated and the not so educated." He says that high growth progress will come from the urban community, because there is not yet enough infrastructure in the rural areas for high growth. "The leaders can't play a zero sum game. They have to take an integrated view." But Murthy is still confident about his country's prospects. "The good thing is that in India, we can stand up and criticize the government," he says.[8]

POWERFUL COMBINATION

Murthy stepped back as executive chairman of Infosys in July 2006, but remains chief mentor. He and co-chairman Nandan Nilekani

(CEO until June 2007) are very much the public face of the company, massaging clients and governments, delivering speeches, and popping up at global events such as the annual World Economic Forum in Davos. For a quarter of a century, Murthy and Nilekani have been the yin and yang of Infosys: one regarded as the cerebral philosopher, the other as an "action man," and together a powerful combination. They and the other Infosys founders are not about to step down from running the company, but Nilekani is already on the succession case. He said recently: "We are making sure we have a whole crop of people who can take charge of this company over the next several years. It is reasonable to assume that leadership will be taken by a new generation of leaders."[9] Beyond what happens at Infosys, on the broader front, Nilekani says there is a fundamental change in the way companies are being run. He sees the world "flattening" from the convergence of such disruptive factors as demographics (workforces aging in the West, getting younger elsewhere), emerging economies, globalization, technology, and regulation.

At Davos 2007, Nilekani described how a successful company of the future would be leaner, flatter, faster, and more adaptable. In his view, these are its likely characteristics: "It may be seen in one location and do most of its business in a completely different location. Distance will finally die, as it won't matter where the company started, where the executive team sits, where the natural resources are from, or where the production lines run. It will treat the whole world as a network of resources and find ways to reallocate work among that network in the most optimal fashion. The work will be taken to the workers, and because of this, the company will do everything faster, better, and cheaper. It will manage operations in a new way using information on a real time basis. And the result is a sharper enterprise, working smarter. It is a company intensely focused on innovation. But it also knows it cannot innovate alone. It will reach beyond its boundaries to tap the ideas of customers and suppliers – bringing them into the lab as co-creators. More than half of its innovations will come from outside its walls."[10]

Nilekani has been vocal about how increased competition for talent is putting pressure on companies. He and Murthy have both been critical of the gap between what India's education system produces, and the quality of people that companies such as Infosys need. Nilekani, like Murthy, advocates broad-scale reform of education to attract more investment into this sector. "We are home to the largest young population in the world. We have to integrate them into the economic engine," he wrote early in 2007.[11]

Addressing a recent "Stanford in India" conference in Mumbai, Murthy told his audience that the Infosys experience was that innovation must be part of the company's DNA. "And the incentive to innovate must percolate down to every level of an organization. From the chairman to the janitor, you have to bring the customer into your mindset." He said Infosys also practiced "eat your own dog food" – extensive testing of a product through internal pilot programs, to iron out any wrinkles before it goes outside.[12] Murthy recalls a potential US customer telling the Infosys team that the United States and India were "like night and day" and there was a low probability of the two working together. "A colleague said, 'Let's use this to our advantage and create a 24-hour workday. At 5 p.m. US time, the American company could send us its problems by electronic file transfer. At 7.45 a.m. Indian time, we could open those files, start work on the problems and hopefully solve most of them by 5.30 p.m. Then send them back to the US so that when the US workers come in, the work is done.' So we combined "prime time" to come up with a 24-hour workday. That struck a wonderful chord with our potential US customers. So we should look to see opportunity in every difficulty." Murthy also noted: "If you encourage people to dream big, you also have to create a safety net for failure as well. This enhances their confidence and enthusiasm."[13]

INNOVATE OR PERISH

The importance of innovation is a theme that resonates with one of Murthy's great competitors, Subramaniam Ramadorai, CEO of Tata Consultancy Services (TCS) and a veteran of the industry. Ramadorai is not a member of India's global wealth club – he holds less than 100,000 shares (worth about US$3 million) in TCS – and is known for his simple, frugal life. "On innovation, if you don't re-invest, you quickly become extinct. That is in every form of process, from branding to delivery," he says. "It all adds to the complexity of our business."[14] Ramadorai points out that India is no longer just a location for Indian companies, but a mainstream base for the world. Every multinational in IT-enabled services (think Accenture, EDS, IBM Global Services) is setting up in India and scaling up for global delivery, he says. He makes the point that global connectivity means it can be done anywhere in the world, not just in India. "How quickly you respond to change is a differentiator. Push your limits," he tells IT industry aspirants. "Five years from now, we expect a complete change in our business. For example, the delivery of software could be a 'pay for service' model."[15]

Like Infosys, TCS is already in the big league: a market cap of more than US$29 billion in mid-2007 (compared with US$9.5 billion when it listed in August 2004), the first Indian IT company to reach an annual revenue of US$4 billion, and a profit of US$1 billion. Ramadorai says the TCS goal is to reach a revenue figure of US$10 billion by 2010 and be one of the world's top 10 consulting companies. He also claims that TCS is "winning the talent game" as Indian IT companies scramble to attract the best staff for a workforce that is becoming increasingly globalized. But, like Murthy and Nilekani, he acknowledges that India's education system needs to be revitalized if it is to keep supplying the IT services sector with suitable graduates. "Education is a challenge in India, as always, not just in IT, but across multiple sectors," he says. "We need investment in training by companies like us, who recruit widely."[16] Plus, TCS is setting up operations in alternative areas – smaller towns outside the traditional IT hubs of Bangalore, Hyderabad, Mumbai, Kolkata, or Delhi. "This provides an alternative employment for rural people and gives them aspirations beyond just menial work," he says. More fundamentally, Ramadorai says the IT industry wants the government to make drastic changes to India's education model that would open it up to competitive forces. "It must be completely unshackled, with affordable loans. Let students have a choice – and let schools be set up freely."

GENERATING AMBITION

On deals in the pipeline so far, TCS should make its global top 10 goal before 2010. The big three Indian companies will rank by market capitalization among the top 10 IT services companies by 2008/09, according to Wipro's Premji, the other grand figure on the Indian IT stage. Over a breakfast shared with Narayana Murthy in Bangalore, Premji told *The Economic Times* that the success of India's software industry had generated an "ambition level" among Indian entrepreneurs and leaders that was spreading across different business sectors such as pharmaceutical, biotechnology, automotive, and – with the Tata acquisition of Corus – steel. "There is an important message in what is happening with global acquisitions. A Corus bid really makes the point," he said. "They [Indian businesses] are willing to take the risk of global expansion. My personal view is that they will succeed."[17]

Murthy backs Premji's view, describing the confidence shown by Ratan Tata and the Tata Steel executives as "a watershed event" in India's commercial life. "When somebody writes the business history of India in the 2000s and 2100s, this will be described as a turning point in the mindset of the Indian entrepreneur. That's what I'm excited about," he told *The Economic Times*.[18] Murthy and Premji share more than a global view – there is some history, too. Back in 1979, Murthy approached Premji for a job, but there was no follow-up call from the Wipro boss. "We just found him too high powered for us. We were not ready for him. And I must have personally felt very threatened also," Premji joked in the interview. Murthy says he is grateful for the way things turned out; after all, the result is that India got two world-class IT companies, rather than just one.

Premji believes India will continue to be a major force globally, including beyond software and BPO, in any service that can be rendered remotely. But like other business leaders, he recognizes that the broader challenge will be to get manufacturing humming if jobs are to be created.

Half a world away, US-based IT services pioneer Bharat Desai of Syntel says he is excited about the future, given the way the internet has transformed the delivery of business services. "Any service can now be performed transparent of location. New industries will emerge that I can't even conceive of now. Look at Google – what a success story!" he says.[19] In Desai's view, the world is still in the initial stages of the services revolution. Desai's own company, Syntel, is an example of how things have changed in the past two decades. He recalls its beginnings in 1980: "We started as a local IT staffing company in Michigan, servicing the auto industry, Blue Cross, utilities. Our staff were largely US nationals. That model proved challenging, because there was growing demand but not a growing supply of workers. So we started importing staff to the US from around the globe. But that model had limitations, too." Desai says that in the next phase, Syntel pioneered remote software development. "It was very expensive to lease lines in those days. For example, it cost US$500,000 a year to get a 9.6K line between Mumbai and the United States. We hung 30 terminals off that line, and had to run two or three shifts to get our money's worth." For Desai, that was the "A-ha!" moment. "We needed to move the work to the people, not the other way around."[20] Today, 90% of Syntel's workforce is India-based. The company has three main locations – in Pune, Chennai, and Mumbai. Its first campus has been launched in Pune, with another on the way in Chennai.

LOOKING FOR SITES

The top IT companies are scouring India for good sites, as the early prime destination of Bangalore gives way to cities with better infrastructure growth prospects. Shiv Nadar's HCL Technologies, for example, is building its next US$220 million campus at a special economic zone in the second-tier city of Nagpur, about 280 miles (450 kilometers) north of Hyderabad. Nadar, perhaps the richest of all the IT members in India's global wealth club, says the project will generate 10,000 jobs in five years. His HCL Group (a contraction of Hindustan Computers Ltd.) is among the largest hardware and software companies in India, growing from a single room in Delhi to annual global turnover in 2006/07 of almost US$4 billion. HCL Technologies alone employs 40,000 people.

In an interview with CNN in December 2005, Nadar recalled what it was like when he first set up in 1976: "The biggest hurdle was government regulations on imports. So what we could do was determined not by what was technically possible, but what the state would allow you to import."[21] Another hurdle was the low level of IT-awareness in India in those days. About five years after starting up as a computer maker, Nadar and his team found that the cost of training their customers in how to use the computers was eating into profits. The result was the decision to set up the National Institute of Information Technology (NIIT), the company that today dominates India's IT training industry.

NIIT is led by wealth club member Rajendra Pawar, who serves as chairman, and his fellow IIT Delhi alumnus Vijay Thadani, who is CEO. According to Pawar, NIIT is now the No. 2 player globally in IT training, behind US-based Skillsoft following the latter's purchase of Thomson Corp.'s NETg for US$285 million in October 2006. NIIT recently made its own acquisition, buying Rochester, New York-based Element K for US$40 million in September 2006. Pawar and Thadani set up NIIT in 1981 with the backing of Nadar (who was NIIT's chairman until 1999); today NIIT operates in 42 countries, from the United States to China to Africa, and has half a million students. Pawar, who is regarded as one of the quiet visionaries of India's IT sector, is interested in identifying trends and crucial inflexion points in how IT is used to make big changes in companies' effectiveness. He says companies must move even more to embrace technology in their approach to training. Pawar notes: "In China, it is mainly a B-to-C [business to consumer] model, where people have to invest in themselves. In developed economies such as the United States (where NIIT has had a presence for more than 30 years), the companies invest in their staff."[22] Hotmail founder Sabeer Bhatia is following that trend. In Haryana state on what is now farmland, Bhatia plans to build a new "knowledge community" known as Nano City – modeled on California's Silicon Valley – that he says will have the finest education facilities in the world, a vibrant culture, and a low environmental footprint for its 500,000 inhabitants. The first residents of Nano City – located about 30 miles (45 kilometers) from the state capital, Chandigarh – are expected in 2010.

DEMOGRAPHIC REALITY

But all the IT training and all the new jobs in IT-enabled services are a mere drop in India's mammoth employment bucket. The demographic reality of a nation where 600 million people are under 25 years of age means that consumers will be looking to spend for 30 years to come, but at the same time more young people are pouring on to the job market. Experts say that India needs to create 40 to 50 million new jobs a year if it is to keep people out of poverty and stop a potentially cataclysmic buildup of social tensions. The downside of India was put forcefully by author Pankaj Mishra, who argued in a *New York Times* article in July 2006 that "triumphalist accounts" ignored or suppressed the poor state of India's public health and primary education, the lack of a manufacturing boom, continuing unemployment, the minuscule number of Indians working in the IT and business processing industries, the agrarian crisis, and the rise of militant Naxalism in north and central India. "The Indian government no longer effectively controls many of the districts where communists battle landlords and police, imposing a harsh form of justice on a largely hapless rural population," Mishra wrote. "The potential for conflict – among castes as well as classes – also grows in urban areas, where India's cruel social and economic disparities are as evident as its new prosperity. The main reason for this is that India's economic growth has been largely jobless."[23]

Part of the answer to Mishra's gloomy summation has to be low-tech manufacturing, better rural education, and a comprehensive change in agricultural practices that boosts output and incomes; in other words, a supply-chain revolution that frees both the farmer and the customer from the tyranny of outdated methods. IT can't fix all of that. What IT *has* done is set the global achievement standard for

Indian business. It has shown what can be achieved with innovation, intelligence, integrity, passion, persistence, curiosity, and, of course, excellence in execution. This is how Professor Amartya Sen, author of *The Argumentative Indian*, described IT in a keynote address to a recent Nasscom forum: "In many ways Indian IT has depended on what we can call TI, that is, 'talkative Indians.' It is not hard to see how a tradition of being thrilled by intellectual altercations tends to do a lot to prepare someone for the challenges of IT interactions."[24]

ENDNOTES

1. Shiv Nadar, "View from the top: Evolve or perish," in *The Times of India*, June 17, 2006.
2. Interview with N.R. Narayana Murthy, Mumbai, January 15, 2007.
3. ibid.
4. Speech by Rajat Gupta to the Wharton India Economic Forum, Philadelphia, November 11, 2006.
5. Murthy, op. cit.
6. Kevin Watkins, director of UN Human Development Report office, "The forgotten other India," *The Guardian*, October 3, 2006.
7. Murthy, op. cit.
8. ibid.
9. Nandan Nilekani, quoted in "New generation of leaders ready," *CyberMedia News*, October 27, 2006 at www.ciol.com.
10. Nandan Nilekani, World Economic Forum, Davos, January 24–28, 2007.
11. Nandan Nilekani, "Hungry, capable and determined. If we play our cards right, we can now influence the global business agenda," *The Financial Express*, January 1, 2007.
12. Murthy, address to the "Stanford in India" innovation conference, Mumbai, January 15, 2007.
13. ibid.
14. S. Ramadorai, panel discussion at "Stanford in India" innovation conference, Mumbai, January 16, 2007.
15. ibid.
16. Ramadorai, TCS press conference, Mumbai, January 15, 2007.
17. Premji and Murthy discussion in *The Economic Times*, February 16, 2007.
18. ibid.
19. Interview with Bharat Desai, Philadelphia, November 11, 2006.
20. ibid.
21. Shiv Nadar, interviewed by Satinder Bindra for CNN's *Talk Asia* program, December 14, 2005.
22. Comments by Rajendra Pawar at Wharton India Economic Forum, Philadelphia, November 11, 2006.
23. Pankaj Mishra, "The myth of the new India," *New York Times*, July 6, 2006.
24. Professor Amartya Sen, in keynote address at Nasscom India Leadership Forum, Mumbai, February 7, 2007.

CHAPTER FIVE

Car Wars: Keeping the Wheels Turning

The Golden Quadrilateral highways will open up,
and out, the closed worlds of India's villages.
   —Goldman Sachs research report on India's
                                    growth potential[1]

Bollywood is in the air at the launch of what the giant Tata Group is pitching as India's first "limousine." The venue is one of the most prestigious in Mumbai: the National Center for the Performing Arts, a stone's throw from the waterfront boulevard of Marine Parade. This is special ground for the Tatas: the center was a gift to the city from the Sir Dorabji Tata Trust, named after the elder son of group founder Jamsetji Tata. Mumbai's good and great gather for the party on a mild January evening. After a splashy multicultural song-and-dance routine that verges hilariously on the politically incorrect, group chairman Ratan Tata unveils a stretched air-conditioned Tata Indigo, a 1.4-liter midsize car with a choice of diesel or petrol engines. The cars are available in manual transmission only, but who is to say a limousine must be automatic? What the Indigo does have is loads of rear-seat legroom – where it matters most, given that the Tata marketers believe this essentially will be a chauffeur-driven car. Under lights in the garden outside, hundreds of guests mill around the Tata cars as the food and drink flow freely. A businesswoman sitting in the back seat with a friend confides that it's roomier than her current Mercedes. A gaggle of media people follow Ratan Tata, keen to get the latest word on a bigger ongoing story, Tata Steel's battle with Brazil's CSN for European steel major Corus. But the wily Tata is having nothing to do with steel questions. It will be another two weeks before that particular US$12 billion deal is resolved in Tata's favor, at the end of January 2007. Still, Tata does offer a response to one question that has kept the Indian automotive world enthralled for years: when will the fabled "one-lakh car" be out? "Production will begin in early 2008, I hope," Tata says.[2] The one-lakh car is Tata's planned entry into a segment now dominated by the Maruti 800 (a Suzuki Alto clone which sells for about US$4,500). One lakh, or 100,000 rupees (US$2,460), is the price – and has been since Tata first mooted it in 2005, astounding competitors who wonder how Tata can deliver a four-door, four- or five-seater car with a 30-horsepower rear engine for that sort of money. This is a project that has been controversial since day one. Its production site in West Bengal's Singur town has been the subject of land protests, sit-ins, and even a hunger strike by a political figure opposed to the Tata plan, Trinamool Congress chief Mamata Banerjee.

Rahul Bajaj, India's billionaire motorcycle and scooter king, says ordinarily he would dismiss the one-lakh car as a figment of media imagination, but "when Ratan Tata says that, I have to listen."[3] Tata is the heavyweight of corporate India; his views on everything from the car industry to investment-friendly policies for NRIs and the health of the relationship with Washington are always much in demand. On the sidelines of an India economic forum in the United States, Bajaj outlines his own automotive ambitions. "We're known for making two- and three-wheelers. But come January 2009, we will launch a low-cost, four-wheel goods carrier, not a passenger car," he says. "Then we'll see if we can do better than Tata."[4]

Bajaj is never one to miss an opportunity to plug his brand. "In my view, going up from two or three wheels to four wheels is cheaper than coming down from trucks, which is what Tata is doing," he says. Tata is best known as a truck brand; although it assembled Mercedes cars, it didn't make its first indigenous car – the Indica – until 1999. Still, it never pays to underestimate the indomitable Ratan Tata, who has carefully piloted the ever-growing fortunes of the US$22 billion (sales) Tata Group since taking over as chairman in 1991. His entreaty to the Tata foot soldiers is: "We must always lead – we must never follow!" By 2007, he had taken Tata Motors' consolidated annual revenue to more than US$9 billion. Tata, a 1962 Cornell architectural graduate who also has an advanced management qualification from Harvard (1975), stepped down as Tata Group executive chairman when he turned 65 in December 2002, as per company rules. But he remains as non-executive chairman, runs the group executive office, and continues to be very much the global face of Tata. The next big marker is December 28, 2007, when Tata turns 70 and is required to step down from all Tata boards. There's no rush to see him go at the venerable house of Tata, established by Jamsetji Tata in Mumbai in 1868. The group is highly diversified, running 96 businesses (including tea, hotels, and watches) across seven industry sectors: chemicals, consumer products, energy, engineering, IT and communications, materials, and services. Three of the Tata Group's listed companies – Tata Consultancy Services (TCS), Tata Motors, and Tata Steel – rank among India's top 30 listed companies and, between them, have a market capitalization of more than US$46 billion. Ratan Tata, often seen as a loner who keeps his own counsel, came in for criticism in his early years as chairman, with some observers saying he was selling off pieces of the Tata empire, such as Associated Cement, too cheaply. But Tata was focused on fixing what he saw as a key problem: the twin holding companies, Tata Sons and Tata Industries, did not have big enough stakes in the main money-spinners, leaving them vulnerable to corporate raiders. Over the past decade and a half, Tata has corrected that. The Tata Group is now leaner, more mobile, and more focused. Tata's rule to his executives is that they must either be one, two, or three in their business, or get out of it. He has also overseen some astute acquisitions, including Tetley Tea in 2000, and led the titanic battle for Corus in 2006/07. But perhaps his greatest success has been the float of Tata Consultancy Services in 2004. The IT services company, valued in mid-2007 at US$29 billion, is one of the shining stars of India Inc., with a global reputation as good as or better than its two great rivals, Infosys and Wipro. Tata Group companies retain a stake of almost 80% in TCS, which is in the US$1 billion a year profit class.

PEOPLE'S CAR

Ratan Tata seems happiest around things that move – he pilots his own helicopter and the group's Dassault Falcon corporate jets, and has co-piloted US fighter jets such as the F-16 and the F-18 Super Hornet. His one-lakh "people's car" has been a dream for some years. In June 2006, Tata told shareholders the styling and design of the car was completed, and prototypes were being tested. He also addressed the competitive pressures the new model might release: "A $2,000 car will surely upset the existing balance in the Indian car industry," he said. "Well, on the other hand, I feel that the competitors do not need to be too much worried about this cheap car. This car will address a market that would never think of buying a car in the first place."[5] Indeed, the advent of the one-lakh car (tipped to be closer to 150,000 rupees once inflation is factored in) is indicative of how much India's automotive sector has changed since the days when the lumbering Ambassador – still the vehicle of choice for some politicians and military bigwigs – ruled the road. It has been a long, long time since the bulbous bonnet of the Morris Oxford III was a familiar sight on its UK home turf. Production of the British-built car stopped in 1959, a year after its Indian clone, Hindustan Motors' Ambassador, was launched at a plant near Kolkata. With judicious tweaking, the spacious old Amby has soldiered on for decade after decade, jostling with all manner of trucks, scooters, carts, bicycles, and a tide of human and animal traffic on India's overburdened roads as it goes about the daily business of conveying ministers, VIPs, bureaucrats, business leaders, generals, and ordinary taxi passengers. The Ambassador was joined in the 1960s by the now-departed Standard, and the Premier Padmini, a clone of Italy's Fiat 1100 that ceased production in 2000. The Amby and Premier remain the staple of the Indian taxi fleet, bolstered more recently by the Tata Indica and Maruti van. The two old-style vehicles got their first serious competition in 1983 with the arrival of the Maruti 800, produced by state-owned Maruti Udyog as a joint venture with Japan's Suzuki. When the first 800 rolled off the production line in December 1983, then-Prime Minister Indira Gandhi shed tears of joy. The controversial Maruti – another "people's car" – was the pet project of her late son Sanjay, who died when his light plane crashed in New Delhi in June 1980. He had been granted the exclusive production license for the car in the 1970s – a decision that brought a storm of criticism at the time. "This is a very long story about a small car," Mrs. Gandhi said later. By mid-2007, Maruti had sold more than six million cars.[6] It has about 45% of the Indian car market, which had total annual sales of 1.2 million cars in 2006 and is expected to hit two million by 2010. Maruti has maintained a clear lead despite a proliferation of new models from Hyundai, Daewoo, Honda, BMW, and Mercedes from the mid-1990s onward, and the arrival of Tata's indigenous cars since 1999. Elsewhere, the clunky Ambassador and Premier may look way behind in style, performance, and appointments, but they keep on keeping on in the taxi sector, where economy of operation outweighs modern convenience. Plus, the Amby has a reputation for safety and ease of servicing, even by a village mechanic working with little more than a spanner.

EXPLOSIVE GROWTH

India's auto market has undergone explosive growth in the past decade
– sadly unmatched by the quality of its roads (see Table 5.1). In 1996,
there were just 10 million vehicles in the country; five years later the
number had reached 40 million and is likely to hit 100 million by 2010.
According to research by investment bank Goldman Sachs, India is
projected to have the largest number of cars in the world, 611 million,
by 2050, outstripping the numbers for China and the United States.
India's total annual production of trucks, utilities, cars, three-wheelers,
scooters, and motorcycles is now more than 10 million units, including
7.8 million two-wheelers and about 1.4 million passenger cars, almost
all of which are sold domestically. Maruti accounts for about 600,000
of the car sales, followed by Tata with 220,000. Tata also has a distribution and manufacturing arrangement with Fiat. Overseas makers such
as Hyundai, Honda, Skoda, VW, Ford, and GM make up the rest.
Toyota, the world's most profitable carmaker, set up a joint venture
with the Kirloskar family in 1997 and says it aims to play a major role
in developing the Indian automotive industry. It wants 10% of the
market and is beginning to make its presence felt with the Innova, a
three-row people mover introduced in mid-2005.

The third domestic force in the automotive sector comes from the
US$3.8 billion (sales) Mahindra & Mahindra Group, maker of SUVs
such as the Scorpio, and a competitor to be reckoned with in the light
of its agreement with Renault to introduce the Logan passenger
car and its alliance with Nissan. In November 2006, Renault and
Mahindra announced they would build a new plant capable of making
half a million vehicles a year. The plant is due to open in 2009, with
an initial capacity of 300,000 vehicles. Mahindra has also moved into

Table 5.1   India's Automotive Sales, 2003–07 (No. of vehicles)

	2003/04	2004/05	2005/06	2006/07
Passenger vehicles	902,096	1,061,572	1,143,076	1,379,698
Commercial vehicles	260,114	318,430	351,041	467,882
Three-wheelers	284,078	307,862	359,920	403,909
Two-wheelers	5,364,249	6,209,765	7,052,391	7,857,548
TOTAL	6,810,537	7,897,629	8,906,428	10,109,037

Source: Society of Indian Automobile Manufacturers, 2007

heavy commercial vehicles through a joint venture with International Truck & Engine Corp. of the United States to set up a 250,000-unit greenfield truck and bus plant by late 2008. Mahindra's total investment in this plant is about US$550 million over five years. Managing director Anand Mahindra (nephew of group chairman Keshub Mahindra) says passenger cars are the glamor end of the automotive industry, but trucks may be more important for India. And he envisions a major export role for Mahindra. "There is no doubt we will succeed," he says.[7] Mahindra is supremely confident; he believes that by 2016 India will be the global destination of choice for the design and manufacture of motor vehicles and automotive components. He expects the automotive sector by then will have an output of US$145 billion, or about 10% of India's expected 2016 GDP, and will employ an extra 25 million people.[8]

While cars, trucks, and buses figure large in Anand Mahindra's expansion plans for the Mumbai-based group, the Wharton-educated industrialist is really a tractor man at heart. "Our goal is to be No. 1 in tractor units sold globally," he says during an interview in his green and airy headquarters in the Mumbai suburb of Worli. "We want to be the largest tractor brand that is sold. We have a thriving business in selling rebranded tractors, such as Mitsubishi and Korea's Dongyang. In the United States, one-third of our sales are Japanese tractors."[9] Mahindra says India is the world's largest tractor market, and international buyers choose his brand simply because they know it can take any kind of beating. "Indian tractors are flogged in the number of hours they work here, so they have a reputation for being very rugged," he says. Boston Consulting Group has identified Mahindra and rival Tata Motors as two of 100 companies from emerging markets such as India, China, Brazil, and Russia with the potential to be top-ranked global corporations. Mahindra says his company has brand power in the US market because US farmers are so knowledgeable. "They spend a lot of time on the internet doing their research." He recounts an example: "We truly understood the power of globalization some time back, when we were able to pass on a price reduction to our Indian customers. We very quickly had US farmers getting on to us, saying they wanted the same discount."[10]

The farming connection is important in more ways than one. Anand Mahindra believes agriculture is the missing link in India's high-growth story, noting that one reason for the rural sector's patchy performance is waste resulting from India's abysmal distribution mechanisms. Bad roads are part of the problem: getting produce from the farmgate to the consumer takes too long and there is no reliable cold chain.

About 70% of goods traffic, borne by Tata trucks or the rival Hinduja family's Ashok Leyland brand, must use India's choked-up roads, which explains why it can take days for goods to travel across the country. Yet, there is no stopping the Indian consumer's quest for mobility. And for many people, the first step to a car is a two-wheeler, typically with an engine of 75 to 125 cc. For that, they turn to the big guns of the bike and scooter world: Bajaj Auto, Hero Honda, and TVS, where three members of India's global wealth club – Rahul Bajaj, B.L. Munjal, and Venu Srinivasan – reign supreme.

SCOOTING ALONG

Harvard-educated Bajaj, a boxing champion at school and since June 2006 a member of India's Rajya Sabha (upper house), has turned over the daily running of the Pune-based business to his sons Rajiv and Sanjiv, but still remains a powerful presence. Bajaj sold a record 2.3 million motorcycles in 2005/06 and wants to be supplying four million of the expected 10 million sales of motorcycles in India in 2010. Bajaj says: "We should clearly establish our leadership in the domestic market, and become a significant player in the global market, among the three largest global producers in two wheelers."[11] But to do that, Bajaj will have to overtake the Munjal family's Hero Honda, which has been No. 1 in two-wheeler sales since 2001. Indicative of Bajaj's aggressive approach is this view, expressed in late 2006: "There is only one guru that teaches efficiency – and that guru is competition."[12] It wasn't always this way: Bajaj, known for his outspoken ways, was a member of the "Bombay Club" of industrialists opposed in the early 1990s to what they saw as a reformist central government giving too much of an open door to multinationals. Bajaj argued that competition was fine, but Indian businesses needed time to bring their operations up to speed after the stultifying years of the "license Raj," when Delhi bureaucrats controlled business decisions. Bajaj says the company has learnt a lot from its Japanese partner Kawasaki, most notably the need to develop its own technology. "We have no choice – the quality bar has been raised." While Bajaj can't overtake Hero Honda on straight numbers, it's aiming to be more profitable by moving higher up the value chain, concentrating on bigger bikes such as its top-selling 150–220cc Pulsar.

Bajaj Auto, which was set up in 1945 and has since become the flagship of the 27-company Bajaj Group, has 20,000 employees, a turnover of US$3 billion a year, and a market capitalization of about US$8 billion. Rahul Bajaj, a tireless networker both domestically and on the global stage, has been the public face of the company since the late 1960s, when he took over from his father Kamalnayan Bajaj (d. 1972). Rahul's grandfather, Jamnalal Bajaj, who founded the group in 1926, was a disciple (and adopted son) of Mahatma Gandhi. Rahul Bajaj is optimistic about his own company's outlook and that for India in general, arguing that the quality of India's human capital will determine its economic performance. "Even in 2025, India will be one of the world's youngest countries. How we educate and train our young people, and bring them into the workforce, is crucial." But he says growth must be inclusive – no other kind will do. "We must give equality of opportunity."[13] Bajaj notes that while the percentage of people in India below the poverty line has fallen from 36% in 1993 to 22% now, "there are still too many pockets of poverty." At a US conference on India's economic outlook, he tells his rich and well-connected audience: "We will do well to remember Gandhi's teaching of the seven social sins: wealth without work, pleasure without conscience, education without character, commerce without morality, science without humanity, worship without sacrifice, politics without principles. We've underachieved because we've ignored these teachings."[14] In the view of some shareholders, Bajaj Auto's share price has also underachieved in recent years. To combat his critics (and maybe keep sibling rivalries contained), in May 2007 Rahul Bajaj unveiled a long awaited de-merger plan in which the automotive manufacturing business and the financial services business are placed in separate companies. The de-merger will see Rahul's elder son Rajiv continue to head the automotive company, while the financial services company will be run by Sanjiv, two years Rajiv's junior. Rahul's younger cousin, Madhur Bajaj (MBA, Lausanne, 1979), is group vice-chairman.

MOTORCYCLE MILESTONE

No such issues confuse the picture for two-wheeler leader Hero Honda, where Pawan Kant Munjal, son of chairman and company founder Brijmohan Lall Munjal, is firmly in place as managing director. Hero Honda is the world's largest motorcycle company, achieving that milestone in 2001 when it sold 1.3 million two-wheelers and helping Munjal senior to the title of Ernst & Young's "Entrepreneur of the Year." It has held the title ever since, with sales topping two million in 2006.[15] Underpinning Hero Honda's success is its complex relationship with Japan's Honda, which goes back to 1984 when the original alliance was set up. That gave Hero access to the latest Japanese technology and put the Munjal family on the path to market leadership. But after 15 fruitful years, in 1999 Honda decided to set up its own subsidiary, Honda Motorcycle and Scooter India (HMSI), to compete in the same sector. Industry observers feared the worst for Hero, expecting the alliance would end for good at the end of the 20-year joint venture term in 2004; instead it has been renewed for another 10 years. HMSI has carved out just 2% of the market and Hero sits firmly on almost 47%, with Bajaj at about 33%.

The entrepreneurial Brijmohan Lall Munjal hails originally from Kamalia, now part of Pakistan. By 1944 the family was in Amritsar. After Partition in 1947, Munjal and his elder brothers Dayanand and Satyanand, and younger brother Om Prakash (who remains a director), moved to the industrial town of Ludhiana in Punjab and set up a bicycle components business. This grew into a manufacturing operation and by 1956 had become Hero Cycles. Munjal and his brothers nurtured relationships with customers and established a network of vendors that would allow Hero to become India's top name in bicycles. By the early 1980s, when scooters and motorbikes were becoming a popular transport mode, Munjal eventually convinced Japan's Honda Motor that cultural compatibility and his deep understanding of the market made Hero its best cycle partner in India. Munjal was keen to get his hands on Honda's four-stroke technology, rather than the two-strokes that had been the market norm. The joint venture rolled out its first CD100 motorcycle in 1985, and has gone on to produce more than 15 million two-wheelers since then from its plants at Dharuhera and Gurgaon in Haryana, on the Delhi–Jaipur road. Om Prakash Munjal is group co-founder, and also chairman and CEO of Hero Cyles. Brijmohan Lall's son Pawan Kant, a graduate in mechanical engineering, handles the day-to-day running of Hero Honda but still finds time to be a passionate golfer. He is a past president of the Professional Golfers Association of India and a board member of the Asian Professional Golfers Association. The Munjal family and Honda Motor each has a 26% stake in Hero Honda (market capitalization: US$3.25 billion), with the remainder publicly held.

GOING IT ALONE

Bajaj, Hero Honda, and HMSI account for more than 80% of India's two-wheeler market. But even the remainder provides reasonable prospects for third-ranked TVS Motor, which concentrates on entry-level bikes. TVS Motor is part of the diversified TVS Group, which began as a transport company established by T.V. Sundram Iyengar in Chennai in 1911 and has since grown to 29 companies with interests in the auto industry, finance, textiles, energy, and electronics. In 1980 TVS Motor rolled out the TVS50, India's first two-seat moped, and in September 1984 it was the first to use Japanese technology in an Indian motorcycle. Where Hero had Honda, TVS had Suzuki as its Japanese partner. But unlike Hero, TVS now goes it alone; the joint venture came to an end in 2001 and the Chennai-based family behind TVS Group, led by chairman Venu Srinivasan and Suresh Krishna (who chairs the family's main auto components company Sundram Fasteners), are in no hurry for fresh joint ventures. TVS won the Deming Prize for quality management in 2002 and its home-grown 150cc Apache, built in its Hosur plant near Bangalore, was India's "bike of the year" in 2006, helping the company emerge from a sluggish patch. TVS says its goal is "top two" status among two-wheeler companies in India and "top five" in Asia. It is currently No. 3 in India and one of the world's top 10. TVS exports mainly to Sri Lanka, Bangladesh, and countries in Africa. TVS notes that while India is the world's second-largest two-wheeler market after China, penetration rates are still low at 45 per 1,000 people, compared to 80 for Indonesia and 150 for Thailand. "This presents ample scope for the industry to grow," it says.[16]

Venu Srinivasan, who has an MBA from Indiana's Purdue University, became CEO of one of the family auto component businesses, Sundaram Clayton, in 1979. That same year, his father started TVS Motor and within five years had set up the joint venture with Suzuki. Later, the company was hit by a debilitating strike by workers and was shut down for several months. In the 1990s, tensions emerged over management style between the joint venture partners, and in September 2001 Venu broke off the alliance with Suzuki. TVS Group (through its Sundaram Clayton unit) bought out Suzuki's 25.97% stake, giving it 58.43% of the company. In 2006 TVS sold 1.34 million two-wheelers and said it envisaged 15% sales growth in the year ahead. Commerce on wheels is a common thread in the Srinivasan household. Venu's wife, Mallika Srinivasan, runs her own family's business,

Tractors and Farm Equipment (TAFE), and in 2006 won the *Economic Times*' Businesswoman of the Year Award for her role in growing the business.

Europe and Japan are the homes of super-cars and super-bikes, respectively, but India has developed core skills in what may be the biggest sectors yet: the global market for bikes under 125cc and cars under 1,000cc. It's not beyond the realm of possibility to imagine the Tata, Bajaj, Hero, and TVS brands emerging in big markets such as China, Brazil, Russia, and Africa. Certainly, that's part of the goals of the Indian government's 2006–16 Automotive Mission Plan. At the other end of the automotive spectrum to the Tata Indica, the Bajaj Pulsar or the TVS Apache are the brands beloved of another wealth club member, business tear-away Gautam Singhania, chairman and managing director of the textile and apparel retailer Raymond. Mumbai-based Singhania just loves fast-moving wheels with a pedigree: Ferrari, Lamborghini, F1 machines. He started in go-karts, graduated to a white Premier Padmini and then a succession of race and rally cars, including a souped-up Maruti and a Honda S2000 drag-racer that he says is the fastest Honda in the country. Building international prestige brands such as Ferrari, Lamborghini, Ducati, and Honda takes time – a great deal of time, but Indian companies such as Infosys, Wipro, and TCS have shown it can be done in IT. The challenge is there for the Tata, Bajaj, Munjal, and Srinivasan families to keep those wheels turning, at home and abroad.

ENDNOTES

1. Goldman Sachs Global Economics Paper No. 152, "India's Rising Growth Potential," New Delhi, January 22, 2007. The Golden Quadrilateral project aims to connect Delhi, Kolkata, Chennai, and Mumbai with 3,625 miles (5,840 kilometers) of multilane highways.
2. Response by Ratan Tata at Tata Indigo launch, Mumbai, January 16, 2007.
3. Interview with Rahul Bajaj, Philadelphia, November 11, 2006.
4. ibid.
5. Ratan Tata, chairman's report in Tata Motors' Annual Report 2005/06, Mumbai, June 13, 2006.
6. Media release, "President visits Maruti Udyog," Gurgaon, May 25, 2007.
7. Anand Mahindra speaking at Mahindra-International Truck press conference, Mumbai, January 16, 2007.
8. Data taken from Automotive Mission Plan 2006–2016, released by Indian Ministry of Heavy Industry, January 29, 2007.
9. Interview with Anand Mahindra, Mumbai, January 18, 2007.

10. ibid.
11. Interview with Bajaj, op. cit.
12. Speech by Rahul Bajaj to Wharton India Economic Forum, Philadelphia, November 11, 2006.
13. ibid.
14. ibid.
15. Media release, "Hero Honda world no. 1 for six years in a row," New Delhi, January 31, 2007.
16. Media release, "TVS Motor Co. records highest two wheeler sales in 2006–07," Hosur, April 2, 2007.

CHAPTER SIX

Pharma: Building the Next Blockbuster

*It is our duty as children of the same God and citizens
of the same planet to pool our energies and banish
the scourge of AIDS.*
    —Former US President, Bill Clinton[1]

Every day, more than 7,500 Indian children die of preventable diseases – everything from malnutrition to malaria, tuberculosis, dysentery, and HIV/AIDS. This annual death toll of 2.8 million is one of the greatest blights on 21st-century India, where access to primary healthcare and affordable medicine remains beyond the reach of 400 million people, or a third of the population. While the problem is far from solved, the sheer scale of that need for cheaper drugs has been behind the rise of India's pharmaceutical industry in the past two decades. It has grown from the simple copying of overseas medicines to the point where, spurred by changes to patent protection laws, Indian makers now have home-grown "blockbuster" drugs in the pipeline. Information technology has a higher international profile, but it is the pharmaceutical and biotechnology sector that has created the most members of India's global wealth club. The founders and owners of Indian drug makers such as Sun, Cipla, Ranbaxy, Dr. Reddy's, Glenmark, Nicholas Piramal, Lupin, Biocon, Aurobindo, Cadila, Wockhardt, Serum Institute, Divis Labs, Torrent Pharma, Matrix Lab, and Jubilant Organosys have become hugely wealthy on the back of an industry that until just a few years ago was known primarily as a maker of "knock-off" generic medicines: a copycat, a cloner, an imitator, rather than an innovator (see Table 6.1).

Table 6.1   Global Wealth Club Members in Pharmaceuticals and Biotechnology, based on Market Capitalization, June 2007

1. Dilip Shanghvi, Sun Pharma	US$3.71 billion
2. Yusuf Hamied, Cipla	US$1.68 billion
3. Malvinder & Shivinder Singh, Ranbaxy Labs	US$1.25 billion
4. Gracias Saldanha, Glenmark Pharmaceuticals	US$1.08 billion
5. Cyrus Poonawalla, Serum Institute of India	US$1.0 billion
6. Habil F. Khorakiwala, Wockhardt	US$838 million
7. Bhiku & Vijay Patel, Waymade Healthcare, UK	US$800 million
8. Desh Bandhu Gupta, Lupin Laboratories	US$750 million
9. Pankaj R. Patel, Cadila Healthcare	US$733 million
10. Kiran Mazumdar-Shaw, Biocon	US$723 million
11. K. Anji Reddy, Dr. Reddy's Laboratories	US$683 million
12. Ajay Piramal, Nicholas Piramal India	US$656 million
13. Shyam & Hari Bhartia, Jubilant Organosys	US$508 million
14. P.V. Ramprasad Reddy, Aurobindo Pharma	US$366 million

Sources: Data from Bombay Stock Exchange and filings with Securities Exchange Board of India

THE PATENT PUSH

Generics remain the most substantial part of the pharma business, but increasingly India's top companies are doing their own research, making their own breakthroughs, creating their own new products. Some of the pressure for change is external; World Trade Organization-mandated changes to patent protection rules that took effect from January 2005 mean Indian makers are having to step up their R&D spending in the search for new drugs and delivery systems. Another reason for the sector's growth is its cost advantage. A part of India's competitive edge in drug discovery is the "affordability of failure," according to Biocon founder Kiran Mazumdar-Shaw, a pioneer of the industry.[2] Mazumdar-Shaw, whose 62% stake in the biotechnology company she set up in 1978 makes her among India's wealthiest women, says that in the cycle of drug development, the "R" is a small part of R&D. "It is the 'D' that is expensive and time-consuming. The clinical cost in India gives you a speed and cost advantage, through access and enrollment of patients." Mazumdar-Shaw says there is no moral hazard in India's drug development practices, and that any reference to human guinea pigs is "just not true." "In India it is the hospital bed and the running costs that are cheap, not the patient," she says.

CUTTING UP THE PIE

A thick slice of the global pharma market is well and truly worth having. Drug companies make sales of more than US$650 billion a year, with consumers in North America, Europe, and Japan accounting for about 85% of that figure. Big pharma companies such as Pfizer, Johnson & Johnson, GlaxoSmith Kline, Sanofi-aventis, Merck, Novartis, Roche, and Astra Zeneca grab the choicest pieces of the pie, but Indian pharma companies exported drugs worth US$3 billion in 2006 and the domestic market is growing rapidly from a relatively small value base. India is already the world's fourth-largest drugs market by volume, though it ranks well down by sales – about US$6 billion in 2006, with a likely size of US$9.5 billion by 2010. In comparison, the Chinese market size is likely to reach US$15 billion in 2007, or about 2.3% of the global total. What worries "big pharma" is that demand for generic products in the West is growing at about 15% a year, compared with just 5% for patented products. As more drugs come off patent protection (estimated at US$60 billion worth between 2006 and 2009), generic makers are poised to swoop in with lower-cost offerings. The search for new molecules is costly and time-consuming for the biggest companies; they simply lack the discovery speed to replace the off-patent drugs with new blockbusters. Consolidation and partnering may be the name of the game as big pharma comes to grips with the problems and possibilities thrown up by the generic makers, whether they be from India, Israel, Eastern Europe, China, or a host of other low-cost countries. Already, multinationals are outsourcing to Indian makers to do contract research and manufacturing. The multinational corporations (MNCs) are also investing heavily in India (see Table 6.2) and plan to speed up the launch of their own patented products within the country, according to a report by consultants KPMG to the Pharma Summit held in Mumbai in September 2006.[3]

Table 6.2   Multinationals Listed in India

1. GlaxoSmithKline
2. Aventis Pharma
3. Pfizer
4. Astra Zeneca

Source: Bombay Stock Exchange

AFFORDABLE AIDS CARE

Healthcare is a massive problem in India, particularly for the most vulnerable groups, such as rural children. When the monsoon rains sweep into the country in June, mosquitoes start to breed more rapidly and the risk of malaria rises. With it, too, rises the demand for anti-infective medicines and antibiotics. Tuberculosis and dysentery are prevalent. Leprosy is on the rise again. The World Health Organization predicts the number of India's diabetes sufferers will rise to almost 80 million by 2030. And in a country of 1.2 billion people where safe sex is practiced all too infrequently, HIV/AIDS is another health scourge. Indeed, India has the world's largest number of HIV/AIDS cases – 5.7 million – and AIDS is regarded as India's biggest health problem. A step forward came in December 2006, when the foundation set up by former US President Bill Clinton struck an agreement with two of the biggest Indian drug companies, Ranbaxy Laboratories and Cipla Pharma, to distribute an array of anti-retroviral formulas to HIV-positive children in India for as little as US$60 a year, or about 16 cents a day. The deal is an extension of one made earlier in the year with several Indian pharma companies to supply rapid HIV tests and anti-AIDS drugs to adults at a discounted price.

Cipla, headed by Yusuf Hamied, has been at the forefront of making cheaper drugs available for HIV-positive patients. In 2001, Cipla was the first to offer the triple drug cocktail, Triomune, at about a dollar a day – a fraction of the international cost.

Hamied says it is important to remove the stigma associated with HIV. In comments made to mark the 2006 World AIDS day, he noted: "We need to recognize that HIV is no longer a death sentence, but can be regarded as a chronic ailment."[4] Hamied, whose stake in the drug company set up by his father Khwaja Abdul Hamied in 1935 is worth almost US$1.7 billion, says it is not important if Cipla sells a few of its 1,000-plus drugs at or below cost. He points instead to Cipla's mission statement: "Success does not make a company great. What really matters is its contribution toward making life better for everyone." Hamied's stance does not go down well with some of his global rivals. Sanofi-aventis chairman Jean-François Dehecq told the *Financial Times* newspaper in January 2007 that generic drug makers in India, Thailand, and Indonesia were taking their cheap drugs to the north (advanced nations) where people could afford to pay more. "They are exploiting people in the south [developing nations]. It's a scandal. They should deal with their own countries first," Dehecq said.[5] He slammed the generic companies, saying they paid their employees "three times nothing" to produce the drugs, and then exported them rather than selling them locally. A few months before Dehecq's remarks, Hamied told the Cipla annual general meeting the company was now getting about 50% of its revenue from exports, compared with just 10% a decade earlier. He said the company is constantly alert to business opportunities. "At the same time, we have not compromised on our basic commitment to promote national interest and humanitarian causes for the poor not only in India but throughout the world."[6]

For years, Indian drug companies were derided as copycats who simply reverse-engineered blockbuster drugs developed elsewhere. Litigation over patents has been a constant of the industry, with Pfizer locking horns with Ranbaxy over the cholesterol drug Lipitor and GlaxoSmithKline clashing with Cipla over the anti-AIDS drug Combivir. Within India, hundreds of patents filed by multinational pharma companies are under review by the patents office. And in the United States, about a third of all drug master filings with the Food and Drug Administration (FDA) in 2006 were from Indian companies. About 70 such Indian companies have FDA approval, and constitute the biggest group outside the United States. But as India adds more FDA-approved R&D centers, it also needs to look at the way it teaches the next wave of pharmaceutical scientists, according to Ajay Piramal, chairman of drug maker Nicholas Piramal. At the 2006 World Economic Forum he noted that India's pharma industry so far had grown through reverse engineering. "We are good at chemistry, but not yet as good in biology. We need to change the way universities teach people."[7]

IN SEARCH OF THE BIG ONE

When India does release its first blockbuster drug, it will most likely come from a new chemical entity (NCE) created either by Ranbaxy Laboratories or Dr. Reddy's Laboratories, the two Indian pharma companies that spend the most on R&D. Innovation, rather than replication, is the name of their game from now on. About 12% of Ranbaxy's and 10% of Dr. Reddy's spending in 2006 went to R&D – well above the domestic norm of 2–4%, but still some way below the 20% or more that big pharma will spend on R&D. The search for NCEs is expensive for Indian companies, but with a drug discovery cost estimated to be still one-third to one-fifth that of the multinationals, it is potentially hugely profitable. Ranbaxy has built three research facilities at Gurgaon, on the outskirts of New Delhi, including one dedicated to new drug discovery research. Ranbaxy CEO Malvinder Singh thinks his malaria molecule will be the first NCE, out by 2011. Hyderabad-based Dr. Reddy's has six NCEs in the pipeline, including two in clinical development. Company founder Dr. K. Anji Reddy believes one of these – most likely an anti-diabetes molecule – may be a blockbuster that will help him achieve his 2010 target of US$2 billion annual revenue, up from US$500 million in 2005. In Reddy's view, money is not the problem in the early stages of research. "You don't need a lot of money in the discovery stage and phase one to pre-clinical," he says. Nor is a huge amount of money needed for phase two clinical tests. But after that, he says, "you need real money."[8] And this is when, he believes, success will bring big pharma running to him. Ranbaxy and Dr. Reddy's are also looking to boost their R&D expertise through acquisitions. Ranbaxy has not been able to buy in the United States but has had more success in Europe. In March 2006, it bought Romania's Terapia, Ethimed in Belgium, and GlaxoSmith-Kline's generic business Allen in Italy. In the same year, Dr. Reddy's bought German generic drug maker Betapharm for about US$570 million, the largest offshore deal to date by an Indian drug company. In May 2007, Mumbai-based Sun Pharmaceutical said it would buy Israeli generic drug maker Taro Pharmaceutical Industries for US$454 million. Taro makes 90% of its generic sales in the rich North American market.

Biocon's Mazumdar-Shaw says that in the last eight years, her company has made the transition from industrial enzymes to an integrated biotech pharmaceutical company. "The excitement in this business is about product development," she says. And the future is in international tie-ups, driven by the knowledge that lower production costs and the availability of skills in India mean the dollars go further. "It is the affordability factor. It extends the runway and means you can go further up the value chain," she says.[9] Biocon's model has been to use the available talent in the best possible ways, including bringing in leadership from the United States if it's appropriate. "Indian talent is not cheap any more," Mazumdar-Shaw says. "But US$100K in India is still about US$200K in the United States. So the affordability is there. But you've got to leverage costs to deliver value. You can't just cut costs as your only strategy. You have to learn to deliver innovation. Our focus is on diabetes, oral insulin, cancer antibodies." Mazumdar-Shaw is bullish about the biotech and pharma outlook for India, particularly when it comes to the economics of clinical trials. "You need large numbers of people in phase 3 trials," she notes. "This is where India has an edge. To do a global trial today, probably about 30% of patients are from India and China. I estimate that in the future 70% of trial data will come from India and China." The KPMG pharma report agrees that Indian companies are well placed to exploit the outsourcing demand, citing their technical and regulatory skills, their cost advantage, and their global relationships. It says that industry sources estimate the global market for contract manufacturing and research will likely be worth more than US$50 billion by 2010. India already has the largest number of FDA-approved drug-making facilities outside the United States.

RISING SUN

Using the experience gained from a wholesale pharmaceuticals business to make generic and specialty drugs is behind the success of India's wealthiest pharma entrepreneur, Dilip Shanghvi, a movie enthusiast who hails originally from Kolkata. He founded Sun Pharmaceutical Industries in 1983 with capital of just US$250 and has taken it to the very pinnacle of the Indian industry, where it vies with Cipla for the title of India's most valuable pharma company (see Table 6.3). Shanghvi's 69% stake in Sun is worth about US$3.7 billion, which puts him well ahead of Cipla's Hamied (about US$1.7 billion), Malvinder and Shivinder Singh of Ranbaxy (about US$1.25 billion), Cyrus Poonawalla and his unlisted Serum Institute of India (about US$1.0 billion), the Saldanha family of Glenmark (about US$1 billion), and Habil Khorakiwala of Wockhardt, on about US$840 million (see Table 6.1 above). Shanghvi, a commerce graduate from Calcutta University, had just a handful of employees and five psychiatry-based products when he began operations in Kolkata. By 1986 he had relocated to Mumbai and a year later was selling nationwide. He launched cardiology products in 1988 and gastroenterology treatments in 1989, the first year that Sun began exporting. By 1993, Sun had opened its first research center. It listed on the stock market the following year after a massively oversubscribed initial public share offer. Shanghvi set out on the international acquisition trail in 1997, buying a slice of US-based generic drug maker Caraco Pharm Labs of Detroit for US$7.5 million. He gradually increased Sun's stake in Caraco to 60% by 2004; it has since risen to about 73%. A sales turnaround at Caraco that began in 2000 has seen the US company pick

Table 6.3   India's Top 15 Pharmaceutical Companies, by Market Capitalization, June 2007

1. Sun Pharma	US$5,339 million
2. Cipla	US$4,121 million
3. Ranbaxy Labs	US$3,585 million
4. Dr. Reddy's	US$2,713 million
5. Glenmark	US$2,004 million
6. Divis Labs	US$1,578 million
7. Lupin	US$1,430 million
8. Nicholas Piramal	US$1,312 million
9. Biocon	US$1,187 million
10. Wockhardt	US$1,137 million
11. Cadila Healthcare	US$1,018 million
12. Jubilant Organosys	US$978 million
13. Matrix Lab	US$911 million
14. Aurobindo Pharma	US$902 million
15. Torrent Pharma	US$529 million

Source: Bombay Stock Exchange

up an increasing share of the huge US generics market. Sun also targets markets in Europe, Latin America, and Africa. In early 2007, Shanghvi said: "We are working to build a competitive global generics business as we pursue expansion opportunities in existing and new geographies."[10] His Taro buy a few months later fitted that template.

FAST MOVER

While Shanghvi's Sun Pharma heads the value list, one of the fastest movers is Glenmark, which has risen rapidly from modest beginnings to the point where it is No. 5 in India by market capitalization. Pharma industry veteran Gracias Saldanha started the Mumbai-based company in 1977 with just three employees and capital of 1 million rupees (then about US$115,000), naming it after his sons Glenn and Mark. Its first product, an antifungal product known as Candid Cream, came out in 1979 and was an early success. It remains the No. 1 product in its category. Glenmark initially targeted markets in Russia and Africa, but has since expanded to North and South America, Japan, and Europe. In 1998, Saldanha's son Glenn returned to India from a stint with PricewaterhouseCoopers and took over as CEO of the company in 2001. Glenmark was floated in 1999, using some of the proceeds to build its first research center on the outskirts of Mumbai in 2000, and by 2003 it had set up a subsidiary in the United States to target the world's biggest market. Major success came in 2005 with licensing deals worth US$250 million for its experimental asthma drug oglemilast, with US-based Forest Labs and Japan's Teijin Pharma. The following year it struck a deal with Germany's Merck to collaborate on an anti-diabetes treatment. It says payments to Glenmark from this deal could potentially top US$200 million.

The pioneering work done by Glenmark, Ranbaxy, Dr. Reddy's, Cipla, Sun, and other makers means that India's pharmaceutical exports could reach US$6 billion by 2010. That's still small compared to other industry sectors such as manufacturing, but it's a huge advance from 30 years ago, when India made only the most basic of drugs. Dr. Anji Reddy is convinced that Indian pharma companies will make more and more of their own discoveries, simply because they have to, driven both by a moral and regulatory imperative. "The goal must be for India – and China – to develop drugs on their own soil at affordable prices for people. They must, or people will die. We will do that one day," he says.[11]

ENDNOTES

1. Statement on the Clinton Foundation website to mark World AIDS Day 2006.
2. Interview with Kiran Mazumdar-Shaw, Wharton India Economic Forum, Philadelphia, November 11, 2006.
3. *India Pharma Inc. – Competing Globally*, KPMG report, Mumbai, September 2006.
4. Statement on World AIDS Day, December 1, 2006.
5. "Sanofi chief 'scandalised' by generic drug makers' exports," *Financial Times*, January 2, 2007.
6. Cipla annual general meeting, Mumbai, September 5, 2006.
7. Remarks at "India's Life Science Revolution" session, World Economic Forum, Davos, Switzerland, January 27, 2006.
8. Interview with Dr. K. Anji Reddy, *Forbes*' Global CEO Conference, Sydney, August 31, 2005.
9. Mazumdar-Shaw, op. cit.
10. "Sun Pharma reports strong performance," media release, Mumbai, January 29, 2007.
11. Reddy, op. cit.

CHAPTER SEVEN

Media and Entertainment: It's Showtime, Folks!

The problem is, basically, that Subramanyam keeps asking producers for ever more outrageous amounts of money, and they astonish us by paying what we ask for.

—Fictional Bollywood superstar Ashok Banjara, in Shashi Tharoor's novel, *Show Business*

What to do with the money? It was a good question back in pre-liberalization 1991 India, when Tharoor published his hilarious novel, *Show Business*.[1] By government edict, banks and other financial institutions had to stay clear of film financing, so Bollywood was a world where dirty money sloshed through the offices of producers, directors, and movie stars like a monsoon flood. Mumbai mobsters were not averse to roughing-up those who didn't get the message about whose interests should be served first. Along with these home-grown gangsters, guns, international terrorists, and offshore accounts were part of the mix, as was the casting couch and formula movie-making: shoot'em-ups, mythological heroes, boy-gets-girl song and dance numbers, and evil dons making off with the leading lady.

A decade and a half on, the plot lines may not have changed too greatly, but the color, quality, and quantity of the money has. High-profile companies such as Anil Ambani's Reliance Entertainment have moved into the film business, top studios such as Yash Raj Films are corporatizing their approach, and international tie-ups are expanding. One reason is that the smart money sees the financial gap between India's film industry now and what it could be a few years down the track as global and domestic audiences grow. Mumbai-based Bollywood, which essentially produces Hindi-language films, and its Tamil- and Telugu-language counterparts Kollywood (based in Chennai) and Tollywood (in Hyderabad, Andhra Pradesh), between them have a turnover of just US$2 billion a year, despite making far more movies than Hollywood. That renders the Indian industry still a financial minnow compared to its US counterpart's US$250 billion weight, and there are plenty of critics who will say most Indian films are "cut and paste" versions of US or European works. Still, the financial growth trajectory is apparent, and movie-making is a significant part of India's media and entertainment scene – an industry that turned over US$10 billion in 2006 and is expected to grow to almost US$24 billion by 2011. Film's slice of the industry will likely double to US$4 billion, making it third to television's US$11.5 billion and print's US$5.5 billion.[2]

According to the latest survey by PricewaterhouseCoopers for the Federation of Indian Chambers of Commerce and Industry (FICCI), growing consumer demand, technological advances such as digital film distribution, greater government encouragement of outside investment, and initiatives by India's rapidly expanding private media companies will help drive the media and entertainment industry at a growth rate of 18% a year until 2011, substantially outperforming the wider economy (see Table 7.1). An early sign of things to come is the move by Raghav Bahl's TV18 Group to set up a London-based film industry company to co-produce, market, and exploit the theater,

Table 7.1   India's Media and Entertainment Industry, Revenue Growth Projections by Sector

	2006 (billion rupees)	2011 forecast (billion rupees)
Television	191.2	519.0
Print	127.9	232.0
Cinema	84.5	175.0
Radio	5.0	17.0
Music	7.2	8.7
Out-of-home	10.0	21.5
Live shows	9.0	19.0
Internet	1.6	9.5
	Total: 436.4 **(US$10 billion)**	**Total: 1,001.7** **(US$23.6 billion)**

Source: FICCI-PwC report, March 2007

television, and DVD rights for Hindi films. Like the IT industry 20 years earlier, a global mindset and corporate discipline are the watchwords for the Indian companies setting out to be the industry champions. Bahl, one of the shining new stars of India's corporate television scene, has also linked up with US entertainment major Viacom (owner of MTV, Paramount Pictures, and DreamWorks) to launch even more channels for Indian viewers. As well, the success of overseas television shows such *as The Kumars at No. 42*, crossover films *Bend it Like Beckham*, *Monsoon Wedding*, and *Bride and Prejudice*, and domestic blockbusters such as *Guru* and *Dhoom 2* are growing the entertainment industry pie. In a sense, they are just among the latest manifestations of how audiences outside India are responding to Indian talent, themes, and creativity. The reality is that Indian entertainment has been going global for two thousand years, particularly when India was at the height of its influence and the world's biggest economy a thousand years ago. Projecting India's "soft power" through art, literature, architecture, and philosophy goes back to the great Sanskrit epics the *Mahabharata* and the *Ramayana*, which were successfully exported to Asia, the Middle East, and Europe by traders and immigrants centuries before *The Tales of Genji* or the Arthurian legends appeared. The *Ramayana*, in particular, is the theme story for much of Southeast Asia's dance and drama, adorning the walls of Thailand's Grand Palace in Bangkok as the *Ramakien*, and being played out in the Wayang puppetry performances of Indonesia.

MEDIA BARONS EMERGE

While a handful of Indian film stars and directors achieve global recognition, it is India's television industry where some of the most important financial, technological, and socially influential decisions are being made. Here, the proliferation of television outlets – including 250 channels on offer to the country's 70 million cable and satellite households – is being accompanied by the emergence of powerful media barons as members of India's global wealth club. All of them have to be mindful of the political environment in which they operate, whether it be navigating India's complex regulatory shoals or dealing with local, state, and central government leaders. To catch the pulse of contemporary urban India, it can be instructive to flick across the 40 or so non-stop news channels available on cable. On the Bloomberg business channel, Mumbai-based stock market guru Rakesh Jhunjhunwala is telling his host why Indian share prices still have plenty of rocket propulsion left in them: "We're not in space yet. We'll get 25–30 times (earnings) in five years – just look at the quality of the profits," he says. On NDTV's morning talk show, author Salman Rushdie is promoting his latest book and lamenting sectarianism, gangsterism in politics, and the terrible violence that continues to afflict the incomparable Kashmir. "India, potentially, is right at the center of the world," he observes. "And Kashmir is so overwhelmingly beautiful, it lifts the heart." On another channel, the "Big B" himself, Bollywood superstar Amitabh Bachchan, is telling the world what a wonderful thing it is to have Aishwarya Rai as a daughter-in-law. Half a dozen other news programs lead with the reaction to a spat involving a UK *Big Brother* contestant and India's heroine and eventual winner Shilpa Shetty. (Shetty would become embroiled a few months later in a separate controversy in New Delhi, when, at an AIDS awareness rally, visiting US actor Richard Gere swept her into his arms and staged a lengthy "lip lock" that had the country's moral guardians in an uproar.) Elsewhere, the pundits are assessing the performance of leading man Shah Rukh Khan as he takes the host's hot seat on Star Plus for the TV quiz show *Kaun Banega Crorepati*, the hugely popular Indian version of *Who Wants To Be A Millionaire*. Channels in English, Hindi, Tamil, Telugu, Malayalam, Urdu, Gujarati, Marathi, Kannada, and Bengali are blossoming. The reason, of course, is money. India is on track to become the world's fifth-largest consumer market by 2025 behind the United States, China, Japan, and the United Kingdom, according to a May 2007 study by the McKinsey Global Institute.[3] Well before 2025, India's growing middle class will have purchasing power of immense proportions – retail spending will likely top US$500 billion by 2010.[4]

SUN SHINES IN THE SOUTH

From his base in Tamil Nadu's Chennai, politically connected TV tycoon Kalanithi Maran has already geared up to make sure those consumers will base their spending decisions on information and entertainment gleaned from the array of TV channels, radio stations, and print media offered by his Sun TV, the country's largest listed media group by market capitalization. With a population of seven million, Chennai is India's fourth-largest city and the south's economic capital, home to extensive automotive and IT industries. It was also where the Indian Ocean tsunami of 2004 delivered one of its many deadly blows, sweeping across the city's long Marina Beach promenade on Sunday morning, December 26, sucking 200 people out to sea and destroying fishing boats, cars, and buildings. The toll was heavier among fisherfolk up and down the Coromandel coast to the north and south of Chennai, and incomparably worse in Sri Lanka, Thailand, and Indonesia's Aceh province. But the shock to Chennai was enormous nonetheless.

The tsunami was the year's biggest story for Sun's news channels; its extensive coverage of the disaster and the relief effort helped bring the reality of the tragedy to global audiences. So, too, did the coverage of rival Tamil-language network Jaya TV, a strong supporter of Tamil Nadu's then incumbent chief minister J. Jayalalithaa. A vocal critic of the central government's handling of tsunami relief funds, Jayalalithaa lost office in May 2006 to a coalition led by Maran's great-uncle, M. Karunanidhi, enabling the veteran politician to take the chief minister's role for a fifth time. Maran, who started Sun in 1992 and is known for running a brutally efficient operation, has had to live with continuing speculation about the network and political influence; his younger brother Dayanidhi Maran was the central government's minister in charge of communications and information technology until he quit in May 2007 over a political spat. Kalanithi Maran was an early mover in offering high-quality Tamil-language TV fare to the citizens of southern India; that success has seen him replicate his offerings to audiences in the Telugu, Kannada, and Malayalam languages. Sun now runs 20 digital television channels in four languages, seven FM radio stations, a cable company, a newspaper, and magazines. In mid-2007, there was speculation of a future newspaper tie-up with global media magnate Rupert Murdoch's US-based News Corp. Despite having virtually no presence in the north of India, Maran is a formidable competitor to national rivals such as Subhash Chandra's Zee Group.

Chandra, another member of the global wealth club, has seen his share of ups and downs in the television industry. For virtually all of the 1990s, Chandra skillfully used Zee's first-mover advantage – he set up Zee TV as the country's first cable and satellite network in 1992 – to rule the overall ratings roost. After Hong Kong entrepreneur Richard Li sold a controlling stake in satellite broadcaster Star TV to Rupert Murdoch in 1993, Chandra's Zee had a joint venture with Star covering its Indian operations. But it was a difficult relationship, and the parties finally split in late 1999. Star and Sony Entertainment Television (SET) gradually overhauled Zee from 2000 onwards, using

innovative programming in sports, game shows, and soapies. Star has
been No. 1 since about 2001, while Zee has since regained the No. 2
spot from SET.

On the comeback trail, Chandra restructured his group in 2007,
splitting it into three listed entities led by Zee Entertainment Enterprises, which contains the broadcast and general entertainment assets.
Dish TV has the direct-to-home business, and Wire & Wireless has the
cable distribution. Chandra had already spun off Zee News in 2006 as
the news-gathering entity. The four companies' combined market
capitalization in mid-2007 was almost US$4.5 billion. Chandra and his
younger brothers Laxmi N. Goel, Jawahar Goel, and Ashok Goel
(Chandra dropped the "Goel" from his name in protest over caste-
based politics) run various parts of the Essel Group, which in turn
controls Zee. Chandra's network and programs have global reach: Zee
TV has been in the United Kingdom and Europe since 1995, and in
North America, Africa, and Asia since 1998. Chandra also has 50% of
Dubai-based Taj TV and 60% of a small Indian news agency, UNI.
After the split with Chandra, Murdoch's television partner in India
for his Star News operation is now the Kolkata-based ABP Group,
controlled by Aveek Sarkar and family. ABP owns the largest Bengali
daily, *Ananda Bazaar Patrika*, the English daily *The Telegraph*, and
TV interests.

MARKET POTENTIAL AHEAD

About 48% of India's households have no access to television, indicat-
ing the potential ahead for Maran, Chandra, Subrata Roy Sahara's
Sahara TV, the listed NDTV Group of Prannoy and Radhika Roy, and
other players, including relative newcomers such as Bahl's TV18
Group. TV18's properties include Global Broadcast News, which runs
the high-rating CNN-IBN news channel and CNBC-TV18. Anil
Ambani's Reliance Capital owns a piece of Bahl's holding company,
Network 18.

Bahl says that rationalization in the media industry is inevitable,
although he expects all the major existing players to survive in some
form or another. "There will be consolidation at the national and
regional level, and between formats such as print and television," he
says.[5] Another big player is the Jain family's unlisted Times Group,
which bills itself as India's largest media and entertainment house.
Along with flagship English-language newspapers *The Times of India*
and *The Economic Times*, the group runs the Zoom lifestyle channel

and the Times Now TV news venture with Reuters, plus a swag of other properties that include Radio Mirchi – India's largest FM radio network, the Planet M chain of music stores, Hindi and Marathi daily newspapers, specialist magazines, and internet portals focused on jobs, real estate, and matrimony. It has also taken stakes in a string of other companies involved in media content and technology. Led by educationalist and entrepreneur Indu Jain, widow of the late Ashok K. Jain, the Jain family controls Bennett, Coleman Co. Ltd. (BCCL), the company that publishes the Times Group newspapers. Although it is unlisted, annual turnover and earnings figures suggest that BCCL could be valued at about US$4 billion, which would put its owners well into the global wealth club. Indu Jain is BCCL's chair, while sons Samir and Vineet are vice-chairman/managing director and managing director, respectively. The brothers hold direct stakes in both BCCL and BCCL's three biggest shareholders, Bharat Nidhi Ltd., Camac Commercial Co. Ltd., and Ashok Viniyoga Ltd.[6]

Competition is everywhere, and newcomers are sniffing around the scene. BCCL's *The Economic Times*, for example, must do battle with another national business daily, *Mint*, launched in 2007 by HT Media – publisher of *Hindustan Times* – with the backing of *The Wall Street Journal*. HT Media is controlled by industrialist K.K. Birla, a member of one of India's greatest business dynasties, the Birla family. K.K.'s daughter, Shobhana Bhartia, wife of wealth club member Shyam Bhartia (founder of Jubilant Organosys), is vice-chairperson and editorial director. K.K. writes occasional opinion pieces for the newspaper in his capacity as a former parliamentarian. Adding to the competition mix is the London-based Pearson Group, publisher of the *Financial Times*, which has a 26% stake in the *Business Standard* newspaper. Another overseas investor is Irish tycoon Tony O'Reilly, whose Independent News & Media has a 21% stake in Hindi publisher Jagran Prakashan Ltd. (JPL), controlled by Mahendra Mohan Gupta and his son Sanjay Gupta. JPL, based in Kanpur, Uttar Pradesh, publishes India's most-read newspaper, *Dainik Jagran*, which has 31 separate editions and about 20 million readers. JPL's Jagran.com claims to be the world's largest Hindi portal, and has joined forces with Yahoo India to further boost the site's reach and influence. JPL has also launched *I-next*, a compact daily in Hindi and English that targets younger readers. The senior Gupta, who is a member of India's upper house (the Rajya Sabha), is JPL's chairman, while son Sanjay is CEO. As a consequence of the equity link, JPL prints a version of O'Reilly's *The Independent* newspaper. The Guptas also have interests in radio and satellite television. Among the other heavy hitters of the Indian print world is Chennai-based Kasturi & Sons, publisher of *The Hindu*, an English-language daily that has been rated among the best newspapers in the world. In a variety of forms, the Kasturi family has owned the newspaper since 1905. Though regarded as conservative in appearance and editorial tone, *The Hindu* was the first Indian newspaper to introduce color, the first to transmit pages by facsimile, and the first to create an internet site, in 1995.

From Bhopal in Madhya Pradesh, Ramesh C. Agarwal and sons Sudhir, Girish, and Pawan run the Bhaskar Group, publisher of the Hindi newspaper *Dainik Bhaskar* (readership 15 million), the Gujarati newspaper *Divya Bhaskar*, and the bright and breezy *DNA* (Daily News & Analysis) English-language newspaper in a joint venture with Zee's Chandra in Mumbai. The Agarwals, dubbed potentially "the masters of middle India" by *India Today* magazine, also have interests in television, FM radio, the internet, and entertainment.[7] *India Today* itself is part of Aroon Purie's The India Today Group, which publishes 13 magazines in six languages, runs three radio stations, and owns the *Today* tabloid newspaper in New Delhi, a book publishing operation, and the listed company TV Today, which runs the top-rating Hindi news channel Aaj Tak and three other channels.

One of the most aggressive players in the media space is T. Venkattram Reddy, whose listed Deccan Chronicle Holdings (DCH) publishes the English-language *Deccan Chronicle* from Hyderabad and Chennai, and its sister paper the *Asian Age* from Delhi, Mumbai, Kolkata, Bangalore, and London. Reddy, who owns the Odyssey India retail book chain, also includes aviation among his business interests, having set up India's first dedicated cargo airline, Flyington Freighters, to run between India and Dubai, China, and Africa. Reddy has committed US$1 billion to buy six Airbus A330–200F jets between 2008 and 2010. Reddy and family hold a stake of about 63% in DCH, which had a market capitalization in mid-2007 of about US$1 billion. DCH is aiming to lift revenue from US$130 million in 2007 to about US$180 million in 2008, after a Bangalore edition of the *Deccan Chronicle* is launched. In one of the largest deals in India's media sector, US private equity firm Blackstone Group has invested US$275 million for a 26% stake in Hyderabad-based Ramoji Rao's Ushodaya Enterprises Ltd., which owns the leading Telugu-language newspaper *Eenadu* and Eenadu TV. Separately, Rao owns Ramoji Film City, a huge production studio located outside Hyderabad.

STRATEGIC PARTNERSHIPS

According to FICCI Secretary General Amit Mitra, the age of convergence is helping create "media powerhouses" as partners all along the value chain join forces to create new products and services.[8] Existing heavyweights such as the Times Group, HT Media, Jagan Prakash Ltd., Deccan Chronicle, Zee Group, and Sun TV are taking strategic stakes in new players, bringing in joint venture partners, and setting up cashboxes that will fund film production and distribution, open more TV channels and radio stations, and create mobile media and what they hope will be money-making internet portals. Newcomers such as Reliance Entertainment – which owns film distribution major AdLabs and has ambitions in music, sports, and gaming – are entering the fray, too, and international media groups are angling to see where they can fit in, as incredibly cool India expands its global footprint. "Increased foreign direct investment in India media groups is a given," says Raghav Bahl. "India now is probably the largest untapped media market in the world, so foreign interest is high."[9]

Essentially, all of India's movers and shakers in the media and entertainment industry are scrambling to take advantage of what will be an explosion in demand from India's cashed-up middle class, and high levels of interest in India from offshore markets such as the Middle East, North America, Europe, and Asia. "Entertainment is no longer a luxury," Percept Holdings managing director Shailendra Singh noted recently as he outlined the Indian advertising, media, and talent management group's goal of becoming a US$1 billion revenue company by 2010.[10] Singh, son of Percept Holdings founder Mangal Singh, says that with India's young adult population having access to "unprecedented levels" of disposable income, the challenge is to identify opportunities and create essential content. It's a view that resonates throughout the industry: content and credibility is to entertainment and media what location is to real estate. Which means the eventual successors to TimeWarner, Viacom, Walt Disney Company, Sony Entertainment, Pearson, and Reuters may well be working up their expansion plans inside a Mumbai studio, newsroom, or coffee house now.

The danger for India's media and entertainment industry is not so much the inroads of piracy or a downturn in the economic growth story. Bahl, for one, believes the size of the Indian economy and its diversity and segmentation by language and region means that it can support multiple media outlets. In television, he sees three financial challenges: first, Indian brands and industries have shown no great propensity to advertise, so it is a tough struggle to grow the advertising base; second, there is huge fragmentation of audiences, which impacts on revenue streams; and third, distribution is "completely disorganized," with what Bahl terms "incorrect technology, entry barriers, and unregulated monopolies" as India ushers in the creation of a genuine subscription-supported cable TV market. He says that among the last-mile operators, there is considerable piracy and underreporting of subscriptions.[11] These operators, often with ties to mobsters and local politicians, want to keep their stranglehold on cable distribution. But they must contend with the advance of direct-to-home (DTH) broadcasting from groups such as state-run Doordarshan, Chandra's Dish TV, the Star and Tata Group joint venture Tata Sky, and new players such as Maran's Sun Direct and Anil Ambani's Reliance Blue Magic.

In the scheme of things, these are the simple technical and financial hurdles any aspiring media baron expects to confront. As always, it is the perpetual tensions of caste, creed, custom, color, ethnicity, poverty, language, and political loyalties that threaten to undo India's creative cascade. In late 2006, *Show Business* author Shashi Tharoor, nearing the end of a distinguished career at the UN that took him almost to the Secretary General's chair, touched on this when he spoke at an Indian economic forum in Philadelphia. "In realizing the Indian dream," Tharoor said, "I hope for an India that is unafraid of the outside world and frees up the creative energy of its people. My dream is for a pluralist land that celebrates its diversity."[12] With hundreds of TV channels and multiple print, radio, film, and internet outlets, India looks to have enough media to handle that diversity.

ENDNOTES

1. Shashi Tharoor, *Show Business* (New Delhi: Penguin Books, 1991).
2. Report by PricewaterhouseCoopers for the Federation of Indian Chambers of Commerce and Industry, *Indian Entertainment and Media Industry: A Growth Story Unfolds,* released in Mumbai, March 26, 2007.
3. Report by the McKinsey Global Institute, *Bird of Gold*, released May 2007.
4. Current Size & Future Projections for Indian Retail Market, analysis by Technopak Advisors, updated March 2007.
5. Telephone interview with Raghav Bahl, May 24, 2007.
6. From draft prospectus for HT Media, lodged with the Securities & Exchange Board of India, April 2005.

7. In "Power List 2007," *India Today*, March 26, 2007.
8. FICCI-Frames conference on Indian entertainment industry, Mumbai, March 26–28, 2007.
9. Bahl, op. cit.
10. Shailendra Singh, media release "Percept headed to become US$1 billion company by 2010," July 31, 2006.
11. Bahl, op. cit.
12. Shashi Tharoor, address to the Wharton India Economic Forum, Philadelphia, November 11, 2006.

CHAPTER EIGHT

Telecommunications: Making the Call

Telecom in India will grow big enough to support voice free. Operators could make money through data services.

—Former Communications Minister,
Dayanidhi Maran[1]

Cheap phones and cheap plans mean that even the hundreds of millions of Indian consumers at the bottom of the pyramid are now able to make a phone call – something that would have been unthinkable a decade ago. Ninety percent of the money flowing into Indian phone companies comes from voice traffic, so Dayanidhi Maran's idea that one day a phone call will be free isn't necessarily something the phone company owners want to see happen soon. So, will consumers pay for data? As the humble mobile phone morphs into a communications hub, India is becoming a testing ground for value-added services: SMS and email, internet access, mobile TV content such as sports and entertainment programs, advertising and shopping destination directions, downloads of ring tones, movie previews and music video clips, and the "point and pay" abilities of the smartest handsets. But a mature data market is still some way off – for now, it's all about voice. Everybody's talking, and everyone wants to be No. 1 in the Indian phone services market, where half a dozen big players jostle for a share of a mobile customer base that is likely to hit 200 million by the end of 2007 and as many as 500 million by March 2010. Third-placed Essar Group vice-chairman Ravi Ruia, who began 2007 with a new partner after Vodafone bought out Hong Kong tycoon Li Ka-shing's Hutchison for US$11.1 billion plus US$2 billion in debt, says he looks forward to building "the most valuable telecom company in India."[2] Second-ranked Anil Ambani says his Reliance

Table 8.1 India's Big Six Telecommunications Companies

	Number of mobile customers (in millions), End May 2007	Market capitalization (US$ billion), June 2007
1. Bharti Airtel	40.70	$39.12
2. Reliance Communications	30.50	$25.64
3. Vodafone Essar (Hutchison)	29.20	Unlisted
4. BSNL	27.99	Unlisted
5. Tata Indicom	16.76	$1.25 (Tata Teleservices)
6. Idea Cellular	15.30	$8.16

Total (all companies): 175.83 million, made up of GSM (global system for mobile communications) 130.6 million, and CDMA (code division multiple access) 45.23 million.
Sources: Celullar Operators Association of India; Association of Unified Telecom Service Providers of India

Communications is one of Asia's five most valuable telecom companies and will take connectivity to the world.[3] But the man who clearly is No. 1 in this fast-growing and hotly contested market is another member of India's global wealth club, Sunil Bharti Mittal, whose Bharti Airtel has 40 million mobile customers and aims to have 125 million by 2010 (see Table 8.1).[4]

HARD TIMES

Mittal, named Asia's "Businessman of the Year" by *Fortune* magazine in January 2007, has been top of the heap for some time, and has no intention of giving ground to other competitors that include such powerful names as Birla (Idea Cellular), Tata (Tata Indicom/VSNL), and state-owned BSNL. "We are delighted to be leading the telecom revolution in the country," Mittal told shareholders after the company reported a profit of US$1 billion on revenues of US$4.35 billion for the year to March 2007.[5] It wasn't always like this. While Mittal could see the potential for a transformational business after India deregulated and threw open the telecommunications sector to private enterprise in 1991/92, the early days were hard. A huge number of domestic and overseas participants crowded into the sector; at one time or another the Hindujas, the Goenkas, the Nandas, Rajeev

Chandrasekhar of BPL Telecom, C. Sivasankaran of Aircel, France Telecom, AT&T, Cingular, Telecom Italia, British Telecom, SingTel, Australia's Telstra, and Malaysia's Maxis have all been active in India's market. Mittal endured a decade of losses as he painstakingly built a cellular phone network across the nation, securing licenses for ever more "circles" (service areas) as other companies went to the wall or sold out to rivals. Mittal didn't see a profit from mobile telephony until 2004. But in the past few years he has ridden the consumer growth wave more skillfully than his competitors. A key reason is that he doesn't have to worry about the detail of Bharti Airtel's network infrastructure, resource management, and maintenance; he's outsourced that to European telecom equipment majors such as Ericsson, Nortel, and Nokia, leaving him free to concentrate on his customers. All his company's energy can go into making the phone user's experience as trouble-free (and profitable to Bharti Airtel) as possible, through services, content, tariff plans, and handset offers. With a market capitalization at June 2007 of more than US$39 billion (up from just US$1 billion in 2003, when the share price began the year at just 23.50 rupees, or about 55 cents), Bharti Airtel is more than 50% larger than second-ranked Reliance Communications. Vodafone Essar is worth perhaps US$20 to US$25 billion, Idea Cellular is valued at US$8 billion, and the yet-to-be-listed BSNL may well come in around US$30 billion.

Mittal plans to invest US$8 billion in rolling out 3G and other services, along with related phone infrastructure, to win and hold a 25% market share by 2010. At mid-2007 he had about 23% of the total mobile market and has a handy lead among companies offering GSM services.[6] In the CDMA sector, Anil Ambani's Reliance dominates, out-punching Tata and small regional players such as Shyam and HFCL. Reliance also has a small presence in GSM. If Mittal hits his target of 125 million customers and keeps his average revenue per user at the current 343 rupees per month, he is looking at revenue of more than US$12 billion a year, making Bharti Airtel a significant global player by any standard. The company is only the 10th in the world (and the first in India) to cross the 40-million mobile customer mark. But telecom is just a part of Mittal's big game plan, which includes such other Bharti enterprises as life insurance, fresh food production, and retail, including a joint venture with Wal-Mart. He says he is stepping back from daily management in October 2007 to scan the horizon for the next big wave to ride.

BUILDING A BACKBONE

Just as Mittal is looking beyond the mobile phone business, so too is Anil Ambani. His goal is the oft-sought one of convergence: integrating his telecommunications interests with his media and entertainment assets, allowing him to produce and distribute content to multiple users on multiple platforms in multiple locations. The 71,400-mile (115,000-kilometer) Internet Protocol (IP) network being built by Reliance Communications subsidiary FLAG Telecom is the backbone that he believes will enable him to reach out to broadband, 3G, and 4G customers virtually anywhere in the globe by the end of 2009. About 40,360 miles (65,000 kilometers) of fiber optic cable is already in place between India, North America, Europe, and the Middle East. Ambani, who plans to list FLAG on the London Stock Exchange, says that once completed, the full network will "democratize digital access" and give five billion people in the world the opportunity to be part of a "massive lifestyle change."[7] Ambani says that his late father, Dhirubhai, dreamt of "a global village where everyone, but most of all every Indian, would have the chance to communicate and connect, compete and collaborate."[8]

Leaving aside state-owned BSNL, which with 64 million mobile and fixed-line customers is by far the biggest telco in India, Vodafone Essar (formerly Hutch Essar) ranks No. 3 behind Bharti and Reliance among private sector players. It had 30 million mobile users at the end of May 2007, well ahead of the Birla Group's Idea Cellular with 15.3 million, and CDMA operator Tata Indicom with 16.76 million. Essar, controlled by the brothers Shashi and Ravi Ruia, finds itself in a good place, with a 33% stake in its telco venture, more than 2,600 transmission towers already built, and a chain of 2,000 retail outlets to help sell its services, handsets, and accessories, in association with Richard Branson's Virgin Group. More importantly, it has the technological expertise of Vodafone, the world's biggest mobile phone operator, as India moves into the 3G world. Nor does it hurt that Vodafone CEO Arun Sarin, a graduate from the Indian Institute of Technology Kharagpur, knows more about India than any of his global competitors. It's not surprising, then, that Ravi Ruia is upbeat about having Vodafone as his new partner after Hutchison sold out. "Together we expect to bring to Indian consumers an entirely new experience in mobile telephony," he says.[9]

Likewise, Kumar M. Birla feels good vibrations from his US$8 billion Idea Cellular, which made a spectacular debut on the Indian

stock market in March 2007 as the first new company listed by the
Birla Group in a decade. Birla, recalling how his late father Aditya
V. Birla envisioned a great company in the making when the Birlas
set up a joint venture with the US telco AT&T, said: "We exult in the
fulfilment of my father's dream."[10] That joint venture in turn became
a three-way relationship in 1995 between Birla, AT&T, and the Tatas,
with the parties each holding a one-third share. After AT&T Wireless
merged with Cingular in 2004, AT&T sold its stake to its Indian partners. But Tata's own ambitions with its CDMA operator Tata Indicom
complicated Idea's move into the key Mumbai market, resulting in
Birla companies buying out Tata's stake in Idea in mid-2006 after
some acrimonious debate. With ownership now sorted, Birla says Idea
is a brand that epitomises "vim, vigour, innovation and customer
care" and is central to the Birla Group's plans. "We will be providing
unflinching support to it," he said on the day of its listing.[11] But with
a national market share of 8.6%, Idea has a long chase ahead if it is
to close the gap on Bharti, Reliance, and Vodafone Essar.

GETTING ATTENTION

India is adding between five and six million mobile customers a month
– the sort of turbocharged growth that means it is destined to challenge China for the mantle of the world's biggest mobile market.
Reliance alone reported it sold a record one million handsets in the
first week of May 2007. Numbers like that get India plenty of attention
from phone makers. When Nokia launched seven new phones in 2007
designed specifically for customers in emerging markets, New Delhi
was a natural launch venue. The Finnish phone maker's 1200 and 1208
series phones are aimed at first-time users, and incorporate phone-
sharing and call-tracking technology – a vital marketing point in India
where mobile phones can expect to be handed around among a group
of rural users. It means village phone entrepreneurs can preset a time
or cost limit that will automatically end a call after the limit is reached.
Nokia backs its Indian manufacturing operations – which churn out
six million handsets a month – with R&D facilities in Bangalore,
Hyderabad, and Mumbai. Other global handset makers such as Sony
Ericsson, LG, and Samsung have similar ambitions.

Despite the mammoth numbers, India's telephone romance
remains a story of two parts in which, as always, the rural market is
the ugly duckling. Teledensity, or the number of phones available to

the population, is 55–65% in the megacities of Mumbai and Delhi, but just 2% for rural India. Nationally, the figure is 18%.[12] By 2010, if government planners are right, rural subscribers should reach 80 million, giving a teledensity of 20%. In urban India, the figure will be above 85% and could reach saturation levels a few years later. Of course, there are challenges aplenty for the private phone companies. One is that internet telephony, with its promise of virtually free calls, is still in its infancy in India but is destined to grow as broadband availability takes off. That, in the view of some players, gives internet service providers a back-door entry to the phone market. Another is that while handset prices are getting low enough for the poor to buy them, the returns may not be there to justify rural expansion. The major constraints are network infrastructure and the cost of delivering phone services. While mobile operators now share transmission towers, many thousands more than the existing 6,000 towers are needed to fill in reception gaps and cope with the increasing number of users. Unstable and erratic power supplies, particularly in the hot summer months and in rural areas, weighs on service availability and network management. Overburdened networks already irritate customers, particularly in Mumbai and Delhi where mobile calls often drop out. A customer satisfaction survey released by *Voice & Data* magazine in January 2007 found only Bharti Airtel and Tata Indicom were above the 90% benchmark set by the industry regulator.

LUXURY ITEM

Before the great deregulation advances of 1991/92, telephones were a luxury in India and waiting times for a home or business connection could stretch for years. But according to comments in a report by the Boston Consulting Group (BCG),[13] the very fact that phones were seen as a luxury, and not a necessity, enabled telecommunications to skirt the sort of political roadblocks that faced the power sector, where state governments and other interests were capable of derailing or delaying investment proposals. The BCG report quotes industry expert Ravi Aron, a senior fellow at the Wharton School's Mack Center for Technological Innovation in Philadelphia, as noting: "A lot more needs to be done. But compared to power, ports and road, [telecom] is an extraordinary fairy tale with a happy ending."[14] For some consumers, though, the happy ending is still a little way off. That will come with rural teledensity of 100%, always-on broadband reaching into the remotest village, stable and crystal-clear reception in the megacities, and free voice calls for all. The next challenge for global wealth club members such as Mittal, Ambani, Ruia, Birla, and Tata will then be to make money in changed circumstances. Adapt, innovate, create. Or as CNN television news founder Ted Turner was fond of reminding himself: "Lead, follow, or get out of the way."

ENDNOTES

1. Comments by then-Minister of Communications & Information Technology Dayanidhi Maran in interview "Rural connectivity is centerstage," *Business India*, May 6, 2007, p. 68.
2. Statement by Ravi Ruia on Vodafone acquisition, May 9, 2007.
3. Statement by Anil Ambani on Reliance Communications' full-year results, April 30, 2007.
4. Statement by Sunil Bharti Mittal on Bharti Airtel's full-year results, April 27, 2007 and media release, "Bharti Airtel breaks into 40 million mobile customer club," May 23, 2007.
5. ibid.
6. Statistics released by Cellular Operators Association of India, May 2007.
7. Statement by Anil Ambani on FLAG Telecom's next generation network, December 28, 2006.
8. ibid.
9. Ruia, op. cit.
10. Statement by Kumar Mangalam Birla in "An idea whose time has come," released by Aditya V. Birla Group, Mumbai, March 9, 2007.
11. ibid.
12. Statement by Dayanidhi Maran on "Vision 2010" at CEOs Roundtable, New Delhi, December 14, 2006.
13. Boston Consulting Group and Knowledge@Wharton, "What's Next for India: Beyond the Back Office," February 15, 2007.
14. ibid.

Industry: Men of Steel

*Do you mean to say that the Tatas propose to make
steel rails to British specifications? Why, I will under-
take to eat every pound of steel rail they succeed in
making.*
        —Sir Frederick Upcott, Chief Commissioner,
        Great Indian Peninsular Railway, circa 1907[1]

Serendipity is a marvelous thing, including for Indian business
tycoons. Ratan Tata had no trouble making a compelling case
to the Tata Group board to take over the much larger European steel
major Corus early in 2007 for US$12 billion. The deal stacked up on
price and potential, but it was the Corus antecedents that added
piquancy to the mix. Peel away a few layers of the London-head-
quartered company, and lurking beneath could be found the old
British Steel, which had rescued itself from troubled times through a
merger in October 1999 with Dutch steelmaker Hoogovens to form
Corus. In Mumbai, Ratan Tata refrained from gloating about
colonial-era myopism, instead observing that the Tata Group was
optimistic that it could "extract benefits from the acquisition in different scenarios."[2] One such scenario is entry to high-end markets in
Europe. With an expected 27 million tonnes of crude steel production
in 2007, the merged Tata–Corus entity becomes the world's fifth-
largest steel producer, with 84,000 employees across four continents.
When the acquisition was formally completed in April 2007, Ratan
Tata called it an exciting time and noted: "I firmly believe that both
Tata Steel and Corus, two companies with long, proud histories, share
a common business culture and a global vision for the business."[3]

Though Lakshmi Mittal's takeover of Arcelor in 2006 was a far
bigger acquisition, Tata Steel's Corus deal is seen by entrepreneurs
such as Infosys founder N.R. Narayana Murthy as a defining moment
in the history of Indian business. Finance Minister P. Chidambaram

says it reflects "the new-found confidence of Indian industry." Within weeks of the Corus deal, Kumar M. Birla's Hindalco bought Canadian aluminum giant Novelis for US$6 billion, while the Ruia brothers' Essar Steel paid US$1.6 billion for another Canadian company, steel-maker Algoma, and committed to buying Minnesota Steel of the US for about US$1.6 billion. In May, Vijay Mallya's United Spirits kept the momentum going, buying Scotch maker Whyte and Mackay for about US$1.1 billion, and Dilip Shanghvi's Sun Pharma followed with a US$450 million takeover of Israeli generic drug maker Taro Pharma. Certainly, the pace of India's global acquisitions has picked up in recent years: Anand Mahindra's M&M, Azim Premji's Wipro, Habil Khorakiwala's Wockhardt, the Singh family's Ranbaxy Laboratories, Baba Kalyani's Bharat Forge, Tulsi Tanti's Suzlon, and K. Anji Reddy's Dr. Reddy's Laboratories are all among the buyers. It runs both ways: Anil Agarwal's London-based Vedanta Resources has bought a stake in Sesa Goa for US$1 billion, and Vodafone created headlines with its acquisition of a majority stake in Hutch Essar that valued the telco at about US$19 billion.

ORIGINS IN JAMSHEDPUR

The Corus deal comes a century after the Tatas began work on a plant in Jharkhand state, 155 miles (250 kilometers) west of Kolkata, from where they produced their first steel in 1912. This became the focus of the town of Jamshedpur, named after the founder of the house of Tata, Jamsetji N. Tata (1839–1904). As a trader and entrepreneur, Tata observed firsthand the impact of the Industrial Revolution on the British economy in the second half of the 19th century, and could see the potential for India in textiles, steel, and power. He devoted much of the last two decades of his life to these projects. In a letter he wrote to his son Dorab Tata in 1902, he discussed not just the site of a steel plant, but his concept for a township to house the workers. "Be sure to lay wide streets planted with shady trees, every other of a quick-growing variety," he told him. "Be sure that there is plenty of space for lawns and gardens. Reserve large areas for football, hockey and parks. Earmark areas for Hindu temples, Mohammedan mosques and Christian churches."[4] Today, the Tata steel plant at Jamshedpur produces four million tonnes a year of hot and cold rolled flat and long products, drawing on iron ore and coal from its own mines and collieries. Tata is just one of half a dozen leading steel-makers in India who, between them in 2007, will produce about 50 million tonnes – much of it for use in meeting the country's growing need for infrastructure.

According to the Brussels-based International Iron & Steel Institute (IISI), India was the world's seventh-largest steel producer in 2006 with 44 million tonnes, up 11.5% from the previous year.[5] China dominates global output, with 419 million tonnes, or 34% of the record 1.24 billion tonnes of crude steel produced in 2006. It is followed by Japan with 116 million tonnes, the United States with 98.5 million tonnes, then Russia, South Korea, and Germany. On a regional basis, the European Union followed China with about 180 million tonnes, with North America third on 132 million tonnes. Among individual companies, Lakshmi Mittal's merged Arcelor Mittal is the top producer with 109.7 million tonnes, a long way ahead of second-placed Nippon Steel. Viewed against that backdrop, the plans of Tata and other Indian steelmakers such as Essar, the Jindals, and Ispat (the family company that Lakshmi Mittal forsook to make his own way internationally) seem puny in comparison. But they are indicative of the mood of optimism that now permeates the Indian industry.

COMEBACK FOR ESSAR

For the Mumbai-based Ruia family, its Essar Steel operation is looking good, with a 50% production boost to its Hazira plant in Gujarat state completed in 2006, a 2.5 million tonne plant under construction in Trinidad and Tobago, a new integrated facility planned for its Minnesota Steel acquisition, and a two million tonne hot strip mill on the drawing board for Vietnam. By 2015, Essar's total annual steel production could reach 30 million tonnes, split half and half between its Indian and overseas plants. Yet, less than a decade ago, steel looked like it might drag the Ruias's Essar Group into oblivion. From US$400 a tonne in the mid-1990s, steel prices plunged to a 20-year low of US$180 a tonne in 1998, and an expansion of the group's production capacity that was funded almost entirely by short-term debt brought terrible pressures at exactly the wrong time. In July 1999, Essar Steel suffered the ignominy of being the first Indian borrower to default on foreign debt – a US$250 million eurobond. Nor did it help that Essar also had embarked on ambitious investment plans in other sectors such as power, oil, and telecom. But the Ruias were patient, and so were their creditors and investors. When the growth cycle picked up again a few years later, Essar Steel was well placed to ride the upturn. Its operations were low-cost, and it had a handle on the entire value chain, from mining its own iron ore to producing pellets and turning out high-quality steel for the automotive industry at the Hazira plant. Today, it is India's largest exporter of flat steel and operates the world's largest gas-based sponge iron plant. Shashi Ruia's elder son Prashant is seen as the driving force on the steel side and the man who brought the US and Canada steel acquisitions to the boardroom table. On the energy front, the surging price of oil has boosted revenue: Essar Oil's refining capacity at Vadinar is being expanded from 10.5 million tonnes to 16 million tonnes. The Ruias like their privacy – so much so, they have decided to take their main Indian-listed companies Essar Steel, Essar Oil, and Essar Shipping private, under their Essar Global Limited. Announcing its delisting plans for Essar Steel in January 2007, the group said: "The delisting of equity shares will offer more flexibility in the operations and management of the company, greater efficiencies and at the same time provide an exit opportunity for the shareholders of Essar Steel."[6]

Another key name on the Indian steel scene is that of the Jindal Group, which is the country's largest producer of stainless steel and a significant overseas investor. A helicopter crash in April 2005 claimed the life of Om Prakash (O.P.) Jindal, known as "the steel man of Hisar" and one of India's most powerful industrialists. His widow, Savitri, now chairs the overall Jindal Group and the four main companies, which were operationally dispersed by O.P. Jindal to their four sons – Prithviraj, Sajjan, Ratan, and Naveen – while he was still alive. The main listed entity is JSW Steel (run by Sajjan), which accounts for about half the group's total US$4 billion annual turnover, though Jindal Stainless is credited as the flagship company. Next in size is Jindal Steel & Power (run by Naveen), followed by Jindal SAW (the former SAW Pipes Ltd.). This is run by the eldest son, Prithviraj, whose daughter Sminu, a graduate of Delhi's Fore School of Management in 1997, is the company's managing director. Ratan runs Jindal Stainless, where his goal is to be among the world's top 10 stainless steel producers by 2010. Ratan also leads the Jindal Group's finance company. The Jindals operate 12 plants in India and two at Baytown, Texas in the United States, producing steel plate and SAW (submerged arc welded) pipes. Jindal Stainless is investing about US$1.4 billion on the first stage of a new integrated stainless steel plant in Orissa state that will have an eventual capacity of 1.6 million tonnes, while JSW Steel plans to raise capacity to 6.8 million tonnes by 2010 and invest about US$1.75 billion between 2007 and 2010 in plant expansion.[7]

MORE OF THE MITTALS

India's biggest private sector producer of hot rolled coils is Ispat Industries, the Mumbai-based steelmaker set up by Lakshmi Mittal's father, Mohan Lal Mittal, in 1985 as Nippon Denro Ispat Ltd. Lakshmi's younger brother Pramod is chairman, while youngest brother Vinod is managing director. Ispat Industries is the flagship of the Mittal family's Ispat Group (*ispat* is the Hindi word for steel), set up in 1952 when M.L. Mittal bought a rolling mill in Kolkata. Mittal senior began experimenting with an electric arc furnace at Vizag, a port city on the Indian east coast, and over the next 20 years set up nine greenfield plants in India using the new technology. In 1974 he made his first venture offshore, establishing Ispat Indo in Indonesia (where Lakshmi would spend some of his formative years in the steel business), and expanded over the next few years with plants in Trinidad and Tobago, Mexico, Canada, Germany, and Ireland. In 1985, Ispat Industries was established and soon became India's largest private sector maker of galvanized steel products. By 1989, Lakshmi Mittal had set up Ispat International, and five years later he split from the family steel business to make his own way globally, with spectacular results that have brought him the title of the world's "Man of Steel." His father and Lakshmi's two younger brothers have kept a mainly domestic focus, running their overseas operations in South Africa, Europe, and Asia through Global Steel Holdings, the majority shareholder in Ispat. They have their own expansion plans nonetheless for the Ispat Group, which also operates in mining, energy, and infrastructure. Ispat's main industrial complex at Dolvi in Maharashtra state houses its three million tonne hot rolled coil plant and a 1.6 million tonne sponge iron plant. Ispat plans to lift capacity at Dolvi to five million tonnes by the end of 2008 and later to 10 million tonnes. It also plans to build a US$1.7 billion steel plant in Jharkand state with a capacity of 2.8 million tonnes.[8]

POWER SHORTAGE

Much of the steel being produced by Tata, Essar, Jindal, and Ispat is going into the construction of Indian infrastructure, including roads, railway lines, ports, dams, and power stations. Though all of India's infrastructure needs are critical, it is perhaps in the power sector where the shortcomings are felt most acutely. It is a problem only too apparent during high summer in Mumbai, when India's "maximum city" can barely cope. As air-conditioning units kick in throughout the high-rise apartments that front the Arabian Sea, the power grid creaks under the strain, then starts load-shedding. That means it's brownout time in the city that aspires to commercial and financial leadership in South Asia – hardly a good starting point. Inadequate infrastructure and incompetent planning similarly mean that Maharashtra state, where power should be plentiful, is on its knees, losing up to nine hours a day. Companies are forced to use costly "captive power" – their own generators – to give them some chance of a reliable supply. Other big cities such as Delhi and Bangalore also face debilitating brownouts during the hot summer months, while the worst-hit states have load-shedding for 12 hours a day and Indian businesses report losing as much as 9% of their production because of power shortages, compared to just 2% in China. Electricity theft, corruption, wastage, inefficient transmission, outdated technology, delays caused by bureaucratic rivalry, poor pricing, natural disasters, and lawlessness all play a part in creating a grim power scenario for consumers and business. A report on India's energy outlook by professional services firm KPMG in May 2007 finds the country will need to spend up to US$150 billion on power sector investments over the next five years to fuel the economy. "Energy transport infrastructure such as ports, railways, pipelines and power transmission networks need significant investment," it notes.[9] India has an installed capacity of about 130,000 MW, which is about 20,000 MW below what it needs to be able to safely meet peak demand and cope with energy losses during transmission. Crucially, the KPMG report is worried about these distribution losses. "Power utilities in India suffer from a very high level of network losses of as much as 30 to 40 percent due to theft, pilferage and non-collection of dues, and also due to the state of the network involving long low voltage lines," it says.[10] KPMG also notes that by world standards, India's energy usage is very low, with per capita consumption of 531 kilograms of oil equivalent (kgoe) in 2004/05. That compares with 1,242 kgoe for China, 4,176 kgoe for Japan, and 7,913 kgoe for the United States.[11] But over the next 25 years it expects India's energy requirement to quadruple. Where will all that power come from, who will build and distribute it, and who will pay for it? And what sort of energy conservation measures should the country be adopting? These are the questions that India's planners need to address. The energy supply base includes coal, oil, gas, nuclear, hydro, renewable sources such as solar, biomass, and wind power, and low-grade sources such as firewood and animal dung, which account for much of the energy generated in rural communities. India has large coal reserves, and about half the power generated in the country comes from coal-fired plants. There have been promising discoveries of oil and gas, but most oil is imported, while constraints on liquefied natural gas (LNG) include the lack of a pipeline network and the security difficulties involved in bringing gas, say, from Iran across Pakistan to India. Nuclear power development will depend largely on how the US–India nuclear deal progresses. India is well endowed with hydroelectric potential – estimated by KPMG at 150,000 MW – but project risks include the resettlement of people affected by new dams. A little over 9,200 MW, or 7.3% of India's total installed capacity, comes from renewable sources, mainly wind power. This is where groups such as Tulsi Tanti's Suzlon hope to become world leaders. With potential for 45,000 MW and installed capacity of about 6,200 MW, India already ranks as the fourth-largest wind user.[12] According to Robert Gleitz, wind general manager at GE Power, wind is nearing the mainstream in terms of cost. In late 2006, Gleitz told a forum in Tokyo: "It's now possible to generate wind electricity at about 7 cents per kilowatt-hour. That explains why wind is growing so fast and why the demand is much larger than the production capacity."[13] Whether it comes from the wind, the sun, biomass, or more traditional sources such as coal, oil, gas, nuclear, or hydro, it's clear that without adequate power generation and distribution, India's enormous economic potential and the quality of life enjoyed by its people are being held back.

INFRASTRUCTURE OPPORTUNITIES

That basic infrastructure need, which is replicated in such other key sectors as water supply, roads, railways, seaports, and airports, is being catered for by a band of business groups that include such traditional names as Tata, Birla, Godrej, Jindal, and Reliance, as well as aggressive wealth club newcomers such as Grandhi M. Rao of GMR Infrastructure, Jaiprakash Gaur of Jaiprakash Associates, and G.V. Krishna Reddy of GVK Group. Understandably, Rao, Gaur, and Reddy all see huge opportunities ahead. But as Rao notes, there can be no success in these sorts of megaprojects without the right management talent, the right IT systems, the best corporate governance, and excellence in execution. That means getting the best people, often recruiting them from offshore, as he has done for his New Delhi and Hyderabad airport projects. Rao says that in the big picture of

India's growth outlook, infrastructure bottlenecks represent the No. 1 problem. "The government itself has said that the infrastructure problem is taking 1.5 to 2.0% off the potential GDP growth," he notes.[14] But even with the political will to make things happen, there is a sense that India – unlike China – is still just in catch-up mode, and not putting in the sort of surplus roads, airports, water, and energy capacity now that the country will need in a decade or two.

Like Rao, Reddy is an entrepreneurial contractor who understands the potential in building the nation's capacity to grow. His GVK Group has two power plants built, and a third on the way, and is handling the complex task of upgrading Mumbai's airport. It also has the Jaipur Expressway, part of the government's grand "Golden Quadrilateral" national highway development project. GMR, GVK, and two other construction groups from Andhra Pradesh state, Nagarjuna Construction and Lanco Infratech, have emerged as infrastructure stars in the past few years, winning key projects in thermal power, hydropower, irrigation, airports, roads, and real estate. Lanco, led by chairman L. Madhusudan Rao, is to build the massive 4,000 MW Sasan power plant in Madhya Pradesh and a 1,000 MW thermal plant in Uttar Pradesh. Nagarjuna, led by managing director Alluri Ranga Raju (son of founder A.V.S. Raju), is concentrating on road construction projects and transmission lines, but is also involved in the 800 MW Parbati hydroelectric project and a real estate development in Hyderabad.

The Indian government's Five Year Plan for 2007–11 includes an estimate of US$350 billion for infrastructure spending, and Prime Minister Manmohan Singh has promised an "enabling environment" for global investors in the sector. The institutional architecture is in place, he says. Whether this rosy prospect will outweigh the inevitable handicaps of delays, cost over-runs, bureaucratic wrangling, corruption, and security concerns is the challenge to be faced by both domestic and overseas players in India's great infrastructure scramble.

ENDNOTES

1. From "The Giant Who Touched Tomorrow," a profile of Jamsetji N. Tata, included in the Tata Group's history at www.tata.com/0_about_us/history/pioneers/jamsetji_tata.htm.
2. Ratan Tata interview in *Business World* magazine, February 6, 2007.
3. Media release, "Tata Steel completes £6.2 billion acquisition of Corus Group," Tata Steel, April 3, 2007.

4. From "The Giant Who Touched Tomorrow," op. cit.

5. Media release, "World produces 1,295 mmt of crude steel in 2006," International Iron & Steel Institute, January 22, 2007.

6. Media release, "ESHL seeks delisting of Essar Steel Limited," Essar Group, January 25, 2007.

7. Media releases by Jindal Stainless and JSW Steel, January 24, 2007 and April 30, 2007.

8. Media release by Ispat Industries, "Ispat Industries unveils expansion plan," January 12, 2007.

9. *India Energy Outlook 2007*, KPMG India, May 2007, p. 5.

10. ibid., p. 40.

11. ibid., p. 9.

12. ibid., p. 37.

13. Robert Gleitz, speaking at Japan Forum 2006 in Tokyo, quoted in "The Power to Innovate," *Fortune* magazine special section, November 27, 2006, p. 12.

14. Interview with G.M. Rao, New Delhi, January 22, 2007.

CHAPTER TEN

Aviation and Travel: Buckle up for the Ride

Everything about travel in India is chaotic. We can't fix that with the internet. The government needs to make huge investments in airports, seaports, and roads to renew infrastructure.
—Sherpalo Ventures founder, K. Ram Shriram[1]

The Jet Airways captain is frank. As the Bangalore-bound B737 taxis out to New Delhi's main runway after an air traffic congestion delay of almost two hours, he tells his 150 frustrated passengers: "Delhi air traffic control has completely lost it today." He cites preparations by the Indian Air Force for a Republic Day fly-past – still four days away – and warns it is unlikely to get better for the rest of the week. The incident is indicative of both the tremendous promise and the problems facing India's fast-growing aviation sector, where in the quest for passengers, a host of low-cost newcomers are battling incumbent carriers for everything from landing slots, qualified pilots and cabin crew, to e-booking systems and parking space for their scores of brand-new jets. Air traffic control is in particularly dire straits; the number of new controllers hired is simply unable to keep pace with the sector's explosive growth rate of 40% in 2006 and as much as 100% in 2007. The government is looking to take air traffic control away from the Airports Authority of India and to put it into a separate organization – a step that can't come too soon for the pilots.

Just a few hours before the Jet Airways captain's succinct explanation of the controllers' woes, billionaire businessman Grandhi M. Rao had given his own assessment of the situation in an interview in New Delhi. Rao, the man who is "Mr Aviation Infrastructure" by virtue of his US$2 billion contract to upgrade Delhi Airport into a regional hub capable of handling 37 million passengers a year in time for the 2010 Commonwealth Games, also sees the need for a dramatic upgrade of air traffic control procedures. "It's no good me building a beautiful airport if it is weighed down by old procedures," he says. "India's air traffic control must be modernized and operate in line with the international model. That means more resources for ATC [air traffic control]. People must be trained, and operating procedures must conform to the best international practice."[2]

Rao says that his goal, both for New Delhi and a US$500 million greenfields airport he is building on the outskirts of Hyderabad (population six million), is to create an "aerotropolis" along the lines of Hong Kong or Dubai. "This concept calls for the construction not just of an international airport, but the creation of a host of supporting facilities, such as shopping malls, entertainment, business centers, hotels, hospitals, a golf course, and a residential component," he says. That ties in with his philosophy of keeping his customers – the airlines – happy. "I don't want to antagonize them with charges. My aim is to reduce charges to airlines, so they will be encouraged to bring in more passengers. With a better environment and facilities at the airport, the passengers will spend more. So, this is where revenue growth will come from. I could make lots of money from parking fees, for example. But we must not abuse our monopoly position."[3]

SIGNIFICANT STAKES

Rao, who started out in the southern Indian jute trade in 1976 in the small Andhra Pradesh village of Rajam before moving to Bangalore and into banking, manufacturing, and now infrastructure and agribusiness, is just one of a swathe of India's wealth club members with a significant stake in the aviation sector. Others include Jet Airways founder Naresh Goyal, whose 80% stake in the dominant domestic carrier is worth about US$1.3 billion; the self-proclaimed "King of Good Times," Vijay Mallya, who set up Kingfisher Airlines in 2005 and runs an Airbus A319 as his own corporate jet; Air Deccan's Captain G.R. Gopinath, a man who went from a small helicopter operation to become the No. 2 domestic carrier; and Air Sahara's Subrata Roy Sahara, whose much-needed merger with Jet Airways came alarmingly unstuck in mid-2006 before the two parties agreed on terms in early 2007, resulting in a makeover for Sahara as Jet Lite. There was more consolidation a few months later, when Kingfisher

announced at the end of May that it was buying a 26% stake in Air
Deccan for US$135 million, though the two would still run as inde-
pendent entities. That meant that as of mid-2007, the Jet/Jet Lite
combination had about 37% of the market, Air Deccan and Kingfisher between them had about 33%, while national carrier Indian
(which has merged with international flag carrier Air India) had just
under 20%. The big players were followed by SpiceJet (backed by the
London-based Kansagara family), the Wadia family's GoAir, and
the tail-ender minnows, all-business Paramount and IndiGo. But it's
largely a case of few frills and even fewer profits in what should be a
red-hot sector. As carriers have added thousands of fresh seats, opened
new routes, and slashed prices (to less than one rupee – about two
cents – in one SpiceJet sales campaign) to keep their competitors at
bay, the red ink has been flowing.

Rakesh Gangwal is a former CEO of US Airways and a co-
founder of IndiGo with Rahul Bhatia. He has lived in the United
States since 1977 and says that after 25 years in the aviation industry,
he swore off airlines in 2001 when he quit US Airways, which at
the time was the sixth-largest US carrier. But then along came the
chance to do something different with IndiGo. Gangwal says IndiGo's
advantage is that it's not a legacy airline; nonetheless, he is sanguine
about the chances of success for his carrier or his competitors. "It's a
dog-eat-dog business. The only way to survive is to kill the other
airline," he says.[4] "Some of them [the new Indian carriers] won't make
it." Gangwal ticks off the prerequisites: "One, a fundamental understanding of the airline business; and two, the size of your pocket-
book." He says linked to that is the size of the aircraft order that a
new carrier can place. "We started with an order for 100 planes –
that's unheard of for a startup."[5] Even so, Gangwal says IndiGo is
losing money. Still, that hasn't stopped some of the big names investing in the sector. The Tata Group, whose 1938–91 chairman J.R.D.
Tata (d. 1993) founded Tata Aviation Service in 1932 and established
Air India International in 1948, has taken a small stake in SpiceJet.

TARGET MARKET

The overwhelming majority of India's 1.2 billion people are destined
never to travel in an aeroplane, just as many of them will never make
a phone call, use a flush toilet, or buy a powered consumer appliance.
India's airline passenger numbers are headed for 30 million in 2007

and 50 million by 2010, but they are the same few million Indians and overseas visitors, shuttling back and forth on the busiest corridors of commerce that link Delhi, Mumbai, Bangalore, Chennai, Hyderabad, and Kolkata. For most domestic travelers in India, the nation's overcrowded trains will remain their long-distance mode. In 2006, India's trains carried six billion passengers. Still, that hasn't stopped the big aircraft manufacturers Boeing and Airbus, along with niche players such as Brazil's Embraer and French turbo-prop maker ATR, salivating over the aviation industry's growth prospects. Boeing sees a need for 600 aircraft over the next 15–20 years in the Indian market, while Airbus envisages a market of 950 planes. The International Air Transport Association forecasts Indian airlines will need US$60 billion of investment by 2030, and airports will need another US$30 billion.

Those are the sorts of numbers that bring a glint to the eye of aviation pioneer Naresh Goyal, a commerce graduate who started behind a counter in his great-uncle's travel agency on a monthly salary of US$6 in 1976. He ran a general sales agency in Delhi for many years, gradually building up his expertise in all areas of the aviation business and making the right contacts for when liberalization would open up the industry. By the early 1990s, the time was ripe. Aided by wife Anita, Goyal launched Jet Airways in May 1993 with a B737 flight from Mumbai to Ahmedabad and the motto, "The Joy of Flying." Jet is now India's most profitable carrier, operating more than 300 domestic flights a day and international flights to Singapore, Bangkok, London, and Kuala Lumpur that go head-to-head with Singapore Airlines and Emirates. Jet code-shares with prestigious carriers such as BA, KLM, Air France, Northwest, South African, and Australia's Qantas. The carrier Goyal most admires – and most wants to beat – is Singapore Airlines. He acted as general sales agent for Singapore Airlines for more than 20 years, but that broke down in 1997. Goyal's goal is simple: he wants Jet to be one of the world's top five airlines.[6] It's a big challenge for a carrier with a market cap of just US$1.5 billion. To do that, Goyal will have to surpass well-established carriers such as Cathay Pacific, BA, Qantas, JAL, Lufthansa, Singapore Airlines, Emirates, American Airlines, and Southwest Airlines, all of which rank at or near the top in fields such as passenger satisfaction, quality of service, and market capitalization. The movie-loving Goyal's ambitions suffered a temporary setback when a proposed 2006 takeover of the rival Air Sahara carrier, owned by enigmatic businessman Subrata Roy Sahara, initially foundered.

There were issues of price, and confusion about what Sahara could bring to the table in the way of airport infrastructure, but within a year the deal was done. Goyal picked up the carrier for an enterprise value of 14.5 billion rupees, or about US$350 million.[7]

While Goyal was busy dealing with Sahara, discount operator Air Deccan had quietly overtaken state-owned Indian Airlines in June 2006 to become India's second-largest airline. Less than three years after starting operations in August 2003 as India's first no-frills carrier, it achieved a market share of 21.2%. With a motto of "No rest till we are the best," Air Deccan's avowed aim was to overtake Jet Airways and become India's No. 1 operator, according to founder and managing director Captain G.R. "Gopi" Gopinath. How that will pan out after Kingfisher moved to take a strategic stake, remains to be seen. As part of Gopinath's plan, Air Deccan in 2006 ordered 96 new aircraft (including 60 Airbus planes worth US$4 billion) for delivery over an eight-year period. Gopinath says the airline's unconventional business model has "brought the luxury of flying to the common man in India," noting that 40% of passengers in 2006 were first-time flyers. Converting even just a small percentage of India's rail travelers to airline passengers figures high on his to-do list. Gopinath, who went to school barefoot in a small village called Gorur in southwest India's Karnataka state, finished his education at a military academy, graduated later from the Indian defense academy, and served on the front in Bangladesh during the 1971 war with Pakistan. In the mid-1990s he decided to start a helicopter service with an old friend from the military. From those humble beginnings would develop a low-cost carrier that has brought air travel within reach of many more Indian travelers. Gopinath is well aware of India's aviation infrastructure shortcomings, but says that "with tenacity, you can make things work."[8] He is also a believer in point-to-point services, believing that connectivity is the key driver of growth. To help India develop, he wants entrepreneurs to find their way to smaller places, rather than immediately concentrating on the major population centers. Indeed, there is a multiplicity of choice when newcomers survey the Indian market. At least 35 cities and urban areas have populations of more than one million people, ranging from the giants Mumbai (17 million), Kolkata (13.5 million), Delhi (13 million), and Chennai (6.5 million), to places like Rajkot, Amritsar, Allahabad, and Jamshedpur that just crack the one-million mark. Early in 2007, Air Deccan said it expected to carry eight million passengers for the year, twice as many as the 2006 figure.

LET THE GOOD TIMES ROLL

Where Gopinath is no-frills, there is no more over-the-top airline figure than his new stakeholder, Vijay Mallya, the flamboyant liquor and aviation tycoon who works hard at building his Kingfisher brand and plays just as hard with an assortment of billionaire-style toys that include a personal Airbus A319 jet, a 95-meter super-yacht, a race-horse stud, his own go-kart track, and mansions across three continents. Indicative of Mallya's style is his annual Kingfisher swimsuit calendar, the "must-have" item that for 2007 was shot on the French Riviera using his latest acquisition, the luxury yacht *Indian Empress*. Formerly *Al Mirqab*, the flagship of the Emir of Qatar, the US$110 million *Indian Empress* features a helipad, car hold, 16 cabins, a crew of 20, and some of Mallya's collection of artworks that include paintings by Renoir and Chagall. The yacht, moving from Monte Carlo to Cannes to Nice, became home base in late 2006 for an array of supermodels, killer whales, photographers, and hangers-on as Mallya, eschewing his usual black garb for the corporate red of his Kingfisher Airlines, oversaw proceedings. Thirteen days of shooting meant 5 a.m. calls for all concerned, but Mallya was ecstatic at the result, terming it a showcase of the "new India's" fashion, style, beauty, and talent.[9]

Mallya, whose Kingfisher "Funliners" are pitched as offering safety, luxury, and value, epitomizes conspicuous consumption. His lavish parties, his sponsorship of fashion shows, rock concerts, and race cars, and his stupendous Kingfisher calendar shoots have made him one of the most talked-about figures among India's new breed of billionaires. That draws some criticism in a country where poverty is endemic and where the gap between rich and poor appears to be widening. But if Mallya is loud and aggressive in flaunting his success, there are other dimensions to the man. He is a member of the Rajya Sabha, India's upper house, representing the pro-farming Janata Party. He says his agenda as an industrialist is to be known as a person who cares about society and people. His UB Group, which includes listed entities United Breweries and United Spirits, funds health and education initiatives. On television talk shows, he cuts an aspirational figure for entrepreneurs on the way up. At a time when business is no longer a dirty word and the country's growth rate is sprinting forward, Mallya shows what can be done in aviation, beer and spirits, engineering, software, media, pharmaceuticals, and chemicals. And some of the spending goes to cultural preservation; Mallya paid about

US$2 million at a Sotheby's auction in London in mid-2005 for a series of items from the armory of the 18th-century Indian warrior king Tipu Sultan. Mallya plans to establish a museum in Bangalore dedicated to Tipu Sultan, the man known as the "Tiger of Mysore."

Mallya is a walking, talking, marketing marvel. A Kingfisher beer – India's favorite brew – is never far from his hand. He is to the Kingfisher brand what UK entrepreneur Richard Branson is to Virgin. In fact, when people tag Mallya with the title of "India's Richard Branson" because of his style, his beard, and a spread of business interests that includes aviation and rock music, his quick rejoinder is that Branson is really "the UK's Vijay Mallya." In reality, aviation is a recent addition to the Mallya empire, which is founded on the UB beer and spirits group. His Kingfisher Airlines began flying only in May 2005, serving domestic Indian routes with a handful of leased Airbus A320s. By 2007 that figure had grown to 24 new aircraft operating 160 flights a day. In typical supersize style, Mallya is gearing up for international routes, such as direct flights to the United States. At the 2005 Paris Air Show, Mallya announced that Kingfisher would buy five new Airbus A380 super-jumbos as part of a US$3 billion package that includes five A330s and five A350s between 2007 and 2012. Two years later at the June 2007 show, Kingfisher upped the ante with a massive US$7 billion order for 50 new planes, including an extra 15 of the new A350s. Earlier in the year, Kingfisher Airlines signed its largest sports sponsorship, a multi-year deal to be an official partner of the Toyota F1 Racing team, reflecting Mallya's passion for motorsports and the marketing chance to bring the "Fly Kingfisher" logo to F1's global TV audience. Mallya says he expects Kingfisher Airlines to be the UB Group's biggest revenue contributor by 2010.

GLOBAL SCALE

For now, though, that mantle rests with the liquor business United Spirits (formerly McDowell) and the beer business United Breweries. Mallya has been running UB for more than two decades, having been forced to take on the chairmanship when his father, Vittal Mallya, died suddenly in 1983, while still in his early fifties. Though Vijay Mallya was born in Bangalore, in the south of India, he spent most of his youth in Kolkata with his mother Lalitha after his parents divorced. Before joining UB, he worked for the pharmaceuticals group Hoechst in the United States and the United Kingdom. He worked in petrochemicals and engineering, along the way acquiring Berger Paints in 1988 and selling it for a substantial profit some years later. But the UB business occupies most of his attention. In March 2005, Mallya paid US$300 million to take over liquor maker Shaw-Wallace from the family of his onetime arch-rival, the late Manu Chhabria, founder of the Dubai-based Jumbo Group. The acquisition, signed off by Manu's widow Vidya Manohar Chhabria, brought an end to a 20-year dispute and turned UB Group into the world's third-largest spirits maker, behind Diageo and Pernod Ricard (which took over Allied Domecq in 2005). Mallya trumped even that deal when he paid US$1.2 billion in May 2007 to buy Glasgow-based Scotch whisky giant Whyte & Mackay, the world's No. 4 Scotch maker. That gives him entrée to the international spirits market and access to Whyte & Mackay's stock of aged bulk Scotch. Spirits – mainly whisky – account for 90% of India's liquor market. The remaining 10% is held by beer, and of that, the Kingfisher brand alone has 30%. So Mallya's global scale in beer – India's domestic market still has plenty of growth potential, with more than half the 1.2 billion population aged under 25 – has brought him a strong international partner: the United Kingdom's biggest brewer, Scottish and Newcastle (S&N). Mallya gives his address as Sausalito, California, but the globetrotting tycoon can be found anywhere his jets and yacht take him – from Bangalore to Mumbai, Dubai, Cape Town, Monaco, or New York.

Airline operators such as Mallya, Goyal, Gopinath, Gangwal, Wadia of Go, and Ajay Singh and Siddhanta Sharma of SpiceJet are seeking to rewrite the rules of Indian aviation, aiming to profit from demand that could reach 100 million passengers a year by 2020. The new planes are ordered and the funding is in place. But in the end, the financial success or failure of the sector may well turn on the quality of India's policy framework and the availability of qualified staff (pilots, ground handlers, cabin crew, air traffic controllers) and support systems. Without the right connectivity in all these areas, the airlines run the risk of over-promising and under-delivering. A good example of this is Delhi airport, which is often closed by fog in winter. But according to one frequent traveler on the Delhi–Bangalore run, the Indian airlines could still use the main runway if their pilots had the right skills. As we wait to board the bus for the short run to the B737 sitting on the tarmac, he confides: "The real reason Delhi is so often closed is the lack of instrument-rated pilots." Industry expert Kapil Kaul, head of the Center for Asia Pacific Aviation's Indian operations, told a recent Singapore conference that India needs up to

3,000 incremental pilots in the next five years. "We view this as a greater obstacle to growth than the shortage of airport infrastructure," he noted.[10]

CONNECTIVITY IS KEY

When it comes to India's physical airport infrastructure, including fast road and rail links to city centers, this is where men like G.M. Rao come in. Even as his team in Delhi races to get the national gateway ready for the 2010 Commonwealth Games, the honor of hosting the first A380s to land in India is likely to go to Hyderabad, where Rao says his new greenfields airport will be ready by mid-2008. A high-speed train will connect the airport to the city center 14 miles (22 kilometers) away. For Delhi, Rao says his goal is to create first-class road and rail connectivity. "We want any corner of the city to be within 20 to 30 minutes of the airport. On the rail front, the government is committing 35 billion rupees [about US$780 million] to a metro line. Although I don't need to do so, I am also investing 10% of the price [or about US$78 million] on this metro line. On the road front, we have called in the best urban planners to identify the city's bottlenecks and how we can best overcome them."[11]

Rao is clear about what needs to be done on the global stage. "The immediate challenge is for the [Indian] airlines. They must meet the standards set by Singapore Airlines, BA, Lufthansa, etc." Rao says India needs an open skies policy if Delhi is to become, an international hub like Singapore, Dubai, or Frankfurt. "That is the way to attract the many Indian passengers now going to the United States, who travel through these hubs and others such as Amsterdam and London."[12] He also wants the government to get behind airlines such as Jet and Kingfisher and help them get slots at international airports.

Rao, who has a degree in mechanical engineering from Andhra University Engineering College, Visakhapatnam, in Andhra Pradesh, sees huge opportunities in infrastructure – not just in aviation, but in sectors such as roads and power. "My main challenge is getting and retaining the right management talent. I'm very selective – because without good management, the right IT systems, the best corporate governance and excellence in execution, you can't do these big projects." As Rao points out, India's government admits that infrastructure bottlenecks alone are shaving potential GDP growth by between 1.5% and 2.0%. But he draws hope from what he says is now the

CHAPTER ELEVEN

Retail: When India Goes Shopping

The great divide between the rich and the poor is not a healthy condition.
— Salman Rushdie, speaking on television during a visit to India in January 2007

Bharti Enterprises chairman Sunil B. Mittal calls India "the last Shangri-la of retail."[1] It's an expansive claim, but the figures bear him out: where else does a retailer find a US$300 billion market that is likely to double by 2011 and almost triple to about US$900 billion by 2015?[2] As such, it is firmly in the sights of Mittal, whose success in telecoms has taken him into the top ranks of India's global wealth club and given his Bharti Group the firepower to focus on "organized" or "modern" retail as the next big growth area. He won't be alone. Along with Mittal's American joint venture partner Wal-Mart, a host of Indian business houses see the same opportunity. Among the top names are Mukesh Ambani with his ambitious Reliance Fresh project, Adi Godrej's Aadhaar rural chain, the Tata Group's Trent and Infiniti arms, the super-aggressive Kishore Biyani's Pantaloon/Future Group, the K. Raheja family's pioneering Shoppers Stop, K.M. Birla spreading his retail wings with the purchase of the 172-store Trinethra chain in the southern part of the country, the Piramal family's Piramyd and Crossroads brands, and the Goenka family's Spencer's supermarkets (see Table 11.1). And salivating on the sidelines are overseas contenders such as Tesco, Carrefour, Metro, ShopRite, and Woolworths.

India's foreign investment regulations limit offshore retailers for now to franchises and multi-brand outlets – hence, the Bharti Group's cash-and-carry joint venture with Wal-Mart will carry the Bharti name

Table 11.1   India's Modern Retail Scene

Major Incumbents
Pantaloon Retail (Biyani)
Shoppers Stop (K. Raheja)
Trent, Westside (Tata)
Spencers (R.P. Goenka)
Foodworld, Health & Glow (R.P. Goenka)
Godrej Aadhaar, Nature's Basket (Godrej)
ITC
Piramyd, Crossroads (Piramal)
Globus (R. Raheja)
Landmark (M. Jagtiani)
Subhiksha (R. Subramanian)
New Players
Reliance Retail (M. Ambani)
Bharti/Wal-Mart (S.B. Mittal)
A.V. Birla Group (K.M. Birla)

out front, even if the back-end systems benefit from the American giant's years of big-store expertise. But the rules may ease before the end of the decade, allowing the global players to open stores in their own right. That could bring in a flood of money, according to industry expert Arvind Singhal, chairman of Delhi-based retail consultants Technopak. Even playing by the existing rules, Singhal expects the leading domestic and foreign retailers to invest US$22 billion over the next five years in India, creating an additional 2.5 million jobs in the process.[3] Bharti is planning to spend US$2.5 billion, and Ambani is talking about a Reliance investment of more than US$5 billion.

Singhal believes the next few years will be "the most remarkable in the evolution of modern retail in India."[4] India, he says, is attempting to do in a decade what took 25 to 30 years in other major retail markets around the world. Modern retail – supermarkets, hypermarkets, "big box" outlets, department stores, and specialty shops in malls – represents only 3–4% (or about US$12 billion) of total retail spending in India, compared with 20% in China and 85% in the United States. But it is by far the fastest-growing segment, powering ahead at 35–40% a year in a country where about 12 million mom-and-pop shops traditionally have dominated the shopping scene. By 2011, the modern retail segment will grow to almost US$100 billion, and it will be approaching US$240 billion by 2015, according to Technopak's research.

THE MALL BOOM

If the future opportunity for modern retail looks bright, the current reality is a little harder to discern. One aspect of it is on display in the boomtown of Gurgaon, on the outskirts of New Delhi. There, amid the high-rise apartment blocks, the office towers for Dell and Amex, the gyms, the tennis courts, the golf courses, and the raggedy huts of itinerant construction workers, the great experimental malling of India is taking place.

Shopping malls by developers such as DLF, Unitech, Sahara, and Raheja are popping up everywhere. On a recent weekend at the MGF Metropolitan Mall next to Gurgaon's Heritage City residential area, a gaggle of hopeful contestants wait their turn for a shot at the Indian capital's biggest talent quest. Saturday shoppers pause briefly to watch the amateur pop singers, then head inside the mall's air-conditioned comfort to browse through a mix of 60 shops, restaurants, cinemas, and a games arcade. Brand names abound: Tommy Hilfiger, Levi's, Benetton, New Balance, Rockport. Across the dusty road at DLF's four-level City Centre Mall, a similar scene of blissful middle-class consumption prevails – the restaurants are busy, the Bombay Bazaar sari shop is humming with mothers, daughters, aunts, and grand-mothers poring over fabric choices. It is a theme being repeated across India's biggest cities: at the Shoppers Stop department store in sub-urban Mumbai, the Pantaloons fashion shop in Kolkata's Gariahat, or the Big Bazaar in Bangalore, the brands are often global, the store layouts familiar to any devotee of consumer dynamics. But with up to 500 malls planned or under construction, is India in danger of being over-malled and over-modernized? Singhal puts it into perspective with some figures: "India's retail sector needs more than 500 million square feet of retail space. All of the malls being built and planned total less than 150 million square feet. So, at the macro level, demand for space far exceeds supply." But at the micro level, Singhal says there could be some mismatching: "Issues such as zoning, parking, the right mix of shops have to be taken into account."[5] A Gurgaon mall that is crowded on weekends can be deserted during the week. Plus, pedestrian traffic doesn't necessarily mean sales, given that window-shopping in air-conditioned comfort can be a cost-free way to pass the time of day. Nor is the situation unique to Gurgaon. Recalling the 1999 launch of Piramyd department store in Mumbai's first mall – the Piramal Group's Crossroads – Piramyd Retail chief executive K.N. Iyer observed in 2005 that catering to a mall's diverse set of customers

can be a challenge. "The issue is not with high footfalls. But all customers are not serious shoppers," he noted.[6] So, to the retailer/prop-
erty developer's first question, "If we build it, will they come?", the
answer seems to be: "Yes, but we're not sure yet how much money
the visitors will spend."

BIGGER PROBLEMS AHEAD

While a lack of turnover might seem a retailer's worst nightmare,
there may be bigger obstacles standing in the way of profitability.
These have to do with India's dysfunctional supply system, a lack of
any meaningful cold storage chain for perishables such as dairy, fruit,
and vegetables, and increasingly scarce management talent. Throw in
market fragmentation, rising prices for commercial property, a fractious body politic that can wax and wane about outside investment,
plus the prospect of hyper-competition from 2008 onwards as the
footprint of the top six retail players starts overlapping in India's top
20 to 30 cities, and the retail outlook can seem less than rosy.

In the view of industry experts, the first challenge is to get the
supply chain fixed. Lack of refrigeration, poor transport links, red
tape at state borders, and too many middlemen means 40% of perishables are spoilt, which is why Reliance Industries is pumping more
than US$5 billion into its "farm to fork" approach. Mukesh Ambani
calls his retail expansion plan a "pathbreaking initiative that will
empower India's rural people."[7] It means he will buy direct from
farmers, cutting out three or four layers of handling, and upsetting
some wholesale merchants in the process. Then Reliance will truck,
pack, brand, and sell the products through food stores it has begun
rolling out in cities such as Chennai, Hyderabad, and Jaipur. All told,
Ambani has ambitions to open 5,000 stores nationally, covering food
and a multitude of other goods. Like Ambani, the Birla, Godrej,
Biyani, Raheja, Tata, Piramal, and Goenka families are snapping up
managers as fast as they can. The war for talent in the retail space is
absolutely critical, in the view of Singhal, and has been largely under-
estimated. The problem is not the quality of the people serving customers, but with middle management, which he describes as "extremely
weak." Nor is hiring expatriates a viable solution. "India is going to
have to train these middle managers. It will take them three to five
years to understand the complexity of the business," he says, and even
then a lot of their knowledge will be theoretical only. He warns that
these middle managers "are going to have to get it right every single

day."[8] Just one slight mistake on stock choices and levels, for example, will see them with a lot of goods unsold. A big player such as Ambani already has a home-grown talent bank inside Reliance, many of whom have had retail experience. Likewise, Sunil Mittal's strategy is to redeploy several hundred telecom executives from his Bharti Airtel business – where rationalization is freeing up staff – to the modern retail business. Whether the skills transfer will be smooth remains to be seen.

The other big problem for modern retail has to do with quality, quantity, and consistency of supply. Singhal says that most Indian suppliers so far have been small companies. Large retailers with a national footprint will want suppliers of a similar large scale, able to deliver consistent quality across the country. Singhal fears that many of the thousands of small suppliers will not be able to cope with the big retailers' requirements. Like the mom-and-pop stores, their future lies in local service and local knowledge of customers' needs.

SLICING THE CONSUMER PYRAMID

Even so, the industry view is that there is space across India for at least 10,000 new outlets of all shapes and sizes; in addition, another 10,000 existing outlets are likely to undergo complete facelifts in the next few years. The streetscapes of cities and towns are being changed as supermarkets, department stores, mini-malls, and brand name advertising become more noticeable. All the ingredients are right for expansion, starting with the consumers. Before the end of the decade, India will have almost 150,000 households that qualify for "super-rich" status – annual incomes of more than 10 million rupees, or about US$230,000.[9] But while they might sit at the top of the consumer pyramid, it's not their money that will drive India's retail revolution. That role belongs to the middle and bottom of the pyramid, where three income groups – known to researchers as "aspirers," "seekers," and "strivers" – reside. They make up "the fortune at the bottom of the pyramid" – the phrase first brought to prominence by influential University of Michigan management expert and author C.K. Prahalad to describe the urban and rural poor. According to India's leading economic think tank, the National Council of Applied Economic Research, these income segments between them will constitute more than 100 million households by 2010, and have about US$500 billion a year to spend.[10] So far, though, modern retail remains the exception to the shopping rule experience for most Indian consumers. Despite the distant buzz of the mall, they continue for now to rely on the "*kirana*," the mom-and-pop corner store that sells them a little of everything.

This is where Adi Godrej's expertise in micro-retailing comes to the fore: his Godrej Group has been active in consumer products, foodstuffs, and household goods for decades, targeting the hundreds of millions of consumers for whom money comes in a daily trickle. Even though Godrej sees micro credit spreading rapidly and driving up household spending, it will take time to change old habits in India's 500,000 villages. "Many people in rural India get paid on a daily basis," he says. "That means most of these consumers don't have a dollar in their pockets on any given day."[11] The response by Godrej and similar companies targeting the rural and urban poor has been to create micro-packages – enough soap or washing powder, say, for a day's use. "Some of our products – cough syrup, for example – are sold for the equivalent of one cent," Godrej says. Another retailer who delves into the rural market is Harish Manwani, chairman of consumer products giant Hindustan Unilever. He sees good returns from empowering his sales force – and consumers – through education. "We trained a large number of rural women to take a simple hygiene measure [washing hands] into rural India with our soap. We've got 28,000 people across rural India, impacting on 100 million people in 80,000 to 90,000 villagers," he told a conference on the Indian economy.[12] Manwani says these women have doubled their household income, while boosting Hindustan Unilever's business. It is a familiar refrain among observers of the Indian shopping scene.

As the economy grows and disposable incomes rise – even slightly – consumption picks up, sometimes in unexpected ways. Occasionally, the aspirational spending of rural consumers defies logic. For example, rather than upgrade their basic necessities of food and drink, they might opt instead for a mobile phone, a motor scooter, or a television set. According to "The Next 4 Billion," a March 2007 global study by the International Finance Corporation and World Resources Institute, India's bottom-of-the-pyramid market, defined as those households with less than US$3,000 a year in local purchasing power, covers more than 900 million people and is worth about US$1.2 trillion a year in purchasing power.[13] Godrej, for one, believes that India's economic success over the next few decades will depend on how well it reaches out to its consumers with suitably priced and packaged products. "If we do that well, there are another 3 to 4 billion consumers like that in the rest of the world," he observes.[14]

CAPTURING ALL THOSE RUPEES

Global wealth club member Kishore Biyani, named 2007 "International Retailer of the Year" by the US National Retail Association, is another player with a weather eye on how the Indian market is changing. He runs his US$700 million turnover Pantaloon Retail business – the listed flagship of his Future Group – on a philosophy of "rewrite the rules, retain values." His stated objective is to "capture every rupee in the wallet of every Indian consumer, wherever they are."[15] To help do that, he has unleashed a veritable barrage of formats on to the Indian market: 30 different store types that cover food, fashion, homewares, electronics, books, music, health, beauty, general merchandise, and e-tailing. Along with the Pantaloons name, some of his best-known formats include Big Bazaar, Food Bazaar, Central Mall, Depot Collection, and Café Bollywood. Plus, he has signed up India's "Little Master" – cricketer Sachin Tendulkar – to help promote new consumer goods. Biyani, who in March 2007 launched his book about his business life, *It Happened in India*, is not afraid of overseas competition. "We excel in what we do," he told a US retailing convention when he accepted his international award in New York. "We have a deep understanding of Indian consumers and we offer everything they need every time, everywhere, through every format of retailing."[16]

While Biyani's Pantaloon and the Raheja family's Shoppers Stop are market leaders for now, industry expert Arvind Singhal sees that situation changing. "None of the current leaders will be in the top 10 by 2010," he says. "But they will be in the next group of 11 to 20." Singhal says he expects six of the top 10 will be Indian, with one or two joint ventures, and three or four will be predominantly foreign, or in partnerships.[17] "Reliance Retail will most certainly be at the top," he says, noting that it has worked hard to get the key ingredients right: logistics, people, farm efficiency. "It will be far ahead of everyone else. Wal-Mart/Bharti will be a very respectable No. 2."

Urvi Piramal, whose Piramal Group was an early starter in modern retail with one of the first malls, Crossroads, sees the potential entry of Wal-Mart in positive terms. "It will only expand the pie and will improve logistics, supply chain and the farm gate," she told a US–India economic forum.[18] Singhal agrees. He says that in its tie-up with Bharti, Wal-Mart is putting a lot of effort into the crucial back end of retailing – the systems and supply side. "It will be a formidable player once it gets all the building blocks in place," he says.[19] By Singhal's calculations, Reliance Retail could be turning over US$20 to US$25 billion by December 2011, and Wal-Mart could be in the range of US$8 to US$10 billion. While these are impressive figures, they also demonstrate that India's market is big enough to accommodate multiple players. With total retail likely to be well over US$500 billion by 2011, even US$25 billion would give Reliance just a 5% share. From his perspective, Reliance's Ambani believes the modern retail sector has space for at least six to eight large players. B.S. Nagesh, who launched Shoppers Stop for the Rahejas in 1991 and remains its CEO, making him possibly India's most experienced modern retail executive, isn't fazed by the competition. Early in 2007, he told the *Business Standard*: "The opportunity is so big it doesn't make too much of a difference whether big foreign players or even big domestic groups like Reliance come in."[20] Nagesh says he's not concerned about being No. 1. What he wants to be is an A-grade player, targeting the high-value end of the retail market where customers have already shown that they are relatively recession-proof. Even in a downturn they will keep buying, he says.

WAITING ON THE MONSOON

For many other participants in India's retail sector, it will all come down to the vagaries of the weather. India's 600 million rural dwellers rely on steady rain from June to September to underpin their winter crops. A good monsoon means a good harvest, which means better returns for farmers and more money to spend. Agricultural advancement is a theme endorsed by bottom-of-the-pyramid guru C.K. Prahalad, who urges a shift from pre-harvest subsidies to a focus on India's post-harvest supply chain.[21] Better logistics would mean better access to markets and reduced handling. Likewise, industrialist Rahul Bajaj notes: "We cannot afford to neglect agriculture. Just too many people are engaged in it."[22] Ambani's farm gate project, along with Sunil Mittal's export-driven fresh food experiment and similar plans by Godrej, ShopRite, and ITC, are all designed to lift farm incomes and improve farming practices. As Adi Godrej says, better agricultural productivity will boost incomes and release people to be absorbed by other sectors, generating more economic growth. "One of our biggest problems – and it will continue to be so – is unemployment. It's a social problem and an economic problem, and the only way we can address it is with a very high growth rate," he says.[23] Godrej has always believed that growth of 10% is feasible for India. The last few years since the mid-2000s have given him good reason to think that a double-digit rate is within India's grasp, opening up the prospect of better living standards. But the statistics show there is still much work to do. According to India's latest National Family Health Survey, almost half the country's children under the age of five are malnourished.[24] Infant mortality, low literacy rates (especially for girls), low school completion rates, and early marriages are the norm for many rural and urban poor. Even so, in their choice of goods, buyers at the bottom of the pyramid often leapfrog what hitherto has been considered the usual pattern of upward consumption – more spending on food. Indeed, research from India's National Sample Survey Organisation charts the changes in consumer behavior between the 1990s and the 2000s: spending on telephones has skyrocketed, and there are solid gains for spending on clothing, education, healthcare, gas and electricity connections, transport, and entertainment.[25] About 26% of rural and 66% of urban households now have a TV, while access to power has risen to 54% in rural areas and 90% in urban areas. Rural buyers say they want TVs, cookers, fans, refrigerators, and a two-wheeler or a light commercial three- or four-wheel vehicle. How many of them complete their aspirational purchases and make the switch to modern retail shopping could well shape the future fortunes of some of India's top business families.

ENDNOTES

1. Sunil B. Mittal, address to the World Economic Forum, New Delhi, November 27, 2006.
2. Retail industry research paper by Technopak, New Delhi, March 2007.
3. Telephone interview with Arvind Singhal, CEO, Technopak, March 15, 2007.
4. ibid.
5. ibid.
6. K.N. Iyer, "Lessons I Learnt from Piramyd," *Rediff/Business Standard*, June 10, 2005.
7. Mukesh Ambani, "Embarking on a Retail Revolution," address to shareholders, Reliance Industries annual general meeting, Mumbai, June 27, 2006, and address to "Stanford in India" innovation conference, Mumbai, January 15, 2007.
8. Singhal, op. cit.
9. *The Great Indian Market*, report by National Council of Applied Economic Research, August 2005.
10. ibid.
11. Adi Godrej, panel remarks in Wharton India Economic Forum, Philadelphia, November 11, 2006, and interview in Mumbai, April 27, 2004.

CHAPTER TWELVE

◆

Financial Services: More Money in the Bank

India's ongoing inflation problem could be the needle that pricks Corporate India's confidence balloon.
—Morgan Stanley's India research
head, Ridham Desai[1]

Bill Clinton loved the name "YES Bank." We know that, because he scrawled it on the name card of the bank's founder, Rana Kapoor, and – smart marketer that he is – Kapoor has put it on the bank's website for all to see. YES Bank is one of the much-needed upstarts of India's financial system. The first new bank licensed since 1994, it only began operating in September 2004 but already has made its presence felt in a country where the banking system is still an unknown concept for almost half the population. Along with the friendly name, YES Bank's totem is the pothos, a popular indoor plant that in India is known as "the money plant" for its growth and climbing ability. Kapoor, a banker for almost 30 years (Bank of America, ANZ Grindlays, Rabo) says his greenfield bank has no legacy issues, so it can make maximum use of technology and draw on best practices from around the world. "We have only two modules: sales and service orientation," he says.[2] Kapoor and co-founder Ashok Kapur floated YES Bank in July 2005 and hold a 37% stake worth about US$320 million – which means they are not yet in the billionaire class, but certainly headed in the right direction. Investors in YES include Rabobank and private equity players CVC-Citicorp, Chrys-Capital, and AIF; in late 2006, Swiss Re also took a stake. Kapoor says he and Kapur chose the name "YES" for a number of reasons:

it projects optimism, and is serious, committed, and service-oriented. But primarily, it is about trust. "The brand name sets exceedingly high delivery standards in the minds of customers relating to both the product and service," he says.[3]

While YES Bank hopes to offer a "delightful banking experience," it is still a minnow among Indian banks. The whale in these particular waters is the State Bank of India (SBI), which dates its origins back to 1806 and the Bank of Calcutta. Today it has more than 14,000 branches, assets of US$156 billion, India's largest network of automatic teller machines (ATMs) (5,800 at January 2007), 23.5 million bank cards, 110 million customers, an annual profit of US$1 billion, and a market capitalization of more than US$17 billion. It is also the only Indian bank in the Fortune Global 500 (though ICICI Bank has a higher market capitalization at US$20 billion). The bank is 60%-owned by the Reserve Bank of India – a stake that is being transferred to the government to overcome the anomaly of the regulator owning the country's biggest bank. SBI's chairman, O.P. Bhatt, wants his staff to get down and dirty in the quest for customers. He told the Wharton India Economic Forum, held in late 2006, that bankers have got to get out into the rural areas, "among the cows." Bhatt believes this is a part of the banking market that isn't growing as fast as it should. "The top of the pyramid is OK, but to make a fortune, look at the middle of the pyramid," is the advice he offered to the swag of financial wannabes who came to hear what India's most powerful bankers had to say.[4]

LOOKING FOR SOLUTIONS

Consulting firm McKinsey & Co. believes more can be done to get India's financial system humming. In 2006 it suggested that an integrated reform program could add US$47 billion a year to India's GDP and raise the annual economic growth rate to 9.4%. India has a relatively high household savings rate of 22% of GDP, plus an estimated US$200 billion in gold stashed away. The problem – and the opportunity – is the country's low debt ratio and low bank penetration rate. Household debt is only 4% of GDP – though even that makes the central bank nervous – and only one household in three in India has a bank account. One reason: a bricks-and-mortar branch can be a rarity for many of the 600 million-plus Indians living in rural areas. That is why SBI, ICICI, and other banks are looking for innovative solutions, using wireless access and ATMs operated by franchisees, such as a local shopkeeper or seed merchant. And to cater for a clientele that is often illiterate, fingerprints and other biometric identification devices are replacing the PIN (personal identification number) of more traditional ATMs. Despite the costs of reaching out to the rural masses with banking services, Bhatt is maximum bullish on the big picture: "We're sitting on top of a huge opportunity over the next 25 years. This country can overtake the economies of Italy, France, and even Japan. The potential is there, but so are the issues that need to be resolved," he says.[5]

That assessment is well and truly shared by the man regarded as India's most astute investment banker, Uday Kotak, founder of Kotak Mahindra Bank and one of the highest-ranking members of India's global wealth club. In 20 years, the sitar-playing Kotak has turned a small finance company into a full service financial institution that ranks among the top four private banks in India, with a market capitalization of US$4.7 billion (see Table 12.1). Kotak, who holds a 56% stake, got early backing from industrialists Harish and Anand Mahindra, hence the Mahindra name. Starting as a bill discounter in 1986 and then moving into lease and hire purchase, car loans, investment banking, brokerage, mutual funds, and life insurance, Kotak converted his operations into a full service bank in 2003. In March 2006, Kotak paid US$74 million to US investment bank Goldman Sachs to buy out its 25% stake in two of Kotak Bank's subsidiaries. Kotak's symbol is the infinity sign ("*ka*" in India), reflecting that "man's needs are unlimited . . . and . . . we have an infinite number of ways to meet those needs."

From his Nariman Point office in Mumbai, Kotak delivers his aggressive outlook: "I believe one of the single largest opportunities anywhere in the world today is the Indian financial sector. I believe financial services will be a core engine of India's growth. It will grow

Table 12.1   India's Biggest Banks, by Market Capitalization, June 2007

1. ICICI Bank	US$20.79 billion
2. State Bank of India	US$17.75 billion
3. HDFC Bank	US$ 9.16 billion
4. Kotak Mahindra Bank	US$ 4.71 billion
5. PNB	US$ 4.24 billion
6. UTI Bank	US$ 4.01 billion
7. Canara Bank	US$ 2.57 billion
8. Bank of India	US$ 2.56 billion
9. Bank of Baroda	US$ 2.49 billion

at a significantly faster pace than the general economy. In real terms, it will grow at least two to two-and-a-half times the general economy. That means with inflation of 5–6%, nominal growth in the sector will be 25%-plus."[6]

But up till now, global investors have preferred to focus on Chinese banks, making a judgment that the billions of dollars in dodgy loans on their books (plus their sometimes capricious attitude to overseas investors and partners) will be more than offset by the share price upside. Kotak says he is stunned by the way China's financial sector is valued, compared with India's. He points out the massive market acceptance of Industrial and Commercial Bank of China (ICBC), which was oversubscribed 26 times in its initial public offer of shares. When ICBC listed in October 2006 it had a market capitalization of US$137 billion – a figure that surged by year's end to more than US$210 billion, making it the third-largest bank in the world behind Citigroup and Bank of America. "I look at the Indian financial sector in that context, and I believe the asset quality of Indian banks is pretty clean. Yet, the market cap for the entire Indian sector is only US$70 billion – SBI, ICICI, Kotak – all of us."[7] One key difference between the top Chinese and Indian banks may be profitability per customer. ICBC made more than US$5 billion profit in 2006 from 150 million customers. SBI, with 110 million customers, made US$1 billion.

Kotak believes China's stellar economic performance is the best thing that has happened to India. "It showed us that we'd better wake up. But it's not about catching China – it's not a race. The winners of the future are those countries which build models of prosperity and strive to build better societies that can be sustained 10 years from now." Kotak says the primary driver of India's recent high growth rate is domestic consumption. As the number of people moving into the "bankable class" makes a hockey stick curve upwards, he sees two big trends: "The first is that a nation of savers is becoming a nation of investors – stocks, commodities, even art. The second is that a nation of savers is becoming a nation of spenders." To define the "bankable class," Kotak points to what is happening in the mobile phone market. "Right now, mobile phone subscribers are growing at a rate of about seven million a month on a base of 110 to 120 million," he says. "That means 200 million subscribers in a year's time. It could be 400 million five years from now. Similarly, look at credit card usage. It's only 20 million now, but it could be 100 million in five years." Kotak says technology gives India a big leap forward in the ability to handle this sort of growth.[8]

Kotak divides India's financial services market into three categories. The first is the big cities such as Mumbai, Delhi, Chennai, Kolkata – perhaps 12 in all. In the second category are between 50 and 60 second-tier cities. "These are going well," says Kotak. "Category two is the biggest opportunity – it will grow to 120 cities." Then, finally, there is the semi-urban and rural category, where the toughest challenges lie for all the banks; existing infrastructure is weak or non-existent, account amounts are small – perhaps only a tenth the size of a city person's account – and illiteracy is a big hurdle. Kotak says about 25% of his bank's branches are in rural and semi-rural areas. The goal is to create financial inclusion, and this is where education – getting people into the mainstream of daily business life – is important. For Kotak, the market opportunity is so large that the initial challenge is just to service the literate group of people.[9]

MUMBAI LAGS

Mumbai, where Kotak is based, clearly is India's financial capital. It is home to the Reserve Bank of India (RBI), the major commercial banks, the biggest business houses and stock market, and the biggest population base. But how does it measure up against other Asian regional financial centers such as Hong Kong, Shanghai, Tokyo, or Singapore? Not well – a fact never more clearly demonstrated than during the great downpour of July 2005, when the city was flooded by 37.2 inches (944 millimeters) of rain in one day. About 1,000 people in and around Mumbai lost their lives, another 150,000 were stranded on train stations, roads were cut, airports shut down, raw sewage contaminated water supplies, bank ATM networks stopped functioning, and muddy water flowed through the lobbies of some of the city's premier office buildings. The drainage system for India's megacity proved woefully inadequate – a testament to the environmental neglect and the haphazard way in which development has been allowed to proceed. Some improvements have been made – stormwater drains have been cleaned, people in low-lying slums relocated, a few more flyovers and link roads built – but the city was flooded again during the 2007 monsoon rains, and Mumbai's amenity and connectivity lag well behind the other key Asian centers. For Uday Kotak, the "big disconnect" is that while Mumbai has the quality of people, its physical infrastructure drags down their ability to do their jobs at the highest level of performance. "The talent is here. But Mumbai needs significantly more schools, more hospitals, improved education and health and social amenity. That is the opportunity and the challenge."[10]

While Kotak believes the raw talent exists in abundance, specialist training is a big issue, given that the demand for skilled people in the financial services sector is growing at a phenomenal rate. At Kotak Bank, for example, staff numbers in 2003 were just 1,500. "Today it is 10,000, and we will add 5,000 this year [2007]," he says. "These are the pangs that come with growth. Market demand is not the problem. It is the scarcity of quality and skills." Kotak notes that the biggest function in his bank is human resources. "The graduates that we take need training – not just 'hard' training in specific skills, but what I call 'soft' training, in things like culture and values. We need strong value systems that cover ethics, corporate governance, and a long-term view rather than short-termism. I believe India's future depends on these values."[11]

Quality of execution is very much the Kotak mantra. "That's why, internally, we say we want Kotak to be the Infosys of financial services," he says. Notwithstanding India's shortcoming, Kotak professes to be "pretty excited" about the country's future. "I feel very good about financial services, which is being driven primarily by the domestic demand story, though also with an international component. But there is a lot to do in civil society beyond the next five years. It will need political will, plus social and physical infrastructure."[12]

GREATEST OPPORTUNITY

For bankers such as Gunit Chadha, CEO of Deutsche Bank India, the infrastructure problem is also the greatest opportunity for the financial services sector. "It is an area that just needs so much capital," he says.[13] Size will be a determinant of who does what in this area, he says, because the numbers are so big: India's Planning Commission puts the funding need at US$320 billion for roads, rail, air and sea ports, energy, water, and telecommunications in the five years from 2007 to 2012.

Technology is critical in India's banking sector, where the size of the market opportunity is almost overwhelming – half of India's population of 1.2 billion is under 25, so their moneymaking ability will extend for at least another 30 years. Or as ICICI Bank CEO K.V. Kamath put it in an October 2006 interview with *The Indian Express*, "To be meaningful in this country, you have to scale up." ICICI is just one of many Indian banks looking to reach the hundreds of millions of people in rural India. In 2005, it began a pilot project using a bio-metric ATM in the tobacco-growing region of Guntur in Andhra Pradesh. Customers log-in via their fingerprints, rather than a personal ID number. Voice recognition is also being trialed, as is the franchise concept, where a shopkeeper becomes the human face of a bank. "It's a myth you need branches to lend," Kamath told *The Indian Express*. He says a bank can find plenty of willing partners in rural areas, including the local micro-credit institution. But a focus on costs is essential. "In rural India, at least on the technology front, we will have to work at one-tenth the cost of working in urban India, as the loan size is much smaller."[14]

YES Bank's Rana Kapoor, who returned to India in 1980 after doing his MBA at Rutgers University in the United States, agrees that technology is vital, both in urban and rural areas. He believes the power of technology will allow banks to keep costs down and deliver more of their services via the internet. (The first wireless bank branches are in India.) But equally, he says banks must commit to technology "with a human face." "Banks have to think differently today. They have to build brand recognition through community engagement, such as programs that focus on water and power conservation, paper recycling, disaster recovery."[15] SBI has been doing just that, according to O.P. Bhatt. "We earmarked 1 percent of our profit for this. We made [US]$1 billion [in 2006], so that's [US]$10 million. It's driven from the bottom up, from the branches," he says.[16] The projects – typically involving water supply, medical equipment, or teaching assistance – have to benefit a community, not an individual.

LONGEST CYCLE

In February 2007, J.M. Morgan Stanley economist Chetan Ahya noted that India was in its longest credit cycle since the early 1970s. He said that credit outstanding had increased by US$250 billion to US$440 billion in the three-and-a-half years since the credit cycle began in September 2003. "Low real rates and a sharp rise in bank credit have been at the heart of India's growth acceleration story over the past three years," he said.[17]

While the banking sector is zooming ahead, already there are worries about the Indian consumer's appetite for debt. The credit card market is only US$4 billion, but is growing at 35% a year as the expanding "bankable class" exercises its newfound freedom to flash the plastic. In January 2007, the governor of the Reserve Bank of

India again raised interest rates and issued a clear warning about what he saw as a personal loan and credit card binge. Noting that bank credit had risen rapidly for the third straight year, Governor Y. Venugopal Reddy said the growth rate was "clearly excessive" and he needed to act to moderate it. Continued high credit growth in the property sector, in credit card debt, and in personal loans is "a matter of concern." Reddy's stance finds backing from Rana Kapoor, who says the one area he is concerned about is real estate, where lending is "completely out of whack" and needs calibrating. Other bankers and commentators also point to the property bubble that has sent the share price of listed property companies such as Unitech soaring. And while bank credit is now easy to get – be it for a home, a new car, scooter, or tractor – the support mechanisms are lagging. For instance, there is no real credit reporting system in India yet for individuals, only corporates. Dr. Anil Khandelwal, chairman and managing director of the state-owned Bank of Baroda, told a financial services panel session recently: "There is definitely a gap there. It will be the next thing to happen."[18]

Banking has thrown up a relatively small number of participants in India's global wealth club: the Hinduja family, Uday Kotak, Grandhi M. Rao (through his early success with Vysya Bank), C. Sivasankaran (who bought Tamilnad Mercantile Bank from the Ruia brothers of Essar Group but sold out in 2004), and newcomers such as Rana Kapoor and Ashok Kapur. Perhaps the next member of India's wealth club will find a fortune in banking's new market niche: running a credit reporting database.

ENDNOTES

1. Ridham Desai, "Powerful Psychology: Corporate India's Winning Formula," *Global Strategy Bulletin* (Morgan Stanley), May 23, 2007.
2. Rana Kapoor, interview at Wharton India Economic Forum, Philadelphia, November 11, 2006.
3. Rana Kapoor, emailed response to author's questions, December 12, 2006.
4. O.P. Bhatt, panel session at Wharton India Economic Forum, Philadelphia, November 11, 2006.
5. ibid.
6. Interview with Uday Kotak, Mumbai, January 16, 2007.
7. ibid.
8. ibid.
9. ibid.
10. ibid.
11. ibid.

12. ibid.
13. Gunit Chadha, panel session, Wharton India Economic Forum, Philadelphia, November 11, 2006.
14. K.V. Kamath, quoted in "After consumer credit, rural lending is the next big opportunity," *The Indian Express*, October 3, 2006.
15. Interview with Kapoor, Philadelphia, op. cit.
16. Bhatt, op. cit.
17. Chetan Ahya, "$250 Billion Credit Party – Drawing to a Close," *Global Economic Forum* (Morgan Stanley), February 14, 2007.
18. Dr. Anil Khandelwal, in panel session, Wharton India Economic Forum, Philadelphia, November 11, 2006.

CHAPTER THIRTEEN

What Does India's Future Hold?

*If schools today mirror tomorrow's society, we need
to be alarmed.*
—Wipro chairman, Azim H. Premji[1]

O n dusty Sarjapur Road, the sign at a laneway entrance reads:
"Now, drive down the road to England." It's an intriguing
entreaty, one of many billboards advertising the housing estates that
rise from the dry plains on the outskirts of Bangalore. This is where
some of India's best and brightest IT companies and their staff make
their home. New office parks, high-rise apartments, and residential
villas in a proliferation of architectural styles (including Olde English)
are springing up everywhere along Sarjapur Road and the Outer Ring
Road that ferries traffic back to the airport and central Bangalore.
These houses have the full complement of amenities: water and sewerage, air-conditioning, TV satellite dishes, tennis courts, gyms, and
playgrounds for the children. But on the vacant blocks between them
are the tents of the itinerant construction workers drawn by Bangalore's frantic building boom. The contrast is stark: no running water
here, no chance to grasp the high life, little prospect of a decent education for their children. A little further along Sarjapur Road is the
corporate headquarters of Wipro, one of the dazzling stars of the
Indian IT scene. Its chairman, Azim H. Premji, is both a champion of
India's human potential and a scathing critic of its education system,
particularly at the primary level. "The focus of schools has to change
from simply preparing children for exams to helping them learn skills
they will use in their lives," he says.[2]

Premji is doing something about it, having decided that education
is the key social area where his money and technology can make a
difference. Next-door to the Wipro campus is a two-story brick and

stone building surrounded by eucalyptus trees, the headquarters of the Azim Premji Foundation. Here, foundation staffers focus on programs aimed eventually at securing a high-quality education for rural children among India's 200 million school-goers in the six- to 14-year age bracket. Statistics cited by the foundation's Anina Chacko illustrate the magnitude of the task: 5.5 million teachers work in 1.3 million schools, where 75% have unplanned, multi-grade teaching. One out of every three children in grade 5 (about 10 years old) cannot read and write. Of 100 children who enter the first grade, 40% will drop out by the fifth grade and 60% by the eighth grade. Teacher absenteeism is high; many of those that do show up simply go through the motions of teaching by rote.

RECOGNITION AND REWARD

The foundation focuses on the potential for changing the system. "In India, everything is based on teaching for a test. We want to reform this process," Chacko says.[3] In conjunction with state governments, the foundation runs pilot programs designed to stimulate and motivate teachers, using technology and research, and the advocacy of key learnings. Recognition and rewards – for the school, the principal, the teachers, and the children – are part of the programs. Accountability and professionalism are stressed.

Chacko says many schools have computers that are not being put to good use because many teachers are technology-averse. The foundation creates CD-based software and trains teachers in its usage through its 1,100 field volunteers. "We use games that have themes such as transport, business, how to use the phone. The kids like to attend computer classes. So, it's not just technology – a lot of non-curriculum changes occur."

Chacko says the foundation gave a couple of schools a digital camera and told them to do a presentation with voiceover. "The children went to the village, interviewed people about the history of the local temple, the customs and the stories behind it. That gives them social confidence."[4] In 2007, the foundation's programs reach 18,250 schools, 56,000 teachers, and 2.5 million children. "We think we can scale up. The target is to reach all children," says Chacko.

Premji's great friend and rival in the IT space, Infosys co-founder N.R. Narayana Murthy, also sees the need to give rural children a better chance at school. For him, nutrition is an important factor. If young children are hungry in class, they are vulnerable to disease and

Table 13.1   India's Human Development Index

Life expectancy at birth: 63.6 years
Adult literacy rate (age 15+): 61.0%
Education – combined gross enrolment for primary, secondary, and tertiary
    schools: 62.0%
Children underweight at age five: 47%
Population living on below US$1 a day: 34.7%
Population living on below US$2 a day: 79.9%
Public health spending as % of GDP: 1.2%
Public education spending as % of GDP: 3.3%
Public education spending as % of government spending: 10.7%

Source: UN Human Development Report, 2006

they cannot study properly, he reasons. He advocates giving them one, two, or even three meals a day at school, and getting company taxes to underwrite it.[5] Another Murthy solution is to bring more private enterprise to education. "The best thing is for the government to give a voucher to poor children – those below the poverty line. I understand it costs 16,000 rupees a year for a primary school student in Bangalore [the home-town of Infosys]. If this was in the form of a redeemable voucher, I believe we could create competition among schools in the private sector," he says.[6] Murthy argues that it is the quality of primary and secondary education that must improve, particularly in the rural areas, so that young people have at least the basic skills to move into manufacturing jobs. "Without this, most people will not be employable," he says (see Table 13.1). Information technology is the glamor industry of high skills and high rewards, but it is not going to solve India's job problem. Only manufacturing can do that, says Murthy.

Another key leader in the IT sector, Tata Consultancy Services chief executive S. Ramadorai, similarly believes education is absolutely crucial to India's future. He says it is poised to undergo the biggest changes yet through the application of technology. He urges a drastic change to the education model. "It must be completely unshackled, with affordable loans. Let students have a choice and let schools be set up freely," he argues.[7]

HOLE IN THE WALL

On the technology front, one of the greatest innovators is NIIT co-founder Rajendra Pawar, who has backed his belief in the learning powers of the human mind with funding for the computer "hole in the wall" program. The concept, nurtured by NIIT chief scientist Dr. Sugata Mitra in the late 1990s, is that groups of uneducated children will learn how to use a computer on their own, without any direct teacher intervention, if the tools are put in front of them. The experiment, which began in 1999 with a single computer at Kalkaji in New Delhi, has grown to more than 120 computers in India and elsewhere, as a joint venture between NIIT and the World Bank's International Finance Corporation.[8]

At the higher education level, business leaders agree that the acclaimed Indian Institutes of Technology (IITs) and Indian Institutes of Management (IIMs) turn out thousands of smart graduates every year, but they are the exception to an otherwise dismal rule. Even these elite students still need special training before they are useful to Wipro, Infosys, or TCS. Infosys, for example, has spent US$120 million on its Mysore training center, where fresh recruits spend 18 weeks in basic training in preparation for their real jobs. Goldman Sachs' report on India's 2020 outlook says the success of elite students from the IITs and IIMs "masks the generally abysmal state of higher education in India." Higher education remains heavily regulated, it says, with little to encourage private sector participation or innovation.[9] There are 18,000 Indian colleges and universities, with 11 million students, but many of them graduate with little more than a piece of paper that is a ticket to low-grade work. Their skills are not those in demand by top employers, who want abilities in English, independent analysis, marketing, human resources, and entrepreneurship, combined with "hard" areas such as maths, chemistry, and electrical engineering.

And yet, India is one of the world's great repositories of knowledge, philosophy, and higher education. Indian mathematicians formalized the concept of zero, its scientists pioneered machine tools, and its hydraulic engineers perfected drainage and irrigation systems thousands of years ago. One of the world's earliest universities was at Nalanda (near Patna in Bihar state), a seat of Buddhist learning that was active five centuries before the birth of Christ and had dormitories for students from around 450 CE. Prime Minister Manmohan Singh is pushing for the creation of a South Asian University on Indian soil – preferably at Nalanda – that will bring together the region's brightest students. Global wealth club member Anil Agarwal, chairman of London-based Vedanta Resources (which controls Indian metals and mining group Sterlite), has his own plans for a

Harvard-like campus in Orissa state, to be known as Vedanta University. Other big business houses, from Birla to Tata, and Bajaj to Reliance, have created their own institutions or, like Bharti, Goenka, Kotak, and scores of others, have set up foundations with an educational focus.

There are seven IITs – at Kharagpur (the first, which started in 1950 in Kolkata), Mumbai, Chennai, Kanpur, Delhi, Guwahati, and Roorkee, which began life in 1847 as an engineering college. Their alumni have gone on to great achievements at home and abroad – wealth club members such as Murthy (IIT Kanpur), NIIT's Pawar (IIT Kanpur), and venture capitalist Vinod Khosla (IIT Kharagpur) are just some of the illustrious names. Among business schools, the six IIMs have the same sort of status. Three of them – at Ahmedabad, Bangalore, and Calcutta (Kolkata) – lead the Indian B-school rankings, with the IIMs of Lucknow and Indore in the top 10.[10] The sixth IIM, Kozhikode in Kerala, is not far behind. Other prominent B-school names are the Symbiosis Institute of Business Management at Pune, the Jamnalal Bajaj Institute of Management at Mumbai, the Xavier Labour Relations Institute at Jamshedpur, the Faculty of Management Studies at the University of Delhi, and the Indian Institute of Foreign Trade, Delhi. IIM Ahmedabad is the world's most selective business school, according to The Economist Intelligence Unit, taking only 250 of the 170,000 who apply for its two-year MBA program. But equally, its students can expect to do well after they graduate; IIM-A's top three job placements in 2006 were with an investment bank in Singapore at a starting salary of US$185,000 each.[11] In an average year, the six IIMs will accept a total of only 1,300 students out of the almost 200,000 who apply. The seven IITs will take just 5,000 of the 240,000 who seek a place on their campuses. Many of those who don't make it to an IIT or IIM will go offshore. Others will simply opt for an overseas university in the first place. Their first country of choice is the US, where 80,000 Indian students drawn by names such as Harvard, Yale, Stanford, Kellogg, Wharton, Duke, and Tuck attend university and have accounted for the greatest number of overseas students in the US for the last five years.

BUILDING QUALITY

India's richest man, Reliance Industries chairman Mukesh Ambani, is a Stanford old boy. Recalling his time there 25 years earlier, Ambani told a Mumbai conference early in 2007: "Stanford taught me leadership, and how to get the best from people."[12] Ambani is another business leader who believes India must invest in higher education institutes. (He plans to build a private university between Mumbai and Pune.) "Education, both primary and higher, must be a priority," he says, calling it India's single most important challenge and the one where action is most needed. "We have to build quality in our education, not just capacity."[13] He also wants the private sector to spend more on research and development. "We must move from a screwdriver mindset to a drawing-board mindset," he says, pointing out that India's total annual R&D spend is just US$5 billion, compared with US$285 billion for the United States and US$85 billion for China. On the positive side, Ambani says four trends are driving world prosperity – globalization, use of technology, demographics, and democracy – and in each one, India is ahead of its peers. Demographically, he says, India is young and getting younger. "Unlike China, which may become old before it becomes rich, India has the opportunity to get rich before it becomes old." Ambani sees democracy as a great competitive advantage. "We have proved we can sustain democracy in a poor country. We have shown we can change governments without bloodshed. That is not easy in a country of 1.1 billion, but it gives the world confidence in India. The tail winds are with us," he says.[14]

Still, the fear of social fracturing is universal among India's business leaders. Shiv Khemka of Sun Group warns that ignoring the poor will lead to social instability and chaos: "We must look to the under privileged. India will have greater problems if they are left out of growth over the next 30 to 40 years."[15]

Former McKinsey global chairman Rajat Gupta worries about "negative forces" that might blight the Indian dream. If economic growth doesn't keep pace in creating jobs, he cautions, the demographic dividend will evaporate. India's population explosion then becomes a tremendous risk that could keep the country poorer. He says India needs a robust manufacturing sector, because information technology and business process outsourcing are not enough to transform rural Indian lives. "India must focus on labor-intensive and skilled jobs, such as food processing, automotive components, electronics, and specialty chemicals," he says.[16] And in higher education, Gupta joins other business leaders in urging India to open itself up to foreign universities. Scooter king Rahul Bajaj echoes his words: "In my view, the entry of foreign educational institutions should be encouraged. Currently there's a bit of a policy vacuum about it, which needs to be corrected," he says.[17]

Infrastructure specialist G.M. Rao is even more specific about the education focus: "It is unnecessary to give education in regional languages," he says. "It has to be job orientated and in the English medium. Vocational training is the key. It's not simply a question of churning out people with a BA, because nobody can get jobs and it's just postponing unemployment."[18] Rao's GMR Foundation has a rural training program and is starting English-medium schools. "We teach them useful job skills: tractor repairs, heavy truck driving, air-conditioning repairs, stitching," he says. "When they finish these programs, they make four or five times as much money as those who graduate from university with a BA." Still, Rao is heartened by India's intellectual talent and by what he says is a growing awareness among businesses that it makes good sense to nurture this brainpower. "The US was built on philanthropy – think of Harvard and the other top educational institutes. India is starting to do this; Indian business leaders are thinking about their philanthropic duty. This is a good change."[19] Industrialist Anand Mahindra, whose M&M group has its own set of education initiatives, says that while the country's schooling ranges from the "sublime to the ridiculous," people who can pay for a top-quality education from the private sector are doing so, and making space in government institutions for others. "Getting a solution to the education problem will take time, but it is happening because of the economic incentive," he says. With the economy doing well, people can afford the fees for a good education, and that in turn is lifting the salary and status of teachers. "Teaching is becoming lucrative, so we have a virtuous circle at the higher level," says Mahindra. "But there is no such circle in primary, although there is no shortage of people trying."[20] Mahindra says the quality of primary education in the rural areas is "pathetic." In his view, the importance of better rural education is not so much the link to better agricultural economic growth. "We had the green revolution in India many years ago when we were an even poorer country," he notes. "No, its importance is more to do with social issues, making rural society more enlightened on issues such as caste and empowering women."[21] Even Adi Godrej, one of the most optimistic of the Indian business leaders, sounds a note of caution. While Godrej believes there is no real cause for worry about India's business story over the next five years, "The only concern would be a major domestic political or geo-political upheaval," he says.[22]

PARAMOUNT PRIORITY

Recent research fortifies the view that fixing education is a paramount priority. "To embark upon its growth story, India will have to educate its children and its young people (especially its women) and it must do so in a hurry. Lack of education can be a critical constraint to the growth of the knowledge-based IT sector, as well as in the move to mass employment in manufacturing. The demographic dividend may not materialize if India fails to educate its people," the authors of the 2007 Goldman Sachs India outlook note.[23] That link to employability is well recognized. In the view of California-based mentor capitalist and Google investor K. Ram Shriram, a rising company should always go for the best people. "When it comes to hiring, bad quality can be a fatal mistake for entrepreneurs," Shriram says.[24] The inconsistency of India's higher education system is a "real problem" for the country, he warns; outside the top IITs and maybe 10 to 15 other science and business institutions, there is a big gap. Still, Shriram is optimistic: "In the next few years I see a huge amount of entrepreneurship coming out of India. The younger generation have ambition, energy, and smarts – and business people are now their heroes," he says (see Table 13.2).[25] Even if action sometimes seems slow in coming, at least the shortcomings are acknowledged at the highest levels of government: "Our higher education system is in need of comprehensive reforms," Prime Minister Manmohan Singh noted in early 2007 when he released a report by the National Knowledge Commission.[26] It is critical that education and the other impediments to India's growth are removed as quickly as possible. As Praful C. Patel, South Asia Region

Table 13.2   Human Development Index, Selected World Rankings

1. Norway
2. Iceland
3. Australia
7. Japan
8. United States
18. United Kingdom
25. Singapore
81. China
126. INDIA
134. Pakistan

Source: UN Human Development Report, 2006

vice-president for the World Bank, pointed out in December 2006, leaving the poor behind means the fault line between the haves and the have-nots in India will only widen. "Eliminating poverty will enlist another quarter of the population in productive economic activity," he noted. "Imagine how much more spectacular India's story could be if it builds the human capital of the 28 percent left outside."[27]

The last word goes to India's pre-eminent member of the global wealth club, Mukesh Ambani. Asked to define his key success factors, this is what he tells budding entrepreneurs: "1. Stick to first principles and have a clear business model. 2. Win the people's hearts and minds. Get them excited so they are loyal to the cause. 3. Maintain absolute diligence and focus. Never give up."[28] That may not be the solution to all of India's myriad challenges, which extend from education and health, to social injustice, environmental degradation, rural poverty, poor infrastructure, lack of resources, corrupt politicians and bureaucrats, rapacious commercial interests, inefficient judiciary, poor policing, lawlessness, terrorism, and discrimination by caste, creed, community, and color. But Ambani's motto may be a good starting point for the continued economic success India needs if it is to have any real chance of fixing its problems.

ENDNOTES

1. Wipro chairman Azim H. Premji, "The Significance of Education," *Azim Premji Foundation Newsletter*, November 2006.
2. Azim H. Premji, in *India Today*, November 27, 2006.
3. Interview with Anina Chacko, Azim Premji Foundation, Bangalore, January 23, 2007.
4. ibid.
5. Interview with Infosys co-founder N.R. Narayana Murthy, Mumbai, January 15, 2007.
6. ibid.
7. Tata Consultancy Services CEO S. Ramadorai, press conference, Mumbai, January 15, 2007.
8. NIIT chairman Rajendra Pawar, in media release on Hole-in-the Wall Education Ltd., May 5, 2007.
9. Global Economics Paper No. 152, "India's Rising Growth Potential," Goldman Sachs, January 22, 2007.
10. "The best business schools," *India Today*, July 17, 2006.
11. "Final Placements 2006 at IIM Ahmedabad," on Indian Institute of Management-Ahmedabad website: www.iimahd.ernet.in.
12. Speech by Mukesh Ambani to "Stanford in India" innovation conference, Mumbai, January 16, 2007.
13. ibid.

14. ibid.
15. Speech by Shiv Khemka, Sun Group, to Wharton India Economic Forum, Philadelphia, November 11, 2006.
16. Speech by Rajat Gupta, McKinsey former global chairman, to Wharton India Economic Forum, Philadelphia, November 11, 2006.
17. Speech by Rahul Bajaj to Wharton India Economic Forum, Philadelphia, November 11, 2006.
18. Interview with G.M. Rao, New Delhi, January 22, 2007.
19. ibid.
20. Interview with Anand Mahindra, Mumbai, January 18, 2007.
21. ibid.
22. Adi Godrej, emailed response to author's questions, February 2007.
23. Goldman Sachs report, op. cit.
24. Interview with K. Ram Shriram, February 15, 2007.
25. ibid.
26. Indian Prime Minister Manmohan Singh, "Comprehensive reforms needed for higher education," *The Business Standard*, January 14, 2007.
27. Praful C. Patel, "30 years ahead. Will every fourth poor person still be Indian?" *India Today*, December 18, 2006.
28. Ambani, op. cit.

PART TWO

The Profiles

India's Global Wealth Club: The Top 100 Names

The Top 100, based on Market Capitalizations and Exchange Rates prevailing at June 1, 2007

Ranking	Name	Country	Main Company	Wealth (US$)
1.	Lakshmi N. Mittal	UK/India	Arcelor Mittal	$35.0 billion
2.	Mukesh D. Ambani	India	Reliance Industries	$30.5 billion
3.	Anil D. Ambani	India	Reliance Communications	$21.0 billion
4.	Kushal P. Singh & family	India	DLF Group	$20.5 billion
5.	Sunil B. Mittal	India	Bharti	$17.75 billion
6.	Azim Hasham Premji	India	Wipro	$15.0 billion
7.	K.M. Birla & family	India	Aditya Birla Group	$7.0 billion
8.	Tulsi Tanti & family	India	Suzlon Group	$6.6 billion
9.	Hinduja brothers	UK/India/ Switzerland	Hinduja Group	$6.5 billion
10.	Ramesh Chandra	India	Unitech	$6.4 billion
11.	Shashi N. Ruia & family	India	Essar	$6.2 billion
12.	P.S. Mistry	India	Shapoorji Pallonji Group	$5.05 billion
13.	Anil Agarwal	UK/India	Vedanta/Sterlite	$4.95 billion
14.	Adi B. Godrej & family	India	Godrej Group	$4.0 billion
15.	Shiv Nadar	India	HCL Technologies	$3.95 billion

**The Top 100, based on Market Capitalizations and Exchange Rates
prevailing at June 1, 2007 (*Continued*)**

Ranking	Name	Country	Main Company	Wealth (US$)
16.	Dilip S. Shanghvi	India	Sun Pharmaceutical	$3.71 billion
17.	Grandhi M. Rao	India	GMR Infrastructure	$3.2 billion
18.	Kalanithi Maran	India	Sun TV	$3.0 billion
19.	Uday Kotak	India	Kotak Mahindra Bank	$2.34 billion
20.	Venugopal N. Dhoot	India	Videocon	$1.72 billion
21.	Rahul K. Bajaj	India	Bajaj Auto	$1.68 billion
22.	Yusuf K. Hamied	India	Cipla	$1.68 billion
23.	Vivek C. Burman	India	Dabur India Group	$1.65 billion
24.	Jaiprakash Gaur	India	Jaiprakash Associates	$1.56 billion
25.	N.R. Narayana Murthy & family	India	Infosys	$1.51 billion
26.	Kavitark Ram Shriram	US	Sherpalo Ventures	$1.5 billion
27.	Amar Gopal Bose	US	Bose Sound	$1.5 billion
28.	Mike Jatania & brothers	UK	Lornamead	$1.5 billion
29.	Subhash Chandra	India	Zee TV	$1.45 billion
30.	Anurag Dikshit	Gibraltar	PartyGaming	$1.45 billion
31.	Savitri D. Jindal & family	India	Jindal Steel	$1.35 billion
32.	Vijay Mallya	India	UB Group	$1.3 billion
33.	Rajan B. Raheja	India	Exide Industries	$1.3 billion
34.	Naresh Goyal	UK/India	Jet Airways	$1.3 billion
35.	Vikas Oberoi	India	Oberoi Constructions	$1.26 billion
36.	Malvinder & Shivinder Singh	India	Ranbaxy Labs	$1.25 billion
37.	Pradeep K. Jain & family	India	Parsvnath Developers	$1.18 billion
38.	Jignesh P. Shah	India	Financial Technologies	$1.16 billion
39.	B. Ramalinga Raju	India	Satyam Computer Services	$1.1 billion
40.	Gracias A. Saldanha	India	Glenmark Pharmaceuticals	$1.08 billion
41.	Murli Kewalram Chanrai	Singapore	Olam/Kewalram Chanrai Group	$1.07 billion

The Top 100, based on Market Capitalizations and Exchange Rates prevailing at June 1, 2007 (*Continued*)

Ranking	Name	Country	Main Company	Wealth (US$)
42.	Bharat Desai	US	Syntel	$1.04 billion
43.	Nandan M. Nilekani & family	India	Infosys	$1.0 billion
44.	Cyrus S. Poonawalla & family	India	Serum Institute of India/ Poonawalla Group	$1.0 billion
45.	Keshub Mahindra	India	Mahindra & Mahindra	$930 million
46.	Senapathy "Kris" Gopalakrishnan	India	Infosys	$930 million
47.	Ashwin C. Choksi	India	Asian Paints	$930 million
48.	Brijmohan Lall Munjal	India	Hero Honda	$903 million
49.	Chinankanna Sivasankaran	Singapore/ India/US	Sterling Infotech	$900 million
50.	Gautam Thapar	India	BILT	$880 million
51.	Anu Aga	India	Thermax	$870 million
52.	Habil F. Khorakiwala	India	Wockhardt	$838 million
53.	Lord Swraj Paul & family	UK	Caparo Steel	$837 million
54.	Gulu Lalvani	UK	Binatone	$810 million
55.	Vijay & Bhiku Patel	UK	Waymade Healthcare	$800 million
56.	Desh Bandhu Gupta	India	Lupin Laboratories	$750 million
57.	Pankaj R. Patel	India	Cadila Healthcare	$733 million
58.	Tom T. Singh	UK	New Look	$732 million
59.	Kiran Mazumdar-Shaw	India	Biocon	$723 million
60.	Venu Srinivasan	India	TVS Motors	$715 million
61.	Vinod Khosla	US	Khosla Ventures	$700 million
62.	K. Dinesh & family	India	Infosys	$700 million
63.	Baba N. Kalyani	India	Bharat Forge	$695 million
64.	Dr. K. Anji Reddy	India	Dr. Reddy's Laboratories	$683 million
65.	Kishore Biyani & family	India	Pantaloon Retail	$670 million
66.	Ajay G. Piramal	India	Nicholas Piramal	$656 million
67.	Jasminder Singh	UK	Edwardian Group	$630 million

The Top 100, based on Market Capitalizations and Exchange Rates prevailing at June 1, 2007 (*Continued*)

Ranking	Name	Country	Main Company	Wealth (US$)
68.	S.D. Shibulal & family	India/US	Infosys	$600 million
69.	Atul C. Kirloskar & family	India	Kirloskar Brothers	$600 million
70.	Karsanbhai K. Patel	India	Nirma	$588 million
71.	Nusli N. Wadia	India	Wadia Group	$575 million
72.	Vikrant Bhargava	Gibraltar	Party Gaming	$550 million
73.	Narendra Patni	US/India	Patni Computer Systems	$545 million
74.	Amin M. Lalji & family	Canada	Larco Group	$520 million
75.	Shyam S. & Hari S. Bhartia	India	Jubilant Organosys	$508 million
76.	Analjit Singh	India	Max India	$500 million
77.	Chandru L. Raheja	India	K. Raheja Corp.	$500 million
78.	Purnendu C. Chatterjee	US	The Chatterjee Group (TCG)	$500 million
79.	Rakesh R. Jhunjhunwala	India	Rare Enterprises	$470 million
80.	Hari N. Harilela & family	Hong Kong	Harilela Group	$450 million
81.	P.R.S. Oberoi	India	Oberoi Group	$445 million
82.	Rana Kapoor	India	YES Bank	$434 million
83.	Gururaj Deshpande	US/Canada	Sycamore	$420 million
84.	Sabeer Bhatia	US/India	Navin Communications	$400 million
85.	Vikram Chatwal & family	US	Hampshire Hotels & Resorts	$400 million
86.	G.V. Krishna Reddy	India	GVK Group	$400 million
87.	R.P. Goenka	India	RPG Group	$395 million
88.	P.V. Ramaprasad Reddy & family	India	Aurobindo Pharma	$366 million
89.	Sudhakar & Sreekanth Ravi	US	Code Green Networks	$345 million
90.	N.S. Raghavan & family	India	Infosys	$320 million
91.	Pradeep Sindhu	US	Juniper Networks	$300 million
92.	Ratan N. Tata & Tata family	India	TCS	$295 million

The Top 100, based on Market Capitalizations and Exchange Rates prevailing at June 1, 2007 (*Continued*)

Ranking	Name	Country	Main Company	Wealth (US$)
93.	Manu Chandaria	Kenya/UK	Comcraft	$280 million
94.	Rajendra S. Pawar	India	NIIT	$250 million
95.	Sanjiv Sidhu	US	i2Technologies	$200 million
96.	Mukesh Chatter	US	NeoSaej	$200 million
97.	Asim Ghosh	India	Vodafone Essar	$200 million
98.	Vidya M. Chhabria & family	Dubai	Jumbo Group	$200 million
99.	Gautam H. Singhania	India	Raymond	$160 million
100.	Karan Bilimoria	UK	Cobra Beer	$150 million

Note: Exchange rates at June 1, 2007: USD = 40.5 rupees, 0.5045 Stg, 0.7438 euro, $1.53 Singapore, $1.06 Canada, $1.2 Australia, $7.81 HK, 67 Kenya shillings.

Profiles of the Top 100

1. Lakshmi N. MITTAL, United Kingdom/India

Estimated net worth: US$35 billion.

Position: CEO, Arcelor Mittal. Founder of LNM Group.

Born: June 15, 1950 in Sadulpur, Rajasthan. Eldest son of Mohan Lal Mittal, founder of Ispat group.

Educated: St. Xavier's College, Kolkata; B.Com.,* University of Kolkata.

Marital status: Married to Usha. Two children: son Aditya (B.Sc. in economics, Wharton School, University of Pennsylvania) is CFO of Arcelor; and daughter Vanisha Mittal Bhatia (B.A. in business administration, European Business School; M.A., School of Oriental and African Studies, University of London) is on the board of Mittal Steel.

Interests: Swimming, yoga.

London-based Lakshmi Niwas Mittal and his family hold a stake of 43.5% in the combined Arcelor Mittal Group, formed in August 2006 as the world's largest steelmaker after the merger of Arcelor and Mittal Steel. The market capitalization of the group is about US$80 billion, and Mittal is confident it will be earning US$20 billion a year by 2008. It employs about 330,000 people in 60 countries, with production capacity of 130 million tonnes of steel a year, or about 10% of world steel output. That makes it three times larger than its closest rival, Japan's Nippon Steel.

*The abbreviations "Com." (commerce), "Eng." (engineering), and "Sc." (science) are used for consistency across the profiles and may differ from the abbreviations adopted by the named institutions themselves.

The 2006 merger, initially dubbed hostile by the Arcelor board, was an exhausting but ultimately triumphant business deal for the tenacious Mittal. Though excoriated by some European critics over the company's ethnicity and the color of its money, Mittal played it cool and straight throughout, gradually convincing key investors that the merger would bring greater value. Mittal Steel, which had become the world's No. 2 steel company after the merger of Ispat International and LNM Group in December 2004, along with its acquisition of International Steel Group of the US, is known as a low-cost producer. Arcelor, world No. 1 after its creation in 2002 from the merger of European majors Aceralia, Arbed, and Usinor, leads the high-end steel segment. Mittal's next targets: the politically difficult China market, the Middle East, and India itself.

Mittal has always had the No. 1 spot as his goal, even as a young man struggling to do well with a steel plant in the testing environment of Indonesia in 1976. That became the launch pad for his own enterprise: in 1989 he set up Ispat International, and five years later he split from the family steel business his father Mohan had started in the 1950s. His father and younger brothers Pramod and Vinod have contined to run domestically focused Ispat Industries from their Mumbai base. Mittal is regarded as a master of timing, knowing when to move in on distressed or under-performing steel businesses. He has been willing to use new technology and processes to squeeze greater productivity from the steel operations he buys around the world. Mittal was named "Person of the Year 2006" by the *Financial Times* after the Arcelor deal, and was awarded a Fellowship by King's College London in January 2007.

The "Man of Steel" isn't afraid to spend money: along with owning a yacht and private jets, in 2004 he paid US$120 million for a 12-bedroom Kensington, London mansion previously owned by F1 racing boss Bernie Ecclestone. Daughter Vanisha's wedding in June 2004 to Amit Bhatia was one of the society events of the year, with a lavish reception at Versailles and performances by pop singer Kylie Minogue and Bollywood star Shah Rukh Khan. Khan also performed at son Aditya's high-profile wedding in Kolkata in 1998.

Mittal Investments holds the family stake in Arcelor Mittal and in other businesses, such as a US$1 billion half-share in a Kazakhstan oilfield venture with Russia's Lukoil.

2. Mukesh D. AMBANI, India

Estimated net worth: US$30.5 billion.

Position: Chairman, Reliance Industries Ltd.

Born: April 19, 1957 in Aden. Siblings are younger brother Anil (b. July 1959), sisters Dipti (b. January 1961) and Nina (b. July 1962). Son of Dhirubhai Ambani (December 1932–July 2002) and Kokila-ben Patel Ambani.

Educated: B.Eng. in chemical engineering, University of Mumbai; studied for MBA, Stanford University, US.

Marital status: Married to Nita; twin boy and girl Akash and Isha, and second son Anant.

Interests: Hindi films; spending time with his children, who are students at the Dhirubhai Ambani International School in Mumbai; visiting Africa, or the temple town of Tirumala-Tirupati in Andhra Pradesh. Personal transport options include Mercedes S class, Maybach sedan, an Airbus corporate jet, or a long-range Bombardier Global Express.

Despite the slow-burning Ambani sibling feud that kept India's corporate world fascinated for much of the mid-2000s after the death of their entrepreneurial father Dhirubhai in July 2002, the brothers, Mukesh and Anil, have been able to grow their separate business empires substantially since the great split was formalized by their mother Kokila-ben in June 2005. Mukesh, who kept his father's flagship Reliance Industries Ltd. (RIL), has seen it prosper mightily under his hand. Already India's largest private sector conglomerate, RIL by mid-2007 had a market capitalization of more than US$60 billion and annual sales of US$24 billion, despite being forced to spin off stakes in Reliance Energy, Reliance Capital, and its telecom interests, as part of the family restructure. Mukesh Ambani, his mother, family, and associated companies control just over 50% of RIL shares. His uncle, Ramniklal H. Ambani, is also a director of RIL.

The future looks bright for Ambani, with his Reliance Fresh project the first of many retail ventures destined to drive Reliance to leadership of this sector. Oil and gas also beckons. But perhaps the biggest business opportunity of them all may be the new Reliance-backed city planned for Navi Mumbai and Maha Mumbai, on the outskirts of India's commercial capital, covering 35,000 acres (14,000 hectares) of land designated as special economic zones. With its own airport on the drawing board, plus a high-speed roadlink across the water to Mumbai and space for apartments, malls, hi-tech industries, and entertainment parks, the megalopolis could be a transforming venture for the Maharashtra government and Reliance. Or it could become snarled in disputes over land, access, and infrastructure costs.

Mukesh, named Ernst & Young's "Entrepreneur of the Year 2000" and the *Economic Times*' "Businessman of the Year 2006," is maximum bullish on India's economic outlook. In January 2007, he stated that the world had once mocked India's growth aspirations. "But today," he declared, "I believe M.O.C.K. stands for market, outsourcing, capital and knowledge. India's Market is big enough for the whole world. India was the first to do large scale Outsourcing. In Capital, India is both a growing target of foreign direct investment and a provider of capital. India was the fountainhead of ancient Knowledge. Today India has knowledge power in KPO, BPO, biotech etc."

After the 2005 business split, the Ambani brothers and their families continued to live under one Mumbai roof with their mother Kokilaben at the 14-story "Sea Wind" building on Cuffe Parade, Colaba. But Mukesh is building a new high-rise house in Altamount Road, Cumbala Hill, due for completion in late 2008.

3. Anil D. AMBANI, India

Estimated net worth: US$21.0 billion.

Position: Chairman, Anil Dhirubhai Ambani Group (ADAG).

Born: June 4, 1959 in Mumbai. Siblings are elder brother Mukesh (b. April 1957), sisters Dipti (b. January 1961) and Nina (b. July 1962). Son of Dhirubhai Ambani (December 1932–July 2002) and Kokilaben Patel Ambani.

Educated: B.Sc., University of Mumbai; MBA, Wharton School, University of Pennsylvania.

Marital status: Married to former film star Tina Munim; sons Jai Anmol and Jai Anshul.

Interests: Marathon running. Tina helps aspiring artists through her annual art exhibition, the "Harmony Show," and supports the Dignity Foundation for the aged. The Ambanis are close pals of Bollywood uberstar Amitabh Bachchan and his family, which now includes daughter-in-law Aishwarya Rai.

In 2003, about a year before the first rumblings of friction in the Reliance empire, Anil Ambani told an audience at India's Entrepreneurship Development Institute in Ahmedabad that "pedigree is no longer of any significance in modern India. It is performance that is crucial." Four years later, and the younger Ambani is performing at full throttle. His business base is the 140-acre (56-hectare) Dhirubhai Ambani Knowledge City – named after his father – in Navi (New) Mumbai. From this hi-tech campus, Ambani can keep tabs on his various business enterprises, which are led by flagship Reliance Communications since the June 2005 split with elder brother Mukesh. By mid-2007, Reliance Communications (Reliance Info-Comm before the restructure) had 30 million customers, including 28 million mobile subscribers, and a market capitalization of about US$25.6 billion, making it India's second most valuable telecoms company behind Bharti Airtel. It will become even more valuable under Ambani's plan to integrate his telecom and media assets through a new global optic fiber cable network that his FLAG Telecom – controlled by Reliance Communications – is building. Ambani says the 72,000-mile (115,000-kilometer) Internet Protocol network, due for completion by late 2009, will "democratize digital access and give nearly everyone in the world the opportunity to be part of a massive lifestyle change." Along with communications and infotainment, Ambani's other interests include financial services, healthcare, power distribution, and big infrastructure projects such as the long-awaited Mumbai metro. His ADAG conglomerate, encompassing Reliance Communications, Reliance Capital, Reliance Energy, Reliance Natural Resources, and Adlabs Films, has a total market capitalization of about US$40 billion. His Reliance Mutual Fund manages assets of about US$10 billion. Ambani and associated family companies control about 66% of Reliance Communications.

A vegetarian and teetotaler, Anil remains very much the family man, honoring his mother and respecting his older brother. He can be found most early mornings pounding the pavements of Mumbai, preparing for the next great race. For when it comes to performance, there's nothing quite like a super-fit marathon man.

4. Kushal Pal SINGH and family, India

Estimated net worth: US$20.5 billion.

Position: Chairman, DLF Group.

Born: August 15, 1931 in Bulandshahar, Uttar Pradesh state. Son of Muktar Singh.

Educated: B.Sc., Meerut College, Uttar Pradesh; Indian Military Academy, Dehradun; Royal Military Academy, Sandhurst, UK.

Marital status: Married Indira, eldest daughter of Delhi Land and Finance founder Raghvendra Singh, on March 6, 1954. Three children: son Rajiv (mechanical engineering, MIT) and daughter Pia (B.Sc., Wharton School of Business, University of Pennsylvania) both work for DLF. Elder daughter Renuka is married to banker and DLF board member Rana G.S. Talwar.

Interests: Golf. Keeps an apartment in London's Grosvenor Square.

DLF Group, which grew out of Delhi Land & Finance Co. – established by K.P. Singh's father-in-law Raghvendra Singh in September 1946 – is India's biggest real estate developer, with a hugely valuable land bank of up to 10,200 acres (4,000 hectares). Its showpiece is DLF City in the New Delhi fringe town of Gurgaon, where more than 3,000 acres (1,200 hectares) have been developed as hi-tech corporate headquarters, shopping malls, upscale apartments, villas, and detached houses for the capital's executives and emerging middle class. K.P. Singh created DLF City through judicious property purchases from farmers in the rural settlements of Ahris and Jats, beginning in 1979–80. Getting the land he wanted meant months of negotiations with hundreds of farming families. Sometimes, getting clear title to one small plot of four or five acres (around two hectares) involved getting the consent of 30 adults. Singh said his strategy in creating DLF City was to give people "compelling reasons" to move there. The ability to walk to work, and to walk to leisure facilities, schools, hospitals, and shops, was the lure – along with a competitive price. In a 2005 interview in the *Business Standard* newspaper, Singh recalled how it was done: "We provided free transport to the site to potential buyers and offered various discounts . . . Bank finance was exorbitant and difficult to obtain, so we created our own finance schemes." DLF has also developed another 20 "urban colonies" in and around Delhi, and has projects under way or planned in Kolkata, Chandigarh, Mumbai, Pune, Bangalore, Chennai, Cochin, and Hyderabad.

Singh comes from a family of lawyers. After graduating from Sandhurst in the UK, he joined The Deccan Horse, a cavalry regiment of the Indian Army. After leaving the military, Singh joined American Universal Electric Company, a joint venture between Universal Electric of Michigan and Singh's family. Later Singh set up Willard India, a joint venture with ESB of Philadelphia, to make automotive batteries. American Universal was merged into DLF in 1979. Singh had joined his father-in-law's real estate company in 1971. Today, DLF's focus is real estate, but the group's related infrastructure services include power, leisure, and entertainment.

In a 2005 essay in *The Economic Times* to mark the 100th birthday of his mentor, George Warren Hoddy of Universal Electric, Singh noted: "As a CEO, it's essential to have big dreams and be a bit of a visionary. But it's equally necessary to be pragmatic and to acknowledge that things don't always work as planned. The key to success lies in being undaunted in the face of setbacks, and indeed, to learn from failure." DLF was forced to withdraw a planned initial public offer in September 2006 when some minority shareholders challenged a rights issue. The revised offer, constituting a 10.2% stake, went on sale in June 2007 at 525 rupees a share. DLF listed on July 5, ending its first trading day with a modest gain of 8 percent and a market capitalization of about $23.7 billion. Singh and family companies hold a stake of 87.5%, most of which is subject to a one-year lock-in before it can be sold.

5. Sunil Bharti MITTAL, India

Estimated net worth: US$17.75 billion.

Position: Founder and chairman: Bharti Enterprises.

Born: October 23, 1957 in Ludhiana, Punjab. Son of parliamentarian Sat Paul Mittal and Lalita. Elder brother Rakesh and younger brother Rajan are vice-chairman and managing director, respectively, of Bharti Enterprises.

Educated: B.A., Punjab University, 1979; Owner/President Management Program, Harvard, 1999.

Marital status: Married to Nyna; daughter Eiesha (b. 1986), and twin sons Kavin and Shravin (b. 1989).

Interests: Yoga, meditation, chess, and various sports, including golf, tennis, and table tennis. His Bharti Foundation funds schools and a technology and management center at the Indian Institute of Technology, Delhi.

Bharti Airtel, the listed flagship of Mittal's Bharti Group, is India's most valuable mobile, broadband, and fixed-line telephone services company, with a market capitalization in mid-2007 of about US$40 billion. Mittal's majority-owned Bharti Telecom Ltd. holds a stake of 45.36%. The other big shareholder is Singapore Telecommunications, with 31%. Bharti Airtel has almost a quarter of India's hotly contested mobile market, doing battle with Reliance Communications, former 10% stakeholder Vodafone (which bought Hutch-Essar), and state-owned carriers BSNL and MTNL to win the business of 180 million subscribers – a May 2007 number that is rising by about seven million customers a month. Mittal says he is confident India will have 500 million mobile phones by 2010, and he wants to hang on to his quarter-share.

While telecoms has been the key driver of Mittal's meteoric rise to prominence in the past decade, he has even bigger ambitions in retail, where his alliance with US giant Wal-Mart looks likely to reshape India's organized shopping sector. A joint venture with France's AXA in life insurance also is tapping into a big new growth opportunity among India's middle classes. A fresh food export venture with the Rothschild family, media, software operations, and a tourism hotel in the Seychelles are all part of the Bharti spread of interests.

Mittal, Ernst & Young's "Entrepreneur of the Year" in 2004 and *Fortune*'s "Asia Businessman of the Year" in 2006, is a self-made billionaire, notwithstanding his privileged upbringing. At the age of 18, with working capital of 20,000 rupees, he started making bicycle parts in his home-town of Ludhiana in northern India's Punjab state. He moved to Delhi and set up his first company, Bharti Healthcare, in 1983, but had an eye for the coming growth in the telecommunications industry. In the mid-1980s, Mittal and his two brothers Rakesh and Rajan went into the manufacture and sale of telephones, fax machines, and cordless phones. They would drive around Delhi on two-wheelers to clinch sales. In 1992 Mittal bid for and won his first mobile phone license for the Delhi metro area. Since then, he has gradually picked up more licenses to have a nationwide presence in India's 23 "circles" or telecom zones, along the way bringing in investors such as Singapore Telecom and the US private equity firm Warburg Pincus. In October 2005, Vodafone paid about US$1.5 billion for a 10% economic interest in the company, then known as Bharti Tele-Ventures, buying shares from Warburg Pincus and Bharti Enterprises. It agreed to sell 5.6% back to Bharti for US$1.6 billion in February 2007.

Mittal says money isn't his driving force; what matters most, he says, is recognition of his work. Plus, he would like to play a larger role in society – not in politics, but to help empower people. He admires the Tata business model, because the Tatas "never compromise," and the Ambanis for their entrepreneurial flair. Talking to business historian Gita Piramal in November 2006, Mittal said: "Speed has always been our biggest weapon. If you start at the curve at the same time, even if the biggies are there at the same time, you have a chance to survive. If you start on that curve four or five years down the road, when the biggies have taken a position, it is almost impossible to compete with them." He tells would-be entrepreneurs not to be content with one job or one product, but to dream big while managing the risk.

Mittal was awarded the Padma Bhushan, one of India's highest civilian honors, in January 2007 for his services to the telecommunications industry, and was elected president of the Confederation of Indian Industry for 2007/08.

6. Azim Hasham PREMJI, India

Estimated net worth: US$15.0 billion.

Position: Chairman, Wipro Corp.

Born: July 24, 1945 in Mumbai. Son of Mohamed Husain and Gulbanoo Premji.

Educated: B.Sc. in electrical engineering, Stanford University, US. Honorary doctorates from IIT Roorkee and Manipal Academy of Higher Education.

Marital status: Married to Yasmeen (B.A. (Hons) in psychology, St. Xavier's College, University of Mumbai; M.A. in psychology, Smith College, Massachusetts, US). Elder son Rishad (MBA, Harvard Business School, 2005) joined Wipro in mid-2007 after a stint as a management consultant and is married to Aditi; younger son Tariq spent time working at the Azim Premji Foundation, and now handles family investments.

Interests: Collecting art, hiking, jogging, his pet dogs, and education for disadvantaged children through his Azim Premji Foundation, where wife Yasmeen also is on the board.

Bangalore-based Azim Premji and companies he controls hold a stake of 79.6% in information technology standard-bearer Wipro, which had a market capitalization in mid-2007 of US$19.4 billion and revenues of US$3.5 billion. Premji, who in 2005 was awarded one of India's highest civilian honors, the Padma Bhushan, is the country's greatest advocate and practitioner of discipline and ethics in the IT sector and in business in general. "Unyielding integrity" is part of the company's mantra. He says he demands of others only what he demands of himself. Premji is famously frugal, declining to fly first class. Out of 68,000 employees, only about 100 Wiproites fly business class internationally; for everyone else, it's economy (coach) class – and it's economy class for everyone for flights within India.

Premji took over the family's Mumbai food company, Western India Vegetable Products, in 1966 at the age of 21, when his father M.H. Premji died suddenly. Premji was forced to cut short his engineering studies at Stanford University (he finished the course years later) and return to India. In the four decades since, he has transformed the family business (renamed Wipro in 1997) from a US$2 million a year processor of cooking oil to an IT hardware and software services giant with an unparalleled reputation for probity. It is one of the world's top three offshore providers of business process outsourcing (BPO), and the world's largest independent R&D services provider. The telecom and finance sectors account for 60% of its BPO revenues, with healthcare and travel in its sights. Along with its mainstream IT work, which accounts for 90% of revenue, Wipro operates in consumer and lighting products, and in infrastructure engineering.

Aside from working 12- to 14-hour days to ensure Wipro charts the right business course, Premji's great passion is education for India's underprivileged children. He is scathing of the Indian educational experience. This is how he described it recently: "Autocratic classrooms, mechanical teaching, negligible intrinsic motivation, and learning that is estranged from reality – these characterize most Indian schools, urban or rural, private or government, elite or impoverished. If schools today mirror tomorrow's society, we need to be alarmed." Premji says the choices India makes in education will determine if its seemingly inevitable rise to global economic powerhouse is "for the greater good of all."

Speculation that Premji's two sons will have a role in Wipro in the years ahead was heightened in mid-2007 after elder son Rishad was approved by the board to join the company. Premji will say only that Wipro is a meritocracy, where family ties should not discriminate for or against anyone.

7. Kumar Mangalam BIRLA and family, India

Estimated net worth: US$7.0 billion.

Position: Chairman, Aditya Birla Group.

Born: June 14, 1967. Son of the late Aditya V. Birla. Mother Rajashree
Birla is chair of the Aditya Birla Centre for Community Initiatives
and Rural Development. Sister Vasavadatta Bajaj (b. June 10, 1976)
is a trustee of the center.

Educated: B.Com., Fellow member, Institute of Chartered Accountants India; MBA, London Business School, 1992.

Marital status: Married Neerja Kasliwal in 1988. Three children: daughter Ananyashree, son Aryaman Vikram, daughter
Advaitesha.

Interests: Collecting art, Hindi movies, discourse on the *Bhagavad Gita*
(the Sanskrit text that is sometimes described as a guide to life).
Sits on the board of the Reserve Bank of India. Sponsors a school
for boys, the Sarala Birla Academy, in Bangalore. Wife Neerja helps
young artists through the Birla Academy of Art & Culture.

K.M. Birla is the great global con-
solidator, lifting revenues of his
Mumbai-based Aditya Birla Group
above US$20 billion a year with
transformational deals such as the
February 2007 takeover of Canadian
aluminum major Novelis for US$6
billion by Hindalco Industries, the
group's metals company. Birla described the buy as part of his vision
"of taking India to the world." Other
key steps include his taking control
in mid-2006 of now-listed mobile
phone company Idea Cellular, and a
recent move into retail through the
buyout of Trinethra Group, which
will be unified under Birla's "More"
brand name. By mid-2007, the market capitalizations of his twin flagships Grasim Industries and Hindalco Industries were about US$5.6
billion and US$4.3 billion, respectively, while the high-flying Idea Cel-
lular, listed in March 2007, is valued by the market at more than US$8

billion. Birla, a noted team-builder, has been running the group for more than a decade. He was thrust to the fore at age 28 when his father Aditya Vikram Birla, then chairman, died suddenly in the US on October 1, 1995. Birla, who quickly renamed the business Aditya Birla Group after his father, began a long process of review and corporate restructuring that culminated in a string of mergers and acquisitions in the late 1990s and has continued to the present day. Commodities such as copper, cement, aluminum, pulp, and viscose stable fiber underpin much of the group's revenues, but telecoms, retail, insurance, BPO, information technology, and branded garments are all part of the Birla mix. The group has 85,000 employees around the world.

Birla stepped down from the board of Tata Steel in August 2006 after eight years, citing a lack of time. But relations with the Tata Group went sour over a dispute about their stakes in Idea Cellular, the end result of a venture that began in 2000 between Tata, Birla, and AT&T. In the end, Birla bought out the 48% Tata stake for about US$1 billion.

Birla has also been a peacemaker for estranged members of the wider Birla clan, which ruptured in 1987 in the wake of great-grandfather G.D. Birla's death in 1983 and a subsequent asset splitting that left grandfather Basant Birla and father Aditya Birla with the best businesses. Like the Bajaj, Goenka, and Khaitan families, the Birlas are Marwaris, whose origins in the harsh Marwar desert area of central India have left them with great commercial instincts. Birla, who spends a lot of time aboard his Gulfstream corporate jet, sees the global war for talent intensifying. Success, he says, will favor those companies "in which the leadership is alchemical and values-driven."

8. Tulsi TANTI and family, India

Estimated net worth: US$6.6 billion.
Position: Chairman, Suzlon Group.
Born: 1958 in Rajkot, Gujarat. Family moved to Ahmedabad and then
    Pune. Younger brothers Vinod, Jitendra and Girish and their fami-
    lies are shareholders in Suzlon.
Educated: B.Com.; diploma in mechanical engineering, Rajkot
    College.
Marital status: Married to Gita; two children, son Pranav and daughter
    Nidhi.
Interests: Going on vacation with his family.

Tulsi Tanti and his family hold
69.75% of Suzlon Energy, the Indian
wind power company that had a
market capitalization of more than
US$9 billion in June 2007. Younger
brother Girish heads Suzlon's international operations. Suzlon has
Asia's largest wind farm – a 201 MW
facility on a mountain plateau at
Vankusawade, about 25 miles (40
kilometers) from Satara in India's
Maharashtra state, about 125 miles
(200 kilometers) southeast of
Mumbai. On the drawing board is
a 1,500 MW-capacity export-driven
turbine manufacturing plant near
Udipi, Karnataka, close to the new
Mangalore port.

India is the world's third-largest producer of wind energy. According to Tanti, the installed cost of wind power is expensive, but because
no fuel is required, there is no escalation in the cost of production.
"We have the potential to have 45,000 MW in the country," he told
The Hindu Business Line in December 2005. Plus he sees exponential
growth in the other big Asian market, China – as high as 250,000 MW.
Tanti is a former textile producer who decided to switch to wind
energy production in the mid-1990s – initially to ease the pressure on
his power costs. He liked the result, and aided by some government

incentives, set up Suzlon Energy in April 1995. The company made its first wind turbine generator in 1996 and within a decade had grown to become India's largest, and the world's fifth-largest, maker. Its key rivals are market leader Vestas of Denmark and Germany's Enercon. In March 2006, Suzlon paid US$565 million to buy Belgian wind turbine gearbox manufacturer Hansen Transmissions and completed another big acquisition in 2007, the German wind turbine maker REpower. According to Tanti, Suzlon's order book of US$1.5 billion at the end of 2006 "clearly reflects our coming of age as a mature, reliable, and technologically sound global supplier." Admirers include Rahul Bajaj, India's scooter king, who invested in wind power with Suzlon in 2002 and saw electricity costs fall at his Bajaj Auto plant. Citigroup was an early Suzlon backer, making a handsome profit from its partial exit through the company's initial public offering. The IPO price of 510 rupees was subscribed more than 40 times, so it was not surprising the stock closed at 690 rupees – a 35% premium on its first trading day, October 19, 2005.

Domestically, Suzlon's fortunes have been helped by favorable government regulations on renewable energy, but it has also looked at export markets. It regards China as a strategically important market and is setting up a manufacturing plant in Tianjin. In what the company described as a reversal of outsourcing jobs to India, it set up its global office in the wind energy hub of Denmark. Its first big windfarm projects in Europe are in the Penamacor region of Portugal.

Tanti is a fervent advocate of wind power. If India is to achieve sustained economic growth above 8%, he believes conventional energy sources will not be enough. "There is no way forward without wind energy." But any significant drop in crude oil prices will put pressure on the economics of wind energy and Suzlon's sky-high valuation. Tanti was named "Most Promising Entrant to the Big League" at the CNBC-TV18 Business Leader Awards in Mumbai in December 2006.

9. Srichand P. HINDUJA and brothers, United Kingdom/India/Switzerland

Estimated net worth: US$6.5 billion.

Position: Chairman, Hinduja Group.

Born: November 28, 1935 in Shikarpur, Sindh. Eldest son of late Parmanand and Jamuna Hinduja. Elder brother to Gopichand (b. 1940 in Kolkata), Prakashchand (b. 1949 in Mumbai), and Ashok (b. 1950 in Mumbai). The four are known as "S.P.," "G.P.," "P.P.," and "A.P." London is home for S.P. and G.P., while P.P. is based in Geneva and A.P. is in Mumbai.

Educated: Graduate, Davar's College of Commerce, Mumbai; University of Westminster, London, 1996. Gopichand was a student of Jain Hind College. Ashok has a B.Com., University of Mumbai and honorary doctorates in law and economics, respectively, from University of Westminster and Richmond College, in UK.

Marital status: All the brothers are married with children, several of whom work in the family business. Srichand married Madhu Menda, in 1963; they have two daughters, Shanu and Vinoo, who is a director of Gulf Oil Corp. A son, Dharam, died in 1992. Gopichand is married to Sunita Gurnani; they have three children, including son Dheeraj, vice-chairman of Ashok Leyland and son Sanjay, chairman of Gulf Oil Corp. Prakash is married to Kamal; their son Ramkrishan is co-chairman of Hinduja TMT. Ashok is married to Jyoti.

Interests: Spiritual activities, yoga. Srichand heads the IndusInd International Federation, a business body that represents overseas and non-resident Indians.

The Hinduja Group is a transnational trading and industrial conglomerate with turnover of about US$15 billion. It has 25,000 employees worldwide and operates in more than 20 countries. Activities include international trading, banking, financial services, chemicals, agribusiness, automotive, infrastructure, media, and IT. Its main companies include Gulf Oil International, Amas Bank, Ashok Leyland, IndusInd Bank, media arm Hinduja TMT, and newly formed HTMT Global Solutions, which houses its business process outsourcing business. On the horizon are big plans for healthcare in India via a Dubai joint venture, and infrastructure business in the Middle East.

The Hinduja Group was founded in 1914 in Mumbai by the brothers' father, Parmanand Deepchand Hinduja, who hailed originally from Shikarpur in the Sindh region of India (now part of Pakistan). Initially, the 14-year-old youngster learnt the entrepreneurial ropes as a moneylender, then entered the import–export business. He expanded to Iran in 1919, trading in tea, dried fruit, textiles, and jute. Parmanand died in 1971. His motto was: "My dharma [duty] is to work, so that I can give."

P.D. Hinduja's eldest sons, Srichand and Gopichand, moved the group's main operations from Iran to London in 1979, where they and their families have a suite of apartments in Carlton House Terrace, near St. James's Park. The Hindujas took a controlling stake in India-based truck and busmaker Ashok Leyland in 1987, and in 1994 their Amas Bank won a banking license in Switzerland, where Prakash is based. Their most valuable asset is the Gulf Oil brand, outside the United States and Spain. The three Europe-based Hinduja brothers have been dogged by controversy, most notably over the 1986 arms deal between Swedish maker A.B. Bofors and the Indian government, then led by Rajiv Gandhi. The Hindujas were alleged to have received US$8 million in corrupt payments as part of the US$1.8 billion deal. In May 2005, the Delhi High Court quashed all charges against the brothers. Srichand Hinduja was at the center of another scandal in 2001, when Peter Mandelson, a minister in the Blair government, was forced to resign after admitting he made misleading statements about Hinduja's British citizenship application. An official inquiry, the Hammond Report, found in March 2001 that second brother Gopichand's 1997 naturalization application was handled properly. The two brothers were first refused British passports by the Conservative government in 1991. Gopichand was given a British passport by the new Labour government in November 1998. Srichand received his in March 1999. The brothers conduct their philanthropic activities in health, education, and social welfare through the Hinduja Foundation.

10. Ramesh CHANDRA, India

Estimated net worth: US$6.4 billion.
Position: Founder, Unitech Ltd.
Born: 1940.
Educated: B.Tech. (Hons) in civil engineering, Indian Institute of Technology, Kharagpur; M.Sc. in structural engineering, University of Southampton, UK.
Marital status: Married to Dr. Pushpa Chandra; sons Sanjay and Ajay.

Property developer Unitech uses the slogan "Dream, believe, create," and that's exactly what Ramesh Chandra has done in a 30-year journey with his company, which had been India's largest listed real estate developer until DLF listed in July 2007. Chandra, the son of a banker, returned from studying structural engineering in the UK (he has a Masters from the University of Southampton) to set up his own consulting business, then moved into housing. With aggressive land banking, Unitech has built a strong position, initially with residential developments around New Delhi and Kolkata, and more recently in cities such as Hyderabad, Chennai, and Kochi. In June 2006, Unitech paid US$350 million for 345 acres (140 hectares) of prime land in Noida, on the outskirts of New Delhi, where it proposes to build 4,000 apartments. Also on Unitech's books for Noida: The Great India Place, a 1.5 million square feet retail development which it says will be India's largest, and a 320-acre (130-hectare) new township at Gurgaon, another fast-growing satellite city to New Delhi. Unitech's wide-ranging business plan targets residential, commercial, retail, and entertainment developments, and it has also tied up with the Marriott hotel group to develop a brand of business hotels in key cities. India's property sector got a push along when the government allowed foreign direct investment in real estate developments in 2005.

Ramesh Chandra told India's *Business Standard* magazine at the time of the Noida deal that his aim was to dominate every new market that Unitech entered. "We have become number one in Noida and Kolkata, and while we started much later in Gurgaon, if you take new acquisition of land and space being constructed there, we are closing in on the competition. That is why we have avoided Mumbai, where there are entrenched players," he said.

The Chandra family is immersed in the Unitech business. Ramesh and wife Pushpa (Bachelor of Medicine & Surgery), and sons Sanjay (University of Massachusetts and Boston University) and Ajay (B.Sc. in civil engineering, Cornell University and MBA, University of North Carolina), are shareholders and directors of the main holding companies, Mayfair Investments and Mayfair Capital. The massive re-rating of India's real estate sector since 2005 means that the Chandra family fortune looks substantial on paper. Its 57.5% holding in Unitech was worth more than US$6.4 billion in June 2007. A December 2005 share purchase offer document lodged with the regulator, the Securities and Exchange Board of India, shows how things have changed for the Chandras. That document puts the net worth figures for Ramesh Chandra as at March 31, 2005 as 3.94 million rupees, for Sanjay as 3.89 million rupees, and for Ajay as 10.75 million rupees, or about US$450,000 between them.

11. Shashi N. RUIA and family, India

Estimated net worth: US$6.2 billion.
Position: Chairman, Essar Group. Younger brother Ravi, who trained as an engineer in Chennai, is vice-chairman.
Born: December 23, 1943 in Chennai. Son of Nand Kishore Ruia and Chandrakala Ruia.
Educated: B.Com., Chennai.
Marital status: Married Manju (now deceased). Two sons: Prashant (B.Com., University of Bombay) and Anshuman, managing director of Essar Steel. Ravi Ruia has a son, Rewant, and daughter, Smiti.
Interests: Executive committee member, Federation of Indian Chambers of Commerce & Industry; former chairman, Indo–US Joint Business Council.

The Ruia brothers, Shashi and Ravi, are the key beneficiaries of India's biggest telecommunications deal so far, the purchase by UK mobile phone giant Vodafone of a 67% stake in Hutchison Essar in early 2007 for US$11.1 billion, plus debt of US$2.0 billion. The deal implied a value of US$18.8 billion for Hutchison Essar (now renamed Vodafone Essar), leaving the Ruias with a 33% stake worth around US$6.2 billion. Ruia Ravi is chair of the phone company, with Vodafone CEO

Arun Sarin as vice-chairman. The deal gives Essar the option to sell out three years hence for at least US$5 billion.

The Ruia family hails originally from Rajasthan, but moved to Mumbai in the 1800s. The brothers' father, Nand K. Ruia, moved on to Chennai and started his part of the family business in 1956, targeting the construction sector. After his death in 1969, the brothers took over the business. Essar (named for the brothers' initials "S" and "R") expanded into other industries – first into marine construction, offshore rigs, and shipping, then steel, oil and gas, power, and, in 1994, into telecommunications when the Ruias bought 51% of Delhi's Sterling Cellular from entrepreneur C. Sivasankaran. The Ruias borrowed heavily during the 1990s to build up their power and steel interests, but liquidity was a problem. Before the epic Vodafone deal, Essar was best known for being the first Indian company to default on an international debt, a US$250 million eurobond that Essar Steel – then India's third-largest steel company – failed to pay on time in July 1999. Those dark days seem to be over, with Essar Oil commissioning its US$2 billion Vadinar oil refinery in western India in November 2006. The refinery's capacity of 10.5 million metric tonnes per annum means its output will add significantly to group turnover. Essar plans to set up more than 5,000 retail gasoline outlets across India by 2008.

Shashi's elder son Prashant is managing director of Essar Steel, and Anshuman is a director of group companies. Ravi Ruia's son Rewant (Hackley School, New York; and Bachelor of Business Administration, Bentley College, Boston) is a director of the major companies, while daughter Smiti (Bachelor of Finance and Marketing, New York) is also a director and runs Mumbai's *Time Out* magazine through her Paprika Media publishing house. Plans are under way to consolidate the Ruia family's stakes in the various Essar Group companies under the umbrella of Essar Global, based in the Caymans.

12. Pallonji Shapoorji MISTRY, India

Estimated net worth: US$5.05 billion.
Position: Chairman, Shapoorji Pallonji Group.
Born: June 1, 1929 in Mumbai.
Educated: Intermediate – arts. Left school before finishing 12th
   grade.
Marital status: Married to Patsy; sons Shapoor (b. September 6, 1964;
   B.A. in business and economics, UK) and Cyrus (b. July 4, 1968;
   B.Eng. in civil engineering, M.Sc. in management, London Business
   School), and daughter Aloo.
Interests: Breeding racehorses at his Manjri Stud Farms near Pune, a
   city about 100 miles (160 kilometers) south of Mumbai. Also enjoys
   yachting and gardening.

When not at his stud farms in Pune, Pallonji S. Mistry, his interior
decorator wife Patsy, and their two sons, Shapoor and Cyrus, can
usually be found in their south Mumbai Georgian mansion overlooking the Arabian Sea. The family also has houses in London and Dubai.
Mistry's daughter Aloo is married to Noel Tata, half-brother of Tata
Group chairman Ratan Tata.

Pallonji S. Mistry's Parsi grandfather came to Mumbai from
Gujarat in 1865 to start a building company. Mistry's father, Shapoorji
Pallonji, extended the thriving business from the 1930s onward, erect-
ing some of Mumbai's landmark buildings along with some residential
developments in south Mumbai. Mistry joined the business in 1970,
and began expanding into the Middle East, where he won a contract
to build the palace of the Sultan of Oman in Muscat. In Mumbai some
of his best-known buildings include those for the Reserve Bank of
India, the State Bank of India, and the World Trade Center.

Pallonji S. Mistry holds a stake of 18.37% in Tata Sons, the
holding company of the Tata Group. Mistry's father began the family's association with the Tatas in the 1930s, and acquired a key
12.5% stakeholding in Tata Sons from the F.E. Dinshaw Estate. The
stake has been added to over the years and today underpins the
Mistry family fortune. Tata Sons, in turn, has a 78.35% stake in
Tata Consultancy Services (TCS), India's biggest IT services
firm. When TCS listed on August 25, 2004, the shares rose 24% on
debut, valuing the company at US$10.8 billion. By June 2007, that
figure had almost trebled to about US$29.4 billion. Mistry's

indirect stake in TCS alone is worth more than US$4 billion, and the Tata Sons holdings in group companies such as Tata Motors, Tata Steel, and VSNL add about another US$900 million. The Mistry family also holds a direct stake in TCS worth about US$130 million. Pallonji is a former chairman of the textile company Forbes Gokak (replaced by his eldest son Shapoor in 2003) and a former chairman of Associated Cement Co. (ACC), where he was a director for 48 years until 2000. The Shapoorji Pallonji Group acquired the Forbes Group (textiles, shipping, engineering, global logistics, travel services, office automation, and consumer durables) in 2002.

In September 2006, Cyrus Mistry, then aged 38, was appointed to the board of Tata Sons. He filled the position left by his father, who retired after he turned 76 in 2005. Cyrus and Shapoor, who is the Shapoorji Pallonji Group managing director, are also on the boards of Indian Hotels (also a Tata company) and Tata Power. The brothers and their wives race a number of horses from the family's 200-acre (80-hectare) Manjri Stud Farms.

13. Anil K. AGARWAL, United Kingdom/India

Estimated net worth: US$4.95 billion.
Position: Chairman, Vedanta Resources, UK and Sterlite Industries, India.
Born: September 7, 1952 in Mumbai. Lives in London. Son of Dwarka Prasad Agarwal, who co-founded Sterlite.
Education: B.Com.
Marital status: Married to Neha; son Agnivesh and daughter Ashima.
Interests: Education initiatives.

Anil Agarwal, a one-time scrap metal trader in Mumbai, now lives in London's Mayfair, runs a private jet, wants to set up a world-class university in India that will "rewrite the history of academia," and is never far from controversy over the activities of his key metals and mining companies, Vedanta and Sterlite. In July 2006, Agarwal signed a memorandum of understanding with Orissa state in eastern India to set up Vedanta University with an endowment of US$1 billion. The proposed university, modelled on the lines of US institutions Stanford and Harvard, is expected to take its first students in 2009 and will offer a multidisciplinary curriculum and a research focus. Agarwal's rationale is that while India has its high-quality IITs and IIMs, they are focused on single disciplines and collectively cater to less than 100,000 students a year.

The money for the education initiative comes from the fortune which Agarwal has amassed from his business activities. He holds a stake of 57.4% in London-listed Vedanta Resources (annual revenue above US$5 billion, market capitalization US$8.6 billion in June 2007) through his Bahamas-domiciled Volcan Investments. Brother Navin (b. 1963), who is Vedanta's deputy executive chairman, father D.P. Agarwal, and Anil's son Agnivesh are also shareholders in Volcan.

Vedanta, which Agarwal calls a "unique growth story," briefly had noted mining industry executive Brian Gilbertson as its chairman after his sudden departure from the helm of resources giant BHP Billiton. Gilbertson stepped down in 2004, to be replaced by Michael Fowle, who made way for Agarwal as executive chairman in March 2005. Vedanta describes itself as a diversified metals and mining group with zinc, copper, and aluminum operations in India and two copper mines in Australia. In April 2007, Vedanta bought 51% of Indian iron ore miner Sesa Goa for about US$1 billion. Vedanta runs its Indian businesses through two local subsidiaries, Sterlite Industries and Madras Aluminium, known as Malco. Sterlite controls Bharat Aluminium (Balco) and Hindustan Zinc, along with two Australian copper mines. Agarwal is chairman and managing director of Sterlite Industries, the current iteration of a company he formed in 1976 and which is now held almost 80% by Vedanta. Sterlite, which had the production of cables for the telecom industry as its main activity for many years, went public in 1988. Agarwal is also a director of Balco, Malco, and Hindustan Zinc (HZL); brother Navin is executive vice-chairman of Sterlite and a director of Balco and HZL. In October 2006 the Agarwal family sold control of its Sterlite Gold to Vedanta.

Agarwal has been in mining and related industries for three decades and has seen his share of controversy, fighting battles with bureaucrats during the push for liberalization in the 1970s, with conservationists opposed to some of his mining activities, and with labor unions unhappy at his employment and industrial safety record. Sterlite's reputation as an employer in India came under scrutiny in the late 1990s and early 2000s because of an industrial accident and its use of contract labor. Privately, Agarwal owns a gold and copper mine in Armenia and a copper smelter in Mexico.

14. Adi B. GODREJ and family, India

Estimated net worth: US$4 billion.
Position: Chairman, Godrej Group.
Born: April 3, 1942 in Mumbai. Son of Burjor and Jai.
Educated: B.Sc. and M.Sc. (in engineering and industrial management), Massachusetts Institute of Technology (MIT), US. Governing board member, Indian School of Business.
Marital status: Married to Parmeshwar; daughters Tanya (b. 1968) and Nisa (b. 1978), and son Pirojsha (b. 1980), all educated in the United States.
Interests: Reading, music, riding, waterskiing, windsurfing, food.

Mumbai-based industrialist Adi Godrej chairs a consumer products, agribusiness, and engineering conglomerate with 18,000 employees, annual turnover of more than US$1 billion, and operations that extend beyond India to Southeast Asia and the Arabian Gulf. Godrej and wife Parmeshwar are gracious stalwarts of the city's social scene. Indeed, an invitation to a Godrej soiree is an event not to be missed. Godrej is one of the great gentlemen of Indian business – unfailingly courteous, a model of commercial probity, ever ready to help a good cause, and prepared to speak his mind about social and economic issues. The family's Pirojsha Godrej Foundation, named for Adi's grandfather, puts money into education, housing, social welfare, and conservation. Like another of India's great business families, the Tatas, the Godrejs are members of the Zoroastrian Parsi religious community that fled Persia for India. Godrej is a great believer in continuing education, both for himself and his managers. Eldest daughter Tanya Dubash is on the board of Godrej Industries, second daughter Nisa also works for the group, and son Pirojsha has taken a break from management training with Godrej Properties to complete his MBA from Columbia University in New York. In November 2006, Godrej was asked about succession planning within the group. He said the family expected to introduce such a procedure in the future, but declined to be more specific. Also in the mix: Adi's younger brother

Nadir (who chairs Godrej Agrovet) has three teenage children; and cousin Jamshyd Godrej (chair of Godrej & Boyce) has two children aged in their twenties.

Godrej is highly optimistic about India's business story, seeing no real cause for concern over the next five years. The only worries, he says, would be a major "domestic political or geopolitical upheaval." Godrej notes that India's GDP is already growing at 9%. He believes that indirect taxation reforms, attention to key areas such as infrastructure, agricultural and rural growth, allied with the prospect of further globalization and liberalization, will only enhance India's economic outlook. With plants in Malaysia, Indonesia, Vietnam, and the Arabian Gulf, globalization is very much a part of the group's business model. The Godrej Group is more than 100 years old (established in 1897) and into the fourth generation of management. Its listed flagship companies are Godrej Industries (held 87%, mainly through Godrej & Boyce) and Godrej Consumer Products (held 68%). These and other companies deal in everything from consumer goods to engineering, agribusiness, information technology, and property development. One key asset for the group is an extensive land bank in suburban Mumbai. Its five-tower Planet Godrej apartment complex near central Mumbai's Mahalaxmi racecourse is due for completion by mid-2008. Godrej and Boyce is the group's main holding company, set up in 1897 when Ardeshir Godrej began a lock-making business. He moved on to build high-quality safes that made the name "Godrej" a byword for security and reliability. Ardeshir next ventured into making soap from vegetable oil and, with his brother Pirojsha, consolidated the group into a powerful business enterprise. The second generation of the family – the brothers S.P., Burjor, and Naval – built on that process. Today the group is eyeing retail tie-ups, agribusiness (including a palm oil joint venture in Malaysia), and property plays.

In July 1999, Adi's late uncle S.P. Godrej, then chairman of the group, rebuked *Forbes* magazine for its estimate of the Godrej family's wealth as both "incorrect and grossly overvalued." More importantly, he said, Godrej wealth belonged to the family as a whole, not to an individual. As for Pirojsha, S.P. wrote, "vulgar displays of wealth were particularly abhorrent to him" – sentiments Adi Godrej would endorse. He noted in 2007: "My family was very clear that business must exist for the greater good of society."

15. Shiv NADAR, India

Estimated net worth: US$3.95 billion.
Position: Chairman, HCL Group.
Born: 1946 in Moolaipozhi, Tamil Nadu. Son of a judge, Sivasubra-
maniya Nadar.
Educated: B.A./B.Sc. in electrical engineering, PSG College of Tech-
nology, Coimbatore, Tamil Nadu, 1967.
Marital status: Married to Kiran; one daughter, Roshni.
Interests: Fine arts; sports, particularly tennis, and attending the
Wimbledon tennis tournament; social issues, including providing
better public health and educational opportunities. Founded Chen-
nai's SSN College of Engineering and SSN School of Advanced
Software Engineering in association with Carnegie Mellon Univer-
sity. Board member, Indian School of Business, Hyderabad.

Shiv Nadar has a simple message for wannabe entrepreneurs:
"Remember, great effort bears the sweet fruit of success." Known as
the wizard of India's information technology sector, Nadar moved to
New Delhi from India's south in 1968 and joined Cooper Engineering
as a systems analyst. He moved on to DCM Data Products, then in
1975 set up a one-room business with five other engineers from DCM
– Arjun Malhotra, Subhash Arora, D.S. Puri, Yogesh Vaidya, and Ajai
Chowdhry – to lay the foundations for a corporate empire that eventually would become the HCL Group. The first venture, Microcomp,
didn't fare too well selling basic calculators, but within a year the six
entrepreneurs had won backing to set up Hindustan Computer Ltd.
(HCL). By 1978, HCL had developed its first computer, and gradually
Nadar transformed it from a simple reseller of IBM machines into a
company making its own hardware. During the 1980s and 1990s, HCL,
aided by Hewlett Packard until a split in 1997, consolidated its position as India's largest computer hardware vendor. Nadar, known as a
visionary with an eye for combining talent and opportunity, turned his
attention from hardware to the more lucrative fields of software
development in the late 1990s. After a period of drifting and not reaching its full potential after the global tech slowdown of the early 2000s,
the various HCL units were restructured by Nadar into two broad
streams: software arm HCL Technologies and HCL Infosystems, which
handles the hardware manufacturing business. It employs 37,000
people and has a presence in 16 countries, including the United States,

Japan, Asia, Australia, and Europe. Business streams include hardware manufacturing and distribution, systems integration, technology and software services, business process outsourcing, and infrastructure management.

In 2006, the 30th anniversary of HCL's founding, Nadar said he had stepped back from HCL Technologies, leaving president Vineet Nayar in charge of operations. Of Nadar's five co-founders, only Chowdhry remains involved as chairman and CEO of HCL Infosystems. Chowdhry believes that, like China, India will become a huge market for locally made PCs, from high-end models down to an entry-level unit that now sells for about US$220. A big focus for Nadar has always been education and training. With Nadar's support, HCL colleague Rajendra Pawar co-founded NIIT with Vijay Thadani and Kiran Nadar in 1981 as a software development and computer training company. NIIT pioneered computer education in India and is among the largest such companies in the world. Apart from his early backing of NIIT, Nadar has funded the creation of two colleges at Chennai – one for engineering, another for advanced software engineering – named "SSN" in honor of his father.

Nadar and his private company HCL Corp. hold about 69% of HCL Technologies and about 44% of HCL Infosystems, which had market capitalizations in June 2007 of US$5.63 billion and US$695 million, respectively; those stakes are worth about US$3.2 billion.

16. Dilip S. SHANGHVI, India

Estimated net worth: US$3.71 billion.
Position: Executive chairman, Sun Pharmaceutical Industries Ltd.
Born: October 1955 in Kolkata. Son of Shantilal and Kumud Shanghvi. Lives in Mumbai.
Educated: B.Com., Calcutta University.
Marital status: Married to Vibha; two children.
Interests: Watching Bollywood films, reading novels, vegetarian food, and nature excursions to Kerala and the hill town of Kodaikanal in neighboring Tamil Nadu.

Dilip Shanghvi and fellow promoters hold 69.6% of Mumbai-headquartered Sun Pharmaceutical, which had a market capitalization of about US$5.34 billion in June 2007 and holds the title of India's most valuable pharma company. The company has 5,000 employees and 15 manufacturing plants on three continents: Asia, North America, and Europe.

Shanghvi is also chairman of Detroit-based Caraco Pharma Laboratories, which makes generic drugs for the US market and is held 73% by Sun Pharma. Caraco, which is Sun's vehicle to tap into the high-priority US market, was the company's first international acquisition, starting in 1997 with a 30% equity-for-technology agreement. Sun moved to a 60% stake in 2004 when it bought out two large shareholders and has added more since. Sun added another US-focused drug maker when it bought Israeli generics company Taro for about US$450 million in May 2007. Taro does about 90% of its sales in North America.

Shanghvi set up Sun Pharma in 1982 in Kolkata, with the goal of transforming his family's wholesale pharmaceuticals business into the more profitable activity of drug manufacturing. Originally a partnership (Shanghvi's father Shantilal was co-founder), Sun Pharma was incorporated in 1993 and first offered shares to the public in 1994. Shanghvi has grown the company through a series of key acquisitions in various segments of the drugs market. Sun sells branded formulations and bulk drugs mainly in Asia, Latin America, and Africa. The US is becoming a valuable market, through Caraco. Sun built its first research center, known as SPARC, in 1993; it also has a drug discovery campus at Baroda and a new R&D center in Mumbai. Sun plans to put its drug discovery and drug delivery systems work into a separate company.

Shanghvi's father, Shantilal N. Shanghvi, served as Sun's chairman until his retirement in 2000.

17. Grandhi Mallikarjuna RAO, India

Estimated net worth: US$3.2 billion.

Position: Founder, GMR Group.

Born: July 14, 1950 in Rajham, Andhra Pradesh. Son of G. China Sanyasi Raju Varalakshmi Nilayam.

Educated: Mechanical engineering, College of Engineering, Andhra University, Visakhapatnam.

Marital status: Married to G. Varalakshmi. Elder son G.B.S. Raju (B. Com., University of Madras, Chennai, 1995) is GMR's director of finance; younger son G. Kiran Kumar (B.Com., Osmania University, Hyderabad, 1996) heads the Hyderabad airport project. Daughter Ramadevi is married to Srinivas Bommidala, who heads the Delhi airport project.

Interests: Spending time with his grandchildren. Awarded honorary doctorate in philosophy, Jawarharlal Nehru Technological University, Hyderabad, for services to industry.

Bangalore-based Grandhi M. Rao began his business career in 1978 with a jute mill in his home-town of Rajham, where his father was a commodities trader and his three brothers worked in the family business. Rao, the first in his family to go to college, gradually diversified into new business sectors. By 1988 he was out on his own, and began to target business opportunities in sugar, ferroalloys, banking (through his role in Vysya Bank), insurance, brewing, information technology, energy, and infrastructure. By the late 1990s, Rao was cashed-up, having sold out of Vysya Bank, along with part of his interest in insurance and brewing. He saw the potential of infrastructure, particularly as the government started to push the upgrading of transport and energy links. Rao won contracts for six big road projects, and has also been active in the energy sector. His GMR Group's Mangalore power plant, for example, is the world's largest barge-mounted combined-cycle power plant. But it is the Delhi and Hyderabad airport projects that have brought him to the fore in India. Rao will spend US$1.5 billion rejuvenating Delhi's airport (in partnership with Germany's Fraport), building a new runway and a new terminal, and chipping in for the much-needed transport links to have it ready for the 2010 Commonwealth Games. The new Hyderabad airport, a greenfield site in which Malaysia Airports is a partner, is much cheaper – about

US$500 million. Rao says he expects the airport will host the first flights of the Airbus A380 superjumbo to India in 2008.

Rao is conscious of the special pressures flowing from generational change within family businesses. He has created a family council and constitution to guide the transition. "In the same way that you must have good corporate governance, so you must have good family governance," he says. "We set up a family constitution and we have a family council of eight members: me, my wife, daughter, son-in-law, two sons and their wives. There is a family office that is separate from the GMR corporate office. It took five years to write down the constitution. We had input from everyone, and also specialist advice."

Rao also set up his GMR Varalakshmi Foundation in 1991 to fund initiatives in health, education, and rural empowerment. Rao holds 79% of GMR Infrastructure, which listed in August 2006 and had a market capitalization in June 2007 of about US$4.1 billion. The group's other listed entity, GMR Industries, houses the sugar and ferroalloys businesses.

18. Kalanithi MARAN, India

Estimated net worth: US$3.0 billion.
Position: Chairman, Sun TV.
Born: 1965 in Tamil Nadu. Son of the late Murasoli Maran (d. November 2003) and Mallika Maran.
Educated: B.Com., Loyola College, Chennai; MBA, University of Scranton, Pennsylvania, US.
Marital status: Married Kavery in 1991; she is Sun's joint managing director. One daughter, Kavya.

South India media mogul Kalanithi Maran, chairman of the hugely successful Sun TV network, might well have followed a different path than television. He is, after all, the son of a politician – the late Union industries and commerce minister Murasoli Maran, who in turn was the nephew of Tamil Nadu chief minister M. Karunanidhi (b. June 1924). Maran's younger brother Dayanidhi Maran (b. December 1966) was Union minister for telecommunications until his shock resignation in May 2007.

Antioch
6060 N Chestnut Ave.
Kansas City, MO 64119-1847
816-454-1306
****

User name: SEARS, DRUSILLA J

Title: New hope for people with bipolar disorder : your
Author: Fawcett, Jan, 1934-
Item ID: 30003006281677
Bill reason: OVERDUE
Amount billed: $.25
Amount paid: .25
Payment type: CASH
Payment date: 9/23/2008,14:13

But rather than politics, a media-tinged entrepreneurial life always called the young Kalanithi Maran. After gaining his MBA at the University of Scranton – a Jesuit institution in Pennsylvania's Pocono region – Maran returned to India in 1987 and began work in the family media business. His first job was as a circulation clerk for the Tamil-language weekly magazine *Kungumam*. Over the next few years Maran learnt the ins and outs of the magazine business. But with cable TV proliferating in the south, Maran sensed an opportunity for a Tamil-language TV channel that would bring big-name stars and blockbuster entertainment to an audience hungry for other than Hindi fare. Maran had the ability to source the programs, but no real distribution outlet. In 1992, he sought unsuccessfully to buy time on Zee TV's satellite transponder, but when this approach failed he struck an agreement with satellite channel ATN, and in 1993 launched Sun TV broadcasting. Its success with the Tamil population has prompted him to launch similar channels, such as Udaya TV in Kannada, Surya TV in Malayalam, and Gemini TV in Telugu.

Today, the Sun Network has 20 digital television channels in four languages, seven FM radio stations, three Tamil weekly magazines, the *Dinakaran* and *Tamizh Murasu* Tamil newspapers, and the cable company Sumangali Cablevision. Maran says the group wants to be in "all spheres of communication."

Maran was named "India's Best Entrepreneur" in 1999, won the Outstanding Businessman in the Entertainment and Information Sector Award in 2004 and the 2005 CNBC's Business Excellence Award. Maran holds just under a 90% stake in Sun TV, which went public in April 2006. The company had a market capitalization in June 2007 of about US$3.4 billion.

19. Uday KOTAK, India

Estimated net worth: US$2.34 billion.
Position: Vice-chairman and CEO, Kotak Mahindra Bank.
Born: 1959. Son of Suresh and Indira Kotak.
Educated: B.Com. (Hons), University of Bombay, 1982; MBA, Jamnalal Bajaj Institute of Management Sciences.
Marital status: Married to Pallavi (also a financial professional); sons Jay and Dhaval.
Interests: Cricket, Indian classical music (plays sitar), philanthropy involving education.

Mumbai-based Uday Kotak, founder of the financial services group Kotak Mahindra Bank, says he believes one of the single largest opportunities anywhere in the world today is the Indian financial sector. "It will be a core engine of India's growth," he says. The group was set up as Kotak Capital Management Finance in 1985 by Uday Kotak, business partner Sydney A.A. Pinto, and Kotak & Co., the cotton, agribusiness and industrial group led by his father, Suresh Kotak. The industrialists Harish Mahindra and Anand Mahindra took a stake the following year, leading to the Kotak Mahindra name. Over the next 18 years, the company developed through a variety of financial services, including bill discounting, lease and hire purchasing, vehicle financing, investment banking, brokerage, funds management, life insurance, online broking, and private equity funding. In 2003, Kotak Mahindra Finance converted to a bank. Its corporate logo is the infinite *Ka* symbol, signifying what it says are the infinite ways to meet man's unlimited needs.

Today the group's business units include Kotak Securities, Kotak Investment Banking, Kotak Life Insurance, and Kotak Mahindra Bank itself, which has about 110 branches across about 50 towns and cities. The group's staff numbers have risen dramatically in recent years – from 4,400 in March 2005 to 6,700 a year later, and then to 10,000 by March 2007, with an expectation it will grow to 15,000 by 2008. Kotak says that when he first visited the United States, he was fascinated by the way in which financial giants such as Goldman Sachs, Merrill Lynch, Morgan Stanley, and JPMorgan had long outlived their founders. He says he believed Indian financial institutions one day would enjoy a similar place in the sun. "Kotak Mahindra was born out of this belief," he says.

In March 2006, Kotak bought out Goldman Sachs, which held a 25% stake in Kotak Mahindra Capital and Kotak Securities, for a total of US$74 million. A few months later, in October 2006, the group bought out partner Ford Credit's 40% stake in Kotak Mahindra Prime for about US$27 million.

Kotak, widely regarded as India's most astute and successful banker, says that as the size of India's "bankable class" grows, a nation of savers is becoming a nation of both investors and spenders.

Uday Kotak holds 51.44% of Kotak Mahindra Bank, while Kotak Trustee Co. holds another 4.5%. The bank had a market capitalization in June 2007 of US$4.5 billion. At the end of 2006, Kotak set up a foundation to promote education among underprivileged children. Its focus is on language training (including spoken English) to help their employment prospects in the IT-enabled services sector.

20. Venugopal Nandlal DHOOT, India

Estimated net worth: US$1.72 billion.
Position: Chairman, Videocon Industries.
Born: September 30, 1951. Son of farmer and sugar-mill operator
   Nandlal Madhavlal Dhoot.
Educated: Firodiya High School, Ahmednagar, Maharashtra state;
   B.Eng. in electrical engineering, Pune Engineering College, Pune.
   Fellow of Institution of Engineers.
Marital status: Married to Rama; son Anirudh, and daughter Surabhi
   (MBA, University of Wales).
Interests: Flute recital, Hindu philosophy, discourse on the *Bhagavad
   Gita.*

Venugopal Dhoot and his two younger brothers Rajkumar and
Pradeepkumar own 70% of Videocon, a consumer electronics group
that had a market capitalization of US$2.43 billion in June 2007. In
addition to electronics and glass shells for TV sets, the group's oil and
gas operations, based on the Ravva field off the coast of Andhra
Pradesh, are a major contributor to profitability. Increased output at
the low-cost Ravva field, coupled with India's growing demand for
energy and high oil prices, helped push turnover to US$2.5 billion in
2006. Dhoot's vision is to be a US$10 billion a year Indian multina-
tional by 2010.

   In partnership with US buyout firm Ripplewood, Dhoot has been
looking to buy South Korea's troubled Daewoo Electronics for about
US$700 million. The on-again off-again deal still has some way to go,
after creditors rejected Videocon's latest offer in May 2007. Daewoo
Electronics has been run by its creditors, led by Woori Bank, since
1999, when parent Daewoo Group collapsed under a debt load of
US$80 billion.

   Videocon has been in acquisition mode for some time. In 2005,
the Mumbai-based company paid about US$290 million for the TV
tube business of French electronics firm Thomson. That made it
the world's No. 4 maker of color picture tubes. It also bought the
Indian operations of Sweden's Electrolux for about US$95 million.
In turn, Thomson and Electrolux bought stakes of about 15% and
5%, respectively, in Videocon. Restructuring and integration of the
offshore businesses is seen as a big challenge for Videocon. But
despite the rise of LCD (liquid crystal display) and plasma screens,
the Dhoots believe there still exists a huge market for cathode ray

tubes in emerging markets such as Russia, India, China, and Latin America.

Venugopal's brother Rajkumar is a member of the upper house, Rajya Sabha, representing the Shiv Sena party. Other brother Pradeepkumar runs Videocon's international operations. Dhoot's son Anirudh works in the business, as managing director of consumer appliances. But daughter Surabhi does not, despite her MBA from the University of Wales. Dhoot says he is no fan of top management roles for women. A hangover from the past for the Dhoot family is the connection with Harshad Mehta, the one-time "big bull" of the Indian stock market who was arrested in 1992 over allegations he manipulated stocks of Videocon and other companies. He died in judicial custody in 2001, the same year that Videocon was barred from accessing the capital markets for three years.

21. Rahul K. BAJAJ, India

Estimated net worth: US$1.68 billion.
Position: Chairman, Bajaj Auto.
Born: June 10, 1938 in Kolkata. Son of Kamalnayan and Savitri Bajaj.
Educated: B.A. (Hons), LLB, MBA, Harvard Business School.
Marital status: Married to Rupa; sons Rajiv (B.Eng. in mechanical engineering, College of Engineering, Pune; M.Sc. in manufacturing system engineering) and Sanjiv (MBA, Harvard), and daughter Sunaina, who is married to Manish Kejriwal, head of Temasek India.
Interests: Cricket, council member of World Economic Forum.

As a young man, Pune-based industrialist Rahul Bajaj was a middleweight boxer. Now nearing 70, he is still a fighter, particularly when it involves the future of his Bajaj Auto or his beloved India. Outspoken in his views on what the country's leaders must do to help India reach its full potential, Bajaj decries what he says are "unspeakable pockets of poverty in rural and urban India." He wants every Indian to have a chance for a better life: "Dreaming is a fundamental human right and the starting point of all change," he says.

Bajaj's own business dream is for Bajaj Auto to be the leader in India's motorcyle market when it crosses the expected 10 million mark by 2010. "We should supply four million of those motorcycles to clearly establish our leadership in the domestic market, and become a significant player in the global market, among the three largest global producers in two-wheelers."

The Bajaj Group was started in 1926 by Jamnalal Bajaj – a confidant of Mahatma Gandhi – and today extends to 27 companies across businesses as diverse as sugar, industrial alcohol, shampoo, Ayurvedic medicines (from Ayurveda, or "science of a long life," which is a healing method based on physical, mental, and spiritual harmony), insurance, and financial services. But it is Bajaj Auto, the two-wheeler and three-wheeler company formed in 1944, that generates about 80% of group revenue and is very clearly the flagship. Jamnalal's son Kamalnayan ran the business from 1942, followed by his brother Ramkrishna until Kamalnayan's son Rahul took over in 1965. Rahul Bajaj remains chairman, but sons Rajiv (CEO of Bajaj Auto) and Sanjiv (CEO of the fast-growing financial side, Bajaj Auto Finance) run the day-to-day operations. In 2001, Bajaj Auto's two-wheelers were losing money and the company ranked only No. 4 in India; today it is No. 2 to Hero Honda. Rajiv is credited with turning around the business, launching new models of cycles, scooters, and three-wheelers, and scouting for global opportunities, particularly in China and Southeast Asia.

Down the years, the clashes between Rahul and Rajiv over the best way to run the business have become legendary; but there is another source of family tension: Rahul's relations with his estranged younger brother, Shishir. The two factions – Rahul and his three cousins Shekhar, Madhur, and Niraj on one side, and Shishir and his son Kushagraha on the other – reached an understanding in 2003 about selling their stakes in Bajaj Auto and sugar producer Bajaj Hindusthan to each other at pre-determined prices. But as of mid-2007, the matter is still in dispute over pricing. Kushagraha, who is married to Vasavadatta Birla, younger sister of A.V. Birla Group head Kumar Mangalam Birla, is CEO of Bajaj Hindusthan and Bajaj Consumercare.

Rahul Bajaj and the other promoters hold 29.85% of the flagship company Bajaj Auto, which had a market capitalization of about US$5.6 billion in June 2007. A de-merger plan agreed in May 2007 will see separate listed companies created for the auto and financial services businesses. Looking ahead, the group's insurance arm, Bajaj Allianz, is seen as a growth engine.

22. Yusuf K. HAMIED, India

Estimated net worth: US$1.68 billion.
Position: Chairman, Cipla.
Born: July 25, 1936. Son of Cipla founder Khwaja Abdul Hamied
  (1898–1972).
Educated: Ph.D in organic chemistry, Cambridge University, UK.
  Elected a Fellow of Christ's College, Cambridge, 2004.
Marital status: Married to Farida.
Interests: Humanitarian issues.

After studying chemistry at Berlin University, Dr. K.A. Hamied returned to India in 1927. Eight years later, in August 1935, he set up the Chemical, Industrial and Pharmaceutical Laboratories Ltd. – later to be known simply as Cipla – in a rented bungalow in central Mumbai. His goal was to establish a modern pharmaceuticals industry in India by "compelling nature to yield her secrets to the ruthless search of an investigating chemist." Today, Cipla is India's No. 2 drug company by market capitalization (more than US$4.1 billion in June 2007) and makes medicines for both the domestic and overseas markets. About 40% of sales are for exports.

Cipla chairman Dr. Yusuf K. Hamied, son of the founder, is regarded as a pioneer in the global fight against HIV/AIDS and was honored with the Indian government's Padma Bhushan award (the third-highest civilian award) in 2005 for his distinguished service to trade and industry. Hamied joined the company in 1960 as a research officer after completing his doctorate in chemistry at Cambridge. He was appointed managing director in 1976 (his father had died in June 1972) and chairman in 1989.

Under Hamied, Cipla has been among the leaders of India's bulk drug industry. The company was the first to offer the triple drug cocktail, Triomune, which can transform the life of an HIV-positive patient, at about a dollar a day – a fraction of the international cost. AIDS is not Hamied's only concern. He worries about diabetes and tuberculosis. In the 1990s, he also helped set up palliative care for cancer patients in Pune.

The Hamied family holds a stake of 39.36% in Cipla, valued at US$1.68 billion in June 2007. Hamied's brother, M.K. Hamied, is joint managing director of the company.

23. Vivek C. BURMAN, India

Estimated net worth: US$1.65 billion.
Position: Former chairman, Dabur India Ltd.
Born: April 28, 1937. Lives in New Delhi.
Educated: B.Sc. in business administration, United States.
Marital status: Married to Monica; sons Mohit and Gaurav.
Interests: Golf, polo, swimming. Honorary consul-general for Nicaragua in India.

Vivek Burman chaired Dabur India, a nature-based consumer goods manufacturer that operates in healthcare, family care products, fruit juices, and food until July 2007. He is the nephew of longtime Dabur patriarch Rattan Chand Burman (who died in May 2006) and great-grandson of Dabur founder Dr. S.K. Burman, a 19th-century Bengal physician who prepared natural cures for villagers at risk of diseases such as cholera, malaria, and plague. In 1884, Dr. Burman set up shop in Kolkata to produce and dispense Ayurvedic medicines. He took the name "Dabur" as a contraction of the way his customers referred to him as "Daktar Burman."

From that first small pharmacy, the business has grown to become the largest nature-based healthcare maker in India, with annual turnover of about US$400 million, a market capitalization in June 2007 of more than US$2 billion, and a marketing network that serves 50 countries. Dabur set up its first R&D unit in 1919, began automatic production of its Ayurvedic medicines in 1930, and shifted its base from Kolkata to Delhi in 1972. For much of the 1980s and early 1990s, Dabur was led by R.C. Burman, father of Pradip, London-based Siddharth Burman, and the late Gyan Chand Burman. He was regarded as a prime mover in Dabur's modernization and expansion in the late 1980s and early 1990s.

In 1989 the Burman family handed over the management of the company to professionals. Following a McKinsey study in 1993 the family took more steps to separate ownership from management. Vivek Burman's brother A.C. Burman stepped down as chairman in 1998, as part of the separation process. G.C. Burman, then vice-chairman and son of third-generation patriarch R.C. Burman, was to become chairman but died in September 2001. The same year the Burmans set up a 10-member Family Council, to further delineate the family business from the operations of Dabur. At least one Family Council member sits on each Dabur company board. The family retains a 74% holding and four seats on the Dabur board: Vivek Burman's son Mohit; his nephew Dr. Anand Burman (who is the new chairman, and also chairman of separately listed Dabur Pharma, which was split off from Dabur India in 2003); cousin Pradip Burman; and Pradip's nephew Amit Burman, who is vice-chairman and also CEO of the wholly owned subsidiary Dabur Foods.

Dabur India's CEO is Sunil Duggal, who joined the company in 1995 and took on the top job in 2002. Dabur de-merged its pharmaceutical business in 2003 to concentrate on consumer goods. It bought oral care company Balsara in 2005 for about US$32 million (Vivek Burman's son Mohit became a Balsara director), and began an expansion program in 2007 targeting the Middle East personal care market from a production facility in the United Arab Emirates.

24. Jaiprakash GAUR, India

Estimated net worth: US$1.56 billion.
Position: Founder, Jaypee Group.
Born: 1931.
Educated: Diploma in civil engineering, University of Roorkee (now Indian Institute of Technology), Uttarakhand (formerly Uttaranchal, until name change in January 2007).
Marital status: Married, with five children. Eldest son Manoj is executive chairman of the listed flagship Jaiprakash Associates. Other sons Sunny and Samir (MBA, University of Wales) are directors of the company. Daughter Rita Dixit is executive general manager.
Interests: Social welfare, education.

Jaiprakash Gaur is a pioneer of private hydropower construction in India and a great believer in India's need for upgraded infrastructure. After completing his education at Roorkee, in the foothills of the Himalayas, Gaur initially worked for the government of Uttar Pradesh, then moved into civil contracting in 1958. He formed his Jaypee Group in the 1970s as a construction and engineering company. Gaur's business focus has been on building roads, bridges, dams, hydropower, and thermal power plants. The group's cement division runs the single largest cement plant in India, and is on track to become India's third-largest cement maker by 2009, with capacity of 20 million tonnes per annum. The group also has interests in hotels, education, and technology.

Apart from its construction work for clients such as the National Hydroelectric Power Corporation, the Jaypee Group has also completed two build-own-operate hydropower projects with a combined 700 MW capacity: Baspa II in Himachal Pradesh, which began operating in 2003; and Vishnu Prayag in Uttarakhand in June 2006. The 1,000 MW Karcham Wantoo build-own-operate project is due for completion in 2011, and two other projects in Arunachal Pradesh are in the pipeline. The group owns and runs four five-star hotels – two in New Delhi, and one each in Agra and Mussorrie, under another listed entity, Jaypee Hotels. It is building the 100-mile (165-kilometer) Taj Expressway, a six-lane highway linking Noida (on the outskirts of Delhi) and Agra.

Gaur sold off part of Jaiprakash HydroPower Ltd. in an initial public offer in 2005 for a profit of about US$80 million. He restructured and amalgamated the listed Jaiprakash Industries with unlisted JCL, creating Jaiprakash Associates as the group's listed flagship. It had revenues of US$850 million in 2007 and a market capitalization in mid-2007 of about US$3.33 billion. Gaur and his family hold just over 42% of the company.

His Jaypee Group set up Jaiprakash Sewa Sansthan trust to provide social welfare, including rural development (drinking water, employment opportunities), animal care, and education (literacy programs for girls). The group aims to expand its education-based infrastructure to cater for up to 100,000 students by about 2015. Gaur noted in October 2006: "I firmly believe that quality education on an affordable basis is the biggest service we can provide as a corporate citizen." The Builders Association of India conferred its Lifetime Achievement Award on Gaur for services to the construction industry in 2005.

25. Nagavara Ramarao (N.R.) Narayana MURTHY and family, India

Estimated net worth: US$1.51 billion.
Position: Co-founder and chairman, Infosys Technologies.
Born: August 20, 1946 in Karnataka state.
Educated: B.Eng. in electrical engineering, University of Mysore, 1967;
    M.Tech. from Indian Institute of Technology, Kanpur, 1969.
Marital status: Married to Sudha; daughter Akshata (MBA, Stanford),
    and son Rohan (computer science graduate, Cornell University;
    Ph.D student, Harvard).
Interests: Classical music, travel, reading.

One-time Marxist student Narayana Murthy has been a huge part of one of India's most successful capitalistic startups, Infosys Technologies. Intellectually, ethically, and technically, Murthy has put down the markers that have seen Infosys rise to the pinnacle of India's IT industry, fabulously enriching the seven founders and thousands of employees along the way. Murthy may be a billionaire, but he recalls how his co-founders – Nandan Nilekani, K. Dinesh, S. "Kris" Gopalakrishnan, N.S. Raghavan, D. Shibulal, and Ashok Arora – all agreed at the outset in 1981 that the company would seek to benefit all stakeholders. The position Murthy put, which was accepted by the others, was: "If we follow the principles of transparency, fairness and goodwill, the rest will come naturally, including profits."

Murthy, who turned 60 in August 2006 and has stepped back from executive duties, remains chief mentor of Infosys. His focus is on innovation, and on motivating people in pursuit of excellence. "Infosys is a hierarchy of ideas, not age," he says. "We create an incentive for every person to participate in innovation." Murthy knows that not every new idea will work. "If you encourage people to dream big, you also have to create a safety net for failure as well. This enhances their confidence and enthusiasm."

Part of Murthy's big dreams are to do with upgrading India's education system, which he says is now not meeting the needs of young people, or indeed, the companies that might seek to hire them, such as Infosys. Murthy wants a bigger role for private enterprise in higher education, saying the market will react well to competition. But in India's often-dysfunctional primary education sphere, he believes a more basic approach is needed: he advocates increased spending by the central government to ensure that underprivileged children, particularly in rural areas, are better-fed. That, he says, is half the battle in getting them to do well at school. Murthy has clashed with politicians over India's other great shortcoming: infrastructure, particularly in Bangalore, the origin of much of India's IT industry and home to the Infosys headquarters. While local, state, and central leaders bicker, Murthy worries the city will founder from a lack of decent power, transport, and water supplies.

Neither of Murthy's two high-achieving children will work at Infosys; nepotism is just not the Murthy way. Akshata is a marketing whizz in San Francisco, while Rohan is a doctoral student at Harvard, most probably headed for a computer science career. Murthy's novelist wife Sudha, whose computer skills rival those of her huband and the other founders, is a trustee and chair of the Infosys Foundation, set up to do good works in education, health, and the arts.

In June 2007, the Murthy family held 5.12% of Infosys, worth about US$1.5 billion. Infosys was the first Indian software company to issue stock options and has created many hundreds of millionaires.

26. Kavitark Ram SHRIRAM, United States

Estimated net worth: US$1.5 billion.
Position: Founder and managing partner, Sherpalo Ventures.
Born: January 1957 in Chennai. Lives in Mountain View, California.
Educated: B.Sc., Loyola College (affiliated with University of Madras), Chennai; MBA, University of Michigan Business School, Ann Arbor, Michigan.
Marital status: Married; two children.

Shriram, a technology industry insider for 25 years, is regarded as one of the top startup investors in Silicon Valley. His Palo Alto-based company Sherpalo Ventures (from "sherpa" the mountain guide and "Palo Alto") has invested in numerous startups including Friendster, Plaxo, Yodlee, Elance, Zazzle, PodShow (online radio) and call center firm 24/7customer.com. He serves on the advisory board of Naukri. com, the leading online site in India for jobs, real estate, and matrimony classifieds.

Shriram was an early investor in – or "mentor capitalist," as he prefers it – and founding board member of online search giant Google, which went public with a high-profile initial share offer in 2004. Despite selling more than half his 5.1 million Google shares, Shriram still owns shares worth about US$900 million at the June 2007 price of US$495. Before setting up Sherpalo in 2000, Shriram ran business development at Amazon, where he grew the customer base from three million to 11 million users. He had moved over to Amazon in 1998, when it bought shopping portal Junglee. Rakesh Mathur, one of the co-founders of Junglee, had invited Shriram – then on a sabbatical from Netscape – to be Junglee's CEO/president. Shriram was with Netscape from 1994, when the internet was just about to take off, and was one of its top executives.

Shriram tells the people who come calling with a business plan that a good vision without good execution is worthless. "Otherwise, you're just another smart guy with a dream. And there are plenty of those." Execution is as important as innovation, he says.

And his advice to startups looking for financial backers: "It's not just about the money; it's also about the quality of the investors and the depth of their pockets. Investors that understand the market space can help the company in innumerable ways."

27. Amar Gopal BOSE, United States

Estimated net worth: US$1.5 billion.
Position: Founder, chairman, and CEO, Bose Corporation.
Born: 1929 in Philadephia. Lives in Framingham, Massachusetts (home of Bose Corp.) and in Hawaii.
Educated: B.Sc., M.Sc., and Ph.D in electrical engineering at MIT, then professor of electrical engineering at MIT for 45 years until retirement in 2000.
Marital status: Married; two children from first marriage: son Vanu and daughter Maya, both educated at MIT. Vanu is a technology entrepreneur; Maya is a chiropractor.
Interests: Electronics, acoustics.

Dr. Amar G. Bose is the son of Nani Gopal Bose, a Bengali revolutionary who was forced to flee Kolkata for the United States because of his campaign against the British rulers of India. The family settled in Philadelphia, where Bose was born and raised. From an early age, Bose was interested in acoustics and electrical gadgets, making pocket money by fixing radios. A Fulbright scholar, Bose spent a year in New Delhi, where he met Prema, the woman who would become his wife. They have since divorced. He is married to a Bose executive, Ursula Boltzhauser.

Bose studied at MIT in the 1950s. After completing his Ph.D there, he began research in 1956 into physical acoustics and the study of the human perception of sound. In 1964, while teaching at MIT, Bose founded the Bose Corporation with the aim of creating loudspeakers that would faithfully reproduce the quality of a live performance. In 1982, he introduced the first factory-installed car stereo systems. He followed that in 1989 with noise-canceling headsets – a boon for pilots initially, and later, for airline passengers. Mobile surround sound arrived for car drivers and their passengers in 2003. Bose's acoustic waveguide technology won him "Inventor of the Year" honors in 1987, shared with Dr. William Short.

Bose was inducted into the Radio Hall of Fame in 2000 and won a distinguished service citation from the Automotive Hall of Fame in 2007. His latest innovation is a car suspension system, unveiled in August 2004 after more than 20 years of research. It uses computer-controlled electric motors to smooth out bumps and dips in the road. Privately held Bose Corporation, which has an annual turnover of about US$1.8 billion, employs around 9,000 people. It has established a software hub in Bangalore, known as Bose Technology Center.

28. Mike (Mitesh) Devshi JATANIA and brothers, United Kingdom

Estimated net worth: US$1.5 billion.

Position: Chief executive, Lornamead Group.

Born: Mike: February 17, 1965; George: August 17, 1950; Vin: November 1, 1955; Danny: February 4, 1959.

Educated: St Marylebone Grammar School, London; Dulwich College; studied accountancy, London South Bank University.

Marital status: Married to Sonal (2005), Lornamead's business development manager for Europe.

Interests: Snow skiing, waterskiing, scuba diving, cricket, opera; food and wines from Bordeaux.

The Jatania family moved from India to Uganda in the 1930s, then to the United Kingdom in 1969 as part of the great exodus of Indians from East Africa as the various former British colonies in Africa became independent. Originally a trading company for brands in Africa, Lornamead now owns a big range of cosmetic products, including Yardley perfumes and various hair, skin, and oral care brands, such as Harmony hairspray (from Unilever), Natural White toothpaste, and Te Tao shampoo. The Jatania business model is to buy well-performing non-core brands and enhance them.

Lornamead, which employs 600 people in the UK/Ireland, Dubai, Canada, and Africa, also has extensive property interests in London, particularly around Paddington.

Mike Jatania started work at the family company in 1985 and became CEO in 1990. There has been talk of selling or floating the company within five years. In 2002, the Jatanias launched EPIC Brand Investments (EBI), a joint venture with London-based fund manager EPIC Investment Partners, specifically to build up a portfolio of consumer brands. EBI, which raised 50 million pounds sterling (US$99 million) on the London Stock Exchange's growth market AIM (Alternative Investment Market), bought six companies. In January 2005, EPIC Private Equity agreed to sell out to Lornamead and EBI was delisted. In May 2006, Lornamead announced it was buying a range of shampoo and conditioner brands from Unilever for US$130 million, following its US$60 million purchase earlier in the year of Yardley perfumes from Procter & Gamble.

Mike Jatania, who owns a Ferrari plus a chauffeur-driven Bentley Arnage, lives in a penthouse apartment in London's West End, next-door to his parents and three brothers. The Jatanias plan to set up a philanthropic foundation to formalize the family's giving.

29. Subhash CHANDRA, India

Estimated net worth: US$1.45 billion.

Position: Chairman, Zee Entertainment Enterprises and Essel Group.

Born: November 30, 1950 in Adampur Mandi, Hisar, Haryana state. Son of Nand Kishore Goenka and the late Tara Devi.

Educated: CAV High School, 12th standard, electrical engineering.

Marital status: Married to Sushila; sons Punit Goenka (University of Bombay, 1995) and Amit; and daughter Pooja. Punit is a director of Zee Entertainment Enterprises and runs Dish TV. Chandra's younger brothers – Laxmi Narayan Goel, Jawahar Goel, and Ashok Goel – are active in Essel Group companies, including Zee.

Interests: Yoga, meditation, music (including songs from Hindi films), philanthropy.

Once a year, India's most visible and voluble media tycoon, Subhash Chandra, takes a vow of silence for 15 days. A follower of Vipassana meditation, Chandra says the experience clears and lightens the mind. "When you come out, you are a much more clear-headed person," he told CNN's Andrew Stevens in 2007. Chandra, the son of a rice trader and the eldest of seven children, has also cleared and lightened the makeup of his up-and-down media empire, splitting his Zee Group into four listed companies in 2006/07 through a de-merger process that he says will "strengthen long-term business prospects of each individual business, by providing focused management attention." After years in the doldrums following flagship Zee Telefilm's share price crash in 2000, that sounds like good news. Messy programming, poor management, and sloppy execution had seen frontrunner Zee, which began in 1992, drop to No. 3 behind Star and Sony in the Indian TV market. Cable was also stagnant, and Zee's much anticipated direct-to-home satellite service didn't deliver the big push that might have been expected when it launched in 2003. Under the restructure in November 2006, Zee Telefilms was renamed Zee Entertainment Enterprises Ltd., concentrating on global broadcasting, entertainment channels, and joint ventures. Zee News Ltd. runs the news and regional language channels; Wire and Wireless India Ltd. runs the cable distribution business (formerly Siticable); and Dish TV India Ltd. (formerly ASC Enterprises) runs the direct-to-home satellite broadcasting business. Shareholders of Zee Telefilms were allotted shares in the other three companies, with Chandra confident the sum of the parts will be greater than the whole. Expansion is in the wings: Chandra says Zee will launch a news and business channel from its Mideast production base in Dubai to target an Arab audience, offering programs in Arabic and English.

Chandra's other media interests include a joint venture in the Mumbai newspaper *DNA* (Daily News Analysis), of which he is co-chairman. In 2006, Zee also bought a 54% stake in Delhi-based United News of India (UNI), with Chandra saying he wanted it to be a viable news agency able to compete with Reuters and to offer an Indian perspective. Zee paid an initial US$7 million, and Chandra said he would pump in another US$22 million to lift UNI's performance. But UNI employees opposed to the deal call Chandra a "media poacher." Chandra is best known for his media ventures, but his Essel Group is where it all started. His working life began in the family's flour mill and cotton trading business, before he moved into vegetable oils, and grain storage and exporting. In 1982 he set up Essel Packaging to make laminated tubes for toothpaste, and in 1986 he opened Essel World, an amusement park on the outskirts of Mumbai, to which he has since added Water Kingdom (1998). Chandra's Essel Group holds 43.9% of Zee Entertainment, which had a market capitalization in June 2007 of about US$3.3 billion.

Chandra has set up an educational foundation, TALEEM (Transnational Alternate Learning for Emancipation and Empowerment through Multimedia), and is a trustee of the spiritual meditation group called Global Vippassana Foundation. His philosophy is: "Paths are made by walking, and walking down beaten paths is for beaten men."

30. Anurag DIKSHIT, Gibraltar

Estimated net worth: US$1.45 billion.
Position: Co-founder, PartyGaming, UK.
Born: 1973 in New Delhi. Lives in Gibraltar.
Educated: B.Tech. in computer science and engineering, Indian Institute of Technology, New Delhi, 1994.
Marital status: Married; one child.
Interests: Chess, antiquities.

Cybersex, tax havens, online gambling, tech wizardry, legal questions, and billions of dollars for the founding four – that, in a nutshell, is the fabulous story behind PartyGaming, until it hit the wall of US anti-gaming legislation in late 2006. The June 2005 flotation of the online casino group delivered an instant windfall to its founders, including a couple of 30-something Indian tech wizards who were students together at the Indian Institute of Technology in New Delhi in the early 1990s. With PartyGaming's market value hitting US$9 billion when it began trading on the London Stock Exchange on June 27, 2005, Anurag Dikshit and Vikrant Bhargava (see profile No. 72) found themselves with a joint stake worth US$3.5 billion, plus another US$685 million cash from shares sold into the float. They had tapped into one of the most lucrative aspects of online business – gambling. It was "clean and inexpensive entertainment" – and best of all, it could be done in secret so that no one need know who was a gambler. But the passage of a new US law at the end of September 2006 targeting online gambling transactions saw share values for PartyGaming and similar companies such as 888.com plummet. PartyGaming immediately lost more than 60% of its value when the London market opened on October 2, and by June 2007 the shares were trading at about 42 pence, down from a year-high of 158 pence. The US was PartyGaming's biggest market by far, but the new legislation effectively shut it down, forcing the company to slash 40% of its jobs, restructure its management, and focus on other markets such as Europe and the Middle East. Before the shakeup, PartyGaming had 1,100 staff, most of them operating from its Hyderabad call center.

Headquartered in the tax haven of Gibraltar, PartyGaming was formed in 1997 by the American husband-and-wife team of James Russell DeLeon and Ruth Parasol. California-based Parasol made her money from phone porn – sex chat lines and cybersex websites – following in the footsteps of her father, Richard Parasol, who once ran a string of massage parlors in San Francisco. DeLeon is a lawyer and software entrepreneur. Dikshit, who joined in 1998, was PartyGaming's operations director and the computer whiz who designed the software for the PartyPoker main brand. Earlier, Dikshit had worked in the US as a software developer and systems analyst. He was followed into PartyGaming by Bhargava in 1999, who became marketing director.

Despite the 2006 downturn, Dikshit remains seriously wealthy, both from his paper holdings and share sales made in June 2005 and again in June 2006, after he stepped down from the PartyGaming board. He holds 28.95% of the company, worth about US$900 million in June 2007. He raised about US$500 million from shares sold into the 2005 float and another US$110 million in June 2006. Dikshit and others may face questions as part of an investigation by the US Department of Justice into illegal internet gambling.

31. Savitri Devi JINDAL and family, India

Estimated net worth: US$1.35 billion.
Position: Chairman, Jindal Steel Group.
Born: March 20, 1950.
Educated: Shree Kanya Pathshala school, Teensukhiya, Assam state.
Marital status: Married Om Prakash Jindal on June 22, 1965. He died in a helicopter crash on March 31, 2005, aged 74. Four sons (Prithviraj, Sajjan, Ratan, and Naveen) and five daughters.
Interests: Social welfare issues: schools, medicine, agricultural development.

Savitri Jindal has chaired the US$4 billion Jindal Group since the death of her husband, O.P. Jindal, the industrialist, agriculturalist, and politician known as the "Steel Man of Hisar" (the district of his birthplace Nalwa, in Haryana state). O.P. Jindal and two other people were killed when his helicopter crashed near Saharanpur in Uttar Pradesh on March 31, 2005. At the time, he was the Jindal Group chairman and power minister for Haryana state. He was elected to the Lok Sabha, the lower house of the national parliament, in 1996. Jindal's mantra was "Where others see walls, I see doors." Savitri Jindal has since been elected as a member of the Haryana legislative assembly and is minister of urban development and housing. Youngest son Naveen (b. March 9, 1970; MBA, University of Texas) was elected a member of the Lok Sabha in 2004, the same year he won a landmark Supreme Court judgment making it a fundamental right to be able to fly the Indian flag.

O.P. Jindal started his industrial career with a small bucket manufacturing plant in Hisar. In 1964 he set up a pipe company, Jindal Ltd., and followed that in 1969 with Jindal Strips. This eventually became the Jindal Group, which today operates in iron and steel, aluminum, mining, and power, and includes India's largest stainless steel producer, Jindal Stainless. The group runs 12 plants in India and two in the United States.

In 2004, the Bengal Chamber of Commerce and Industry conferred its Lifetime Achievement Award on O.P. Jindal for his contribution to India's steel industry.

In the decade before his death, O.P. had stepped back from the daily operations of the business group to concentrate on his philanthropic endeavors. He divided the main group companies among his four sons: Saw Pipes Ltd. (now Jindal SAW) went to Prithviraj; Jindal Iron & Steel and Jindal Vijaynagar Steel to Sajjan; Jindal Stainless to Ratan; and Jindal Steel & Power to Naveen.

As part of a strategic review by the group, Sajjan Jindal (b. December 5, 1959 in Kolkata; B.Eng., Bangalore University, 1982) amalgamated the companies under his control into Jindal South West Holdings in 2005. The main listed entity is JSW Steel. JSW accounts for about half the total US$4 billion annual turnover of the Jindal Group. The main promoter company, Jindal Strips, has been restructured into a non-bank finance company, led by Ratan Jindal.

The Naveen Jindal-led Jindal Steel & Power won the rights in June 2006 to develop one of the world's biggest iron ore mines, El Mutun in Bolivia, with reserves of 40 billion tonnes. At Jindal Stainless, Ratan Jindal says his goal is for the company to be among the top 10 stainless steel producers by 2010.

Savitri Jindal chairs the four main companies controlled by her sons. The biggest of those by market capitalization is JSW Steel (US$2.5 billion in June 2007), followed by Jindal Steel & Power on US$2.4 billion. The Jindal family and associated companies hold 47% of JSW Steel and 51% of Jindal Steel & Power.

32. Vijay MALLYA, India

Estimated net worth: US$1.3 billion.
Position: Chairman and chief executive, UB Group.
Born: December 18, 1955 in Kolkata. Son of UB founder Vittal Mallya
   (d. 1983) and Lalitha. Raised in Kolkata by his mother after her
   divorce from Vittal.
Educated: St. Xavier's College, Kolkata. Honorary Ph.D in business
   administration from University of Southern California.
Marital status: Twice married. First wife Sameera lives in London with
   son Sidhartha (b. May 7, 1987), who is a college student in the UK.
   Second wife Rekha and two daughters Rehana (Leana) and Tanya
   live in Sausalito, California, but Rekha is frequently in Bangalore.
Hobbies: Horse racing, motor racing, yachting, collecting exotic cars,
   military antiques.

Liquor baron Vijay Mallya, king of bling, branding, and good times,
has more facets than the diamond earrings he often wears. A member
of India's parliamentary upper house (Rajya Sabha) with a mission
to help India's rural poor, he is founder of the "funliner" Kingfisher
Airlines, a supporter of Formula 1 racing, a collector of art and
antiques, a fashion promoter, an intensely religious man, a breeder
of champion racehorses, and the owner of residences in California,
Bangalore, London, New York, and South Africa. Anywhere else he
happens to be, there's either his 95-meter super-yacht *Indian Empress*,
or his corporate transport, an Airbus A319, as a place to bed down.
He has big aspirations for Kingfisher Airlines, which has taken a strategic stake in low-cost rival carrier Air Deccan. But for now his main
business is the UB Group, which dominates the Indian beer and spirit
market through its United Breweries and United Spirits divisions. His
Kingfisher beer brand alone accounts for more than a 30% market
share. He took over UB's running in 1983, after his father Vittal
Mallya's sudden death, and has grown it into the world's third-largest
liquor group, behind Diageo and Pernod-Ricard. Along with his
US$1.1 billion acquisition of Scotch major Whyte & Mackay, Mallya
has wine in his sights next: there are big plans for a domestic winery
near Pune, and he has already bought another in France.
   The UB Group's other activities encompass agrochemicals, engineering, life sciences, media, information technology, and infrastructure development. The listed flagships United Breweries (held 37.5%

by Scottish & Newcastle) and United Spirits had market capitalizations of US$1.31 billion and US$1.83 billion, respectively, in mid-
2007. Mallya's UB Holdings, which consolidates various subsidiaries
and has significant stakes in the two flagships, had a market value of
about US$1 billion. Mallya has seen his share of litigation related to
securities, tax matters, and sometimes-bitter commercial ventures, but
remains unfailingly ebullient and in good spirits.

33. Rajan Beharilal RAHEJA, India

Estimated net worth: US$1.3 billion.
Position: Founder, R. Raheja Group.
Born: 1953. Son of Dr. Beharilal S. Raheja.
Educated: B.Com.
Marital status: Married to Suman; sons Akshay and Viren. Brother
    Satish is based in Switzerland.
Interests: Education and charitable trusts.

Rajan Raheja has been involved in the family's real estate business
for more than three decades and lives in the family's "Rahejas" compound in Mumbai's beach suburb of Juhu. In the last 20 years he has
ventured into new business sectors, including manufacturing (petrochemicals, batteries, ceramic tiles), financial services, retailing, media,
and information technology. He holds stakes in several hotel groups,
including EIH, Indus Hotels, and Juhu Beach Resorts. The group's
flagship listed enterprise is battery maker Exide Industries, where a
majority stake was acquired in 1994. Rajan Raheja is Exide's vice-
chairman. Exide is the market leader in India and supplies to top
carmakers including GM, Honda, Hyundai, Maruti Suzuki, and
Toyota. Exide also makes batteries for tractors, two-wheelers, and
commercial vehicles, and supplies markets in the UK, Australia,
and Asia.

In manufacturing, the group acquired ceramic tile maker H & R
Johnson (India) in 1993 and has lifted it to market leadership. Raheja
also chairs Prism Cement. In the hospitality sector, Raheja has a joint
venture operating the J.W. Marriott Hotel in Mumbai, and is co-pro-
moter with Oberoi Hotels in setting up a chain of medium-priced
hotels in Chennai, Udaipur, Jaipur, Agra, and Cochin under the brand
name "Trident Hilton."

The group's retail arm runs under the Globus Stores name. It also holds a 25% stake in Dairy Farm's Foodworld Supermarkets Ltd., which runs 50 stores in Bangalore and Hyderabad, with plans to expand to more than 250 stores in the next few years. One of the group's joint ventures with the greatest prospects for success is ING Vysya Life Insurance Co., held 50% by Exide. It paid about US$50 million in July 2005 to buy the 49.13% held in the venture by Grandhi M. Rao's GMR Group. Raheja's goal is to capture a greater share of India's growing life insurance market.

Including joint ventures, Raheja's group has an annual turnover of about US$1.6 billion and employs around 17,000 people. Flagship Exide Industries had a market capitalization of about US$880 million in June 2007.

34. Naresh GOYAL, United Kingdom/India

Estimated net worth: US$1.3 billion.
Position: Executive chairman, Jet Airways.
Born: March 8, 1949 in Patalia, Punjab. Lives in London and Mumbai.
Educated: B.Com., Bikram College of Commerce, Patiala, 1967.
Marital status: Married to Anita; one son, one daughter.
Interests: Watching Bollywood films; vegetarian food. Anita heads fund-raising for Save the Children India.

Goyal grew up in humble circumstances in Patiala, Punjab state, where his father was in the jewelry business. Finding the money for Goyal's school fees was often a struggle, and he recalls how as a youngster he would walk several miles to school. After finishing his education, he got a job in his uncle's travel business in Delhi, initially as a cashier and later as sales agent for Lebanese International Airlines. Goyal worked his way through all aspects of the travel business, to the point where in 1974 he was able to set up his own general sales agency, representing airlines such as Air France, Cathay Pacific, and Austrian Airlines. With India's economy opening up in the early 1990s, Goyal saw an opportunity to take the next step. By May 1993 he was ready, launching Jet Airways with a single Boeing 737–300. Today the airline has a fleet of 42 aircraft, with more on the way. Goyal floated the company in March 2005 and owns 80% of the stock, worth about US$1.3 billion in June 2007.

Wife Anita, formerly with the Oberoi Hotels Group, plays a big role in the running of the airline, and is involved in marketing, pricing, and scheduling. When Goyal started, he was competing against the state-owned monopoly Indian Airlines. Now, with deregulation and the emergence of low-cost carriers, he must do battle with half a dozen competitors – Vijay Mallya's Kingfisher Airlines, Air Deccan, SpiceJet, IndiGo, Indian, GoAir, and Paramount. He has finally snared rival Air Sahara, the subject of a failed merger attempt by Jet in 2006 that eventually came to fruition in the first half of 2007. Air Sahara will emerge as a low-cost carrier under the JetLite brand. Jet expanded into international services in 2005, flying initially to London, Singapore, and Kuala Lumpur. It has since added services to Bangkok and Colombo. A born leader, Goyal says the person at the top must be able to give direction and take responsibility if things go wrong. He says money is not his motivation. What he wants are satisfied customers who will tell others that Jet Airways is a good airline.

35. Vikas OBEROI, India

Estimated net worth: US$1.26 billion.
Position: Chairman, Oberoi Constructions.
Born: 1970.
Educated: Harvard Business School's Owner/President Management
   Program, 1997.
Marital status: Married Bollywood actress Gayatri Joshi (b. March 20,
   1977) in August 2005. They have a son (b. September 2006).
Interests: Travel, music, reading, films, extreme sports such as skydiving
   and bungee jumping.

Vikas "Vicky" Oberoi runs the Mumbai-based property development company his father started in 1985, Oberoi Constructions. His target customers are high net worth individuals looking for luxury apartments in India's financial capital. Oberoi Constructions first came to prominence when its Kingston Properties successfully bid about US$30 million in 2002 for the former Novartis site in the western Mumbai suburb of Goregaon, where Oberoi has built a retail mall, and commercial and residential development. That was followed in December 2003 by the acquisition of the former GlaxoSmithKline headquarters at Worli in Mumbai for about US$24 million, in a consortium with ICICI Ventures. The company's latest big purchase, made in 2005, is a US$50 million block in Mumbai's northeast at Mulund, which was an old Glaxo factory. At Worli, Oberoi is building a 65-story luxury residential tower. Plans for Mulund call for a mixture of residential and retail space. A five-star hotel is also on the books.

In one of the biggest foreign direct investments into the Indian property sector, Morgan Stanley's real estate arm paid US$152 million in January 2007 for a 10.75% stake in Oberoi Constructions, valuing the company at US$1.414 billion. A major attraction for Morgan Stanley is Oberoi's urban land bank, estimated at about 15 million square feet.

Oberoi told the Indian magazine *Business Traveller* in 2005 that being an effective leader is an exercise in people management. "Empower them with the authority to get work done," he said. "But most importantly, make your people accountable for their actions." Oberoi's business goal is to see the company's various property projects generate cash flow of US$1 billion a year by 2010. When he's not eyeing property deals, Oberoi is happy being a family man. His wife Gayatri Joshi starred in the 2004 film *Swades* opposite Shah Rukh Khan, and represented India in the Miss International contest in Japan in 2000.

36. Malvinder and Shivinder SINGH, India

Estimated net worth: US$1.25 billion.

Position: Malvinder: chief executive, Ranbaxy Laboratories. Shivinder: managing director, Fortis Healthcare.

Born: Malvinder: 1972; Shivinder: 1975. Sons of the late Parvinder Singh (d. July 4, 1999) and Nimmi Singh. Grandsons of Ranbaxy's early driving force, Dr. Bhai Mohan Singh (b. December 30, 1917 at Jhelum and d. March 27, 2006).

Educated: Malvinder: B.Econ., St. Stephen's College, New Delhi, 1993; MBA, Fuqua School of Business, Duke University, US, 1998. Shivinder: Doon School; B.A. (Hons) in mathematics, St. Stephen's College, New Delhi; MBA, health sector management, Fuqua School of Business, Duke University, US.

Marital status: Malvinder is married to Japna; daughters Nimrita and Nanaki. Shivinder is married to Aditi; four sons.

Interests: Malvinder is a photography fan.

When Parvinder Singh died on July 4, 1999 at the age of 56, just a few weeks after he said he would step down as managing director of India's biggest pharmaceutical company because of the effects of cancer on his health, he had chosen an insider – but not a family member – to succeed him. With the Singh family holding a substantial stake in Ranbaxy, there might have been an expectation that Parvinder's elder son Malvinder would take the helm. But it was too early; instead, Singh chose Davinder Singh (D.S.) Brar, the company's president.

Brar's brief was to take Ranbaxy to the next stage in the industry: to move from a generic producer to a research-based internationally competitive pharmaceutical company. Brar's tenure as CEO lasted five years. Brian Tempest became CEO in July 2004, with Malvinder Singh as CEO-in-waiting. Malvinder finally moved into the top job in January 2006 when Tempest became executive vice-chairman and chief mentor. Ranbaxy's revenues crossed the US$1 billion threshold in 2004 and will reach US$1.5 billion in 2007, with a target of US$5 billion by 2012. Ranbaxy also plans to lift R&D spending from 6% to 10% of revenues. It operates in 45 countries and is one of the biggest suppliers of generic HIV/AIDS drugs.

It is all a far cry from the company set up in post-Partition India by Ranjit Singh and Gurbax Singh, whose names provided the basis for Ranbaxy. When they were stretched financially in 1952, Bhai Mohan Singh, Parvinder Singh's moneylender father, took over the company. It was incorporated as a private limited company in 1961 and went public in 1973. Parvinder, who studied pharmacology at the University of Michigan in the United States, took over operationally in 1982. There was a family split in 1989, when Parvinder's brothers Manjit and Analjit left the company. Their father, Bhai Mohan Singh, resigned from the board in 1993, leaving Parvinder in full control. Over the next six years he built Ranbaxy into a company that could not only copy drugs, but improve them, and through research, develop its own new drugs. Ranbaxy's research center is seen as the most likely spot from where India's first blockbuster drug will emerge.

Malvinder Singh worked for American Express after graduation, in New Delhi and Mumbai, before doing his MBA in the United States and then coming back to India to work at Ranbaxy from 1998 onwards. He is a member of the National Council for the Confederation of Indian Industries (CII) and the World Economic Forum's Young Global Leaders group. Shivinder is managing director of Fortis Healthcare and Escorts Heart Institute & Research Centre, bought from the Nanda family for US$150 million in September 2005. With the healthcare market growing rapidly in India, Fortis Healthcare listed in May 2007 and has a market capitalization of about US$450 million. The Singh brothers also control Oscar Investments and pathology company SRL Ranbaxy. In June 2007, Ranbaxy Laboratories had a market capitalization of about US$3.58 billion; the Singh family holds a stake of almost 35%, worth US$1.25 billion.

37. Pradeep Kumar JAIN and family, India

Estimated net worth: US$1.18 billion.
Position: Founder and chairman, Parsvnath Developers.
Born: 1964. One of 13 children of industrialist Sheetal Prasad Jain.
Educated: B.A.
Marital status: Married to Nutan (M.Com., Raheja College, Mumbai and postgraduate degree in hospitality administration, SNDT College, Mumbai). Two children: daughter Neha and son Pranav.
Interests: Chess, collecting statues of Hindu god Ganesha. Trustee of Moradabad Institute of Technology. Member, Institute of Marketing & Management.

Delhi-based Pradeep Jain and his family hold 80.3% of Parsvnath Developers, a real estate company valued in June 2007 at about US$1.5 billion. In a sign of the property boom gripping the country, Parsvnath listed on Indian markets on November 30, 2006 at an 80% premium to its issue price (540 rupees vs. 300 rupees). Pradeep, his wife Nutan, and his younger brothers Sanjeev (B.Eng., B.V. College of Engineering, Pune) and Rajeev (MMBS, J.N. College, Wardha, Nagpur University) are all members of the board. Pradeep sets strategic direction; Sanjeev looks after architectural, construction, and purchasing matters; while Rajeev runs marketing and commercial operations. Other members of the Jain family are part of the promoter group, including Pradeep's father S.P., brothers S.K., V.K., and Ajay; sisters Trishla, Sumitra, Manorama, Shashi Bala, Savita, Rekha, Neelam, and Minu. Nutan Jain's mother, two sisters, and two brothers are also part of the group.

Parsvnath began business in 1990, although the Jains have been active in real estate for more than two decades. The company raised about US$220 million in its initial public offer, which it intended to use to fund projects in its property development pipeline. Jain said in

2007 that Parsvnath owned or held development rights for more than 100 million square feet of saleable area. Its project lineup, covering 41 cities, includes malls, commercial complexes at the New Delhi satellite cities of Gurgaon and Noida, development of Delhi metro (subway) stations, four information technology parks, 13 hotels, and 20 integrated townships across India. In March 2007, Parsvnath announced it would develop a multimedia and film city at Sarangpur, near Chandigarh. About 40% of its planned projects are in north India. Jain's awards include the Jawaharlal Nehru Award for Excellence (1992) and the World Economic Progress Award for Entrepreneurship (1997). According to the Parsvnath share offer prospectus, income tax notices were issued to Sanjeev, Rajeev, and Nutan Jain in 2006 over alleged non-filing of tax returns.

38. Jignesh P. SHAH, India

Estimated net worth: US$1.16 billion.
Position: Founder and executive chairman, Financial Technologies Group.
Born: 1967. Son of Prakash Shah.
Educated: B.Eng. in electronic engineering, University of Mumbai; post-graduate studies, New York Institute of Finance.
Marital status: Married to Rupal; one daughter.
Interests: Reading, Hindi movies, education.

"Exchange king" Jignesh Shah may well be India's youngest first-generation billionaire, courtesy of the 47.43% stake he and associates hold in his listed Financial Technologies Ltd., the online trading software company he set up in Mumbai in January 1995 with partner Dewang Neralla. Financial Technologies had a market capitalization in June 2007 of about US$2.4 billion. Neralla is the chief technology architect.

Shah, who hails from a Gujarati family that traded in iron and steel, is seen as standard-bearer for India's Web 2.0 brigade. He joined the Bombay Stock Exchange (BSE) as a computer engineer in 1990 to work on its trade automation project, and in 1993 was sent on a study tour by the BSE to look at stock exchanges in London, New York, Tokyo, Hong Kong, and Singapore in the search for technological excellence. Shah left the BSE at the end of 1994 to go out on his own.

In the early 2000s, fresh from the success of his online trading software, Shah saw an opportunity to set up a new online commodities trading exchange in India. He won the requisite license from the authorities and established Multi Commodity Exchange (MCX) in November 2003 as a subsidiary of Financial Technologies. MCX has since established links with other commodity exchanges around the world, including London, New York, Tokyo, and China. Shah also has set up a digital currency-trading platform, IBS-Forex, and owns a half-share of Dubai's gold and commodities exchange.

In November 2006, US Senator Hillary Clinton presented Shah with the US–India Business Leadership Award in Washington, DC, to mark his pioneering work in integrating rural India with global markets. In January 2007, the World Economic Forum chose Shah as a "Young Global Leader of 2007," identifying him as one of 250 people aged under 40 whose professional accomplishments and commitment to society marked their potential to contribute to the future of the world.

Shah's Financial Technologies Group sponsors a number of educational research initiatives at Indian Institutes of Management, covering currency, commodities, equities, and debt.

39. B. Ramalinga RAJU, India

Estimated net worth: US$1.1 billion.
Position: Founder and chairman, Satyam Computer Services.
Born: September 15, 1955 in Bhimavaram, Andhra Pradesh. Son of Satyanarayan Raju.
Educated: B.Com., Andhra Loyola College, Vijayawada; MBA, Ohio University, US; Owner/President Management Program, Harvard.
Marital status: Married to Nandini; sons Teja and Ramu.
Interests: Yoga; reading philosophy, science, and management subjects.

B. Ramalinga Raju, eldest son of a well-to-do farmer, returned to India in 1977 after studying in the United States, but didn't immediately venture into the infotech world. In 1987, after a couple of ventures in manufacturing and construction, he set up Hyderabad-based Satyam Computer Services. Younger brother B. Rama Raju

(M.Econ., Loyola College, Chennai; MBA, Laredo State University – now Texas A&M International University) has been on the Satyam board since its inception and became CEO in 1991. Cousin C. Srini Raju was chief operating officer from 1992 until he left in 2000. As the outsourcing movement in the United States gathered steam, Satyam in 1992 became the first Indian company to set up satellite communications to help it tap into the market for offshore software development, then rode the year 2000 debugging wave. In the 2000s, it set up bases and development centers in the Middle East, Southeast Asia, Australia, and Europe, and established a range of alliances with international companies.

In two decades, Satyam has grown to a global consulting and IT services company with 38,000 staff, revenues of around US$1.4 billion a year, and a market capitalization of US$7.7 billion in June 2007, which puts it No. 4 in India behind TCS, Infosys, and Wipro. Satyam was ranked No. 1 in India and No. 2 globally among 872 outsourcing vendors by industry analysts the Brown-Wilson Group in 2006. Its internet service provider Sify (formerly Satyam Infoway until a name change in January 2003) began commercial operations in April 1998 and was the first Indian internet company to list on the US Nasdaq exchange, in October 1999, behind software services rival Infosys, which got the inaugural Indian listing on the Nasdaq in March 1999. Satyam, which itself listed on the New York Stock Exchange (NYSE) in May 2001, has also set up a business processing subsidiary, Nipuna. Ramalinga Raju heads the family's Byrraju Foundation, which was set up in 2001 to help promote education and sustainable development in rural India.

Raju, his brother, and their spouses hold a stake of 8.54% in Satyam, through SRSR Holdings, and other promoters have about 5.5%. Raju, who was named Ernst & Young's "Entrepreneur of the Year for Services" in 1999, says the company needs to face global competition, and for that, it needs the best people, recruited from around the world. At corporate headquarters in Hyderabad, Satyam has its own nine-hole golf course, health center, shopping complex, deer park, and aviary to help keep the staff happy. Satyam has its biggest offshore development center in the Australian city of Melbourne. Aside from Satyam, Ramalinga Raju, brother B. Rama Raju, and youngest brother B. Suryanarayana Raju also own Hyderabad infrastructure company Maytas Infra Ltd., where Ramalinga Raju's son Teja Raju is vice-chairman.

40. Gracias Antony SALDANHA, India

Estimated net worth: US$1.08 billion.
Position: Founder and chairman, Glenmark Pharmaceuticals.
Born: 1937.
Educated: M.Sc., University of Mumbai; diploma in management
   studies, Jamna Lal Bajaj Institute of Management Studies, Mumbai.
   Wife Blanche has a B.Sc. and B.Ed. from University of Mumbai.
Marital status: Married to Blanche Elizabeth Saldanha. Elder son
   Glenn is Glenmark's CEO. Younger son Mark runs a separate
   company, Marksans Pharma Ltd.
Interests: Horse racing.

The Saldanha family holds a stake of almost 54% in Mumbai-based
Glenmark Pharmaceuticals, which had a market capitalization of just
over US$2 billion in June 2007. Pharma industry veteran Gracias
Saldanha founded the company in November 1977 with three staff
and capital of about US$120,000, after more than a decade spent
working with multinational pharma companies. He named the new
business "Glenmark" after his sons Glenn and Mark. Glenn (B.Phar-
macology; MBA from the Leonard Stern Business School, New York
University) joined the company in 1998 as a director, and took over
as managing director and CEO in 2001. The company was floated in
1999.

   Glenmark had sales of about US$250 million in 2006/07, with
India accounting for about 40% of that. It sees buoyant growth coming
from its US and Latin American businesses (currently accounting for
17% and 14%, respectively, of revenue) in the years ahead. Key licens-
ing deals will see Forest Labs in the United States and Japan's Teijin
Pharma pay it about US$250 million for the rights to test and com-
mercialize Glenmark's experimental drug oglemilast, which is designed
to treat asthma and chronic obstructive pulmonary disease. Glenmark
bought a Brazilian pharma company in 2004, one in South Africa in
2005, and has a 2006 development and marketing agreement with
Germany's Merck covering diabetes treatment in North America,
Europe, and Japan. A second deal with Merck involves dermatologi-
cal products in Europe. In March 2007, Glenmark expanded its
European presence, by buying Medicamenta of the Czech Republic,
in what Glenn Saldanha called a "landmark event" for its European
business.

Though generic drugs still constitute a large part of its revenue base, Glenmark is regarded as a leader in new molecule discovery in India, with a focus on asthma, pulmonary disease, diabetes, and obesity disorders. It is working with partners in the US and Europe to test, develop, and commercialize molecules for asthma and Type 2 diabetes. Other molecules, for dental pain and obesity treatment, are in early stages of development.

41. Murli Kewalram CHANRAI, Singapore

Estimated net worth: US$1.07 billion.
Position: Chairman, Kewalram Chanrai Group.
Born: 1922 in Hyderabad, Sind (now Pakistan).
Educated: Matriculated in 1938 from Navalrai Hiranand Academy, Hyderabad, Sind.
Marital status: Married; five children. Nephew Narain Girdhar Chanrai is group CEO.
Interests: Social causes, including supporting the Jaslok hospital in Mumbai. Was president, Singapore Indian Chamber of Commerce & Industry, 1992–96.

The story of the Kewelram Chanrai family empire goes back to 1860, when it began trading handloom fabrics in India. It expanded initially to Africa and later to Southeast Asia. It now runs textile manufacturing plants in Nigeria, Indonesia, and the Philippines, and has invested heavily in cotton growing and processing in Africa and Asia. The group's business interests today span international trading, commodities, textiles, information technology, and property development. It operates in 45 countries and employs more than 10,000 people. M.K. Chanrai has been involved with the group for more than 60 years, working in Africa, India, Indonesia, the United Kingdom, and Singapore. He served as executive chairman from 1976, and as non-executive chairman since 1992.

Flagship of the group is Singapore-listed Olam International, which runs a global food-related commodity business. It trades in edible nuts, cocoa, coffee, cotton, rice, sugar, spices, and timber, and supplies customers such as Kraft, Nestlé, Mars, and Lavazza. Olam, which the Kewalram Chanrai Group set up in 1989 to handle agribusiness, raised about US$132 million in its 2005 initial public offer, some of it earmarked for expansion plans in Brazil, China, and the United States, targeting markets in those countries plus Russia. In March 2007, it bid about US$110 million for the Australian cotton grower Queensland Cotton Holdings, which provoked a bidding war with French commodity trader Louis Dreyfus. Olam increased its offer in May, as did Dreyfus. But a June 2007 bid by Olam that valued Queensland Cotton at about US$137 million proved a winner, with Dreyfus agreeing to accept the sweetened price for its 20% stake. The Australian bid followed Olam's announcement in February 2007 of a cotton and oilseeds joint venture with Chinese cotton grower China-tex. A successful Australian acquisition would make Olam the world's third-largest cotton business.

M.K. Chanrai stepped down as Olam's non-executive chairman in February 2006 but the group retains a stake of 33% valued at just over US$1 billion. Olam had a market capitalization of US$3.26 billion in June 2007 and expected 2007 revenues of about US$4 billion. Chanrai's nephew, Narain Girdhar Chanrai, 57, is a non-executive director of Olam, managing director of Kewalram Singapore, and CEO of the Kewalram Chanrai Group. He holds a B.Sc. in economics, University of London, 1970. He worked in various group operations in Africa, the United Kingdom, and Singapore, and was overseeing its global treasury and accounting functions before taking over as group CEO in 2005.

42. Bharat DESAI, United States

Estimated net worth: US$1.04 billion.
Position: Co-founder and chairman, Syntel Inc.
Born: November 20, 1952 in Mombasa, Kenya.
Educated: St. Xavier's High School, Ahmedabad; B.Tech. in electrical engineering, Indian Institute of Technology, Mumbai, 1975; MBA in systems and finance, University of Michigan, 1981.
Marital status: Married to Neerja Sethi, who plays a key role in the company. She has masters degrees in computer science (Oakland University) and operations research (Delhi University) and a bachelor degree in mathematics (Delhi). Two children: son Saahill (Princeton graduate) and daughter Pia (Harvard), both born and educated in the US.
Interests: Running, yoga, cricket, bridge.

Desai's family fled East Africa for India in 1964 as independence swept through the African continent. The family initially went to Ahmedabad, 400 miles (640 kilometers) north of Mumbai. It was a struggle to make ends meet, but Desai was able to get a good education. He graduated from the Indian Institute of Technology in Mumbai and joined Tata Consultancy Services (TCS) as a programmer in 1975. TCS sent him to the United States to work on a project. He opted to stay on in the US, going to the University of Michigan to begin a dual MBA program, paying his way via a part-time job. In 1980, Desai started Systems International (later to become Syntel) with his wife Neerja. They had US$2,000 to put into the company, and Neerja kept her job at TCS to keep some money coming in. Even then, Desai knew he wanted to create a global company. But initially, the focus was more prosaic: IT staffing work for the auto industry in Michigan. It would be more than two decades before Syntel completed the swap from a US staff focus to an Indian one. In late 2006, Desai noted: "Ten years ago we had 1,500 people in the US and 100 in India. Today the figure is 500 people in the US and 7,000 in India, growing to 10,000 next year [2007]." Syntel's main Indian operations are in Pune, Mumbai, and Chennai. Today, Desai is proud to proclaim Syntel "a truly global company." He points to a client base that includes some of the world's best brands: DaimlerChrysler, American Express, AIG, FedEx, JP Morgan.

Desai says entrepreneurs have to believe in and love their cause. "And they have to be ready for a long, hard road," he warns. In 2005, Desai was named "Entrepreneur of the Year" by his alma mater, the Stephen M. Ross School of Business at the University of Michigan. Syntel had revenue of US$270 million in 2006 and a market capitalization in June 2007 of about US$1.55 billion. Bharat Desai and Neerja Sethi hold a stake of about 60% after selling just over four million shares for about US$118 million in January 2007.

43. Nandan Mohan NILEKANI and family, India

Estimated net worth: US$1.0 billion.
Position: Co-founder, Infosys Technologies.
Born: June 2, 1955 in Bangalore. Son of Durga and Mohan Rao Nilekani.
Educated: Bishop Cotton Boys School, Bangalore; B.Tech. in electrical engineering, Indian Institute of Technology, Mumbai, 1978.
Marital status: Married to Rohini; daughter Jahnavi and son Nihar.
Interests: Rock music (Dire Straits, Pink Floyd).

Nandan Nilekani became co-chairman of IT services company Infosys Technologies on June 22, 2007, relinquishing the chief executive role he held from March 2002 to chief operating officer S. "Kris" Gopalakrishnan. Nilekani, one of the seven Infosys co-founders, was awarded one of India's highest civilian honors, the Padma Bhushan, in 2006 for services to science and engineering.

Nilekani was born and did his early schooling in Bangalore. He left his parents at age 12 (his father was an on-the-move textile executive) to go and live with his uncle at Dharwad in northern Karnataka. After graduating from the Indian Institute of Technology (IIT) in Mumbai with an electrical engineering degree, Nilekani's first job was with Patni Computers, where he met Narayana Murthy, the man who would invite him to co-found Infosys a few years later. When Nilekani entered IIT he was just "a middle-class kid from a small town," he told CNN's Todd Benjamin in a 2006 interview. "Going to IIT and meeting some very bright people helped me get a lot of confidence and figure out how the world worked." Murthy once said of Nilekani: "He is smarter than me . . . and the best communicator among all of us." His workplace slogan is: "Be less busy and more effective." Thomas Friedman's bestseller on globalization, *The World is Flat*, takes its title from Nilekani telling Friedman during an interview at the Infosys headquarters in Bangalore in early 2004: "Tom, the playing field is being leveled."

Time magazine rated Nilekani one of the world's 100 most influential people in 2006, and in 2005 he was awarded the Joseph Schumpeter prize for innovative services in the field of economy, economic sciences, and politics. He and his family hold a 3.55% stake in Infosys (down from 7% in 2003) worth just under US$1 billion in June 2007. Wife Rohini runs a foundation that promotes health and education.

44. Cyrus Soli POONAWALLA and family, India

Estimated net worth: US$1.0 billion.
Position: Chairman, Serum Institute of India Ltd./Poonawalla
  Group
Born: May 11, 1941 in Pune.
Educated: B.Sc., University of Pune; Ph.D, University of Pune,
  1988.
Marital status: Married to Villoo; one son, Adar.
Interests: Classic cars, breeding racehorses. Charity support extends
  to leprosy rehabilitation, hospitals, and public gardens.

Racing identity and owner Dr. Cyrus Poonawalla is widely known for
the champion racehorses bred at his 500-acre (200-hectare) Poonawalla Stud Farms at Pune, but the role that gives him most satisfaction – and wealth – these days is as chair of Serum Institute of India
Ltd. (SIIL), an unlisted company that is the world's fifth-largest
vaccine manufacturer and India's largest biotech company by turnover. Poonawalla set up SIIL in 1967 next to the Poonawalla Group's
stud farm to make anti-snake venom serum and tetanus anti-toxin.
He has grown the company over four decades to the point where it is
the world's largest producer of measles and DTP (diptheria, tetanus,
pertussis) vaccines, and has brought down the price of these and
hepatitis-B vaccines in India and around the globe because, he says,
his products must be affordable to the masses. Serum Institute was
the first company accredited by the World Health Organization to
supply vaccines in bulk to United Nations agencies such as Unicef.
The company says its vaccines are exported to 145 countries and help
protect half the world's newborn children. Poonawalla set up Serum
Bio Pharma Park, India's first biotech special economic zone, near
Pune in February 2006, and estimates the group's total investment
there will eventually reach about US$270 million.

   Poonawalla won the 2002/03 Hall of Fame Award from the Turf
Authorities of India, the 2004 BioSpectrum Person of the Year Award,
the 2005 Sabin Vaccine Institute Humanitarian Award, and a Padma
Shri (one of the highest Indian civilian awards) in the 2005 Indian
President's Republic Day honors list.

   Poonawalla's younger brother Zavary works with him in running
the Stud Farms (set up by their father Soli A. Poonawalla in 1946)
and Serum Institute, as does Poonawalla's son Adar, who is executive

director of operations. Zavary's son Yohan – known for his collection of Rolls-Royces, which includes a 1937 Phantom and a 2005 model – is overall group chairman. The Poonawallas so far have resisted entreaties to float Serum Institute, which had turnover in 2006/07 of about US$200 million. In 2006, Serum Institute struck an alliance with US specialty pharmaceutical maker Akorn Inc. to develop and distribute an anti-rabies treatment in North, Central, and South America, and to work on a second monoclonal antibody product known as Anti-D. Akorn estimates markets for the two products are worth US$600 million. The Poonawalla Group sold its 75% stake in a joint venture making mechanical seals for industrial equipment back to its Japanese partner, Eagle Industry, for US$50 million in mid-2006.

Along with Serum Institute and Stud Farms, other companies in the Poonawalla Group are automatic valve control maker EL-O-Matic (India), butterfly and check valve maker Intervalve (India), and Hotels & Resorts, which has an interest in two UK-based hotels, Grayshott Spa in Surrey and Fawsley Hall, near the Silverstone F1 car racing track. Yohan Poonawalla is looking to expand the hospitality side of the business, striking an agreement in late 2006 with the InterContinental Hotels Group to manage a 200-room luxury property in Pune. The Poonawallas use a Cessna Citation XL business jet to commute between business interests in Delhi, Pune, Bangalore, Dubai, and Goa.

45. Keshub MAHINDRA, India

Estimated net worth: US$930 million.

Position: Chairman, Mahindra & Mahindra. Nephew Anand G. Mahindra is vice-chairman and managing director.

Born: October 9, 1923 in Shimla, Himachal Pradesh. Anand Mahindra was born May 1, 1955.

Educated: Keshub: B.Sc., Wharton School, University of Pennsylvania, US. Anand: MBA, Harvard Business School, 1981, where he studied film-making.

Marital status: Keshub is married to Sudha; three daughters. Anand is married to magazine editor Anuradha; two daughters.

Interests: Anand collects old maps, likes films, and drives a Mahindra Scorpio SUV. His latest boat is named *Dreamcatcher*.

Keshub Mahindra has been chairman since 1963, but nephew Anand runs the sprawling Mahindra Group (M&M), which has interests that range from financial services, telecommunications, software, and real estate to the key automotive and farm equipment businesses. These last two activities make up 80% of the group's turnover of about US$3.2 billion a year, which puts M&M in the top 10 industrial houses in India. M&M has 34 subsidiaries and employs about 25,000 people, with a presence in 20 countries. Main listed entities are Mahindra & Mahindra, which had a market capitalization of about US$4.6 billion in June 2007, and Tech Mahindra, its 46%-held IT joint venture with British Telecom, which went public in August 2006 and is valued at about US$4.4 billion. The Mahindra family and associates hold a stake of about 15% in M&M.

Anand Mahindra's vision for M&M is to be the world No. 1 in tractors and utility vehicles. After buying an 80% stake in China's Jiangling Tractors, M&M is the world No. 4 in tractors. The Scorpio, M&M's home-grown SUV, is being sold overseas in markets such as Europe and Australia. Mahindra also engineered an alliance with Renault to make mid-size cars for the Indian market. Under that deal, the two partners have committed to build a new 500,000-car plant by 2009. In early 2007, Mahindra also linked with International Truck & Engine Co. for a US$500 million greenfield truck and bus plant. The Mahindras were co-promoters of Uday Kotak's Kotak Mahindra Finance, which in 2003 became the Kotak Mahindra Bank, one of the top private sector banks in India. A Mahindra-promoted special economic zone in Chennai, once scorned by competitors as a white elephant, has blossomed into success. In 2004, Anand Mahindra won the Rajiv Gandhi Award for his contribution to business. He won the American India Foundation Leadership Award in 2005, and in 2006 was named "CEO of the Year" at the India Brand Summit. He says India's economy is now large enough that it cannot be derailed. But he worries about the social landscape: "We don't want dreams of wealth allowing the toggle switch to flick over to the side of depravity rather than divinity."

Anand Mahindra's passion for education and social justice is reflected in roles such as his trusteeship of the K.C. Mahindra Education Trust, which provides student scholarships, and his membership of the board of governors of the Mahindra United World College of India.

Keshub Mahindra, who joined the company in 1947, has been one of the giants of the Indian corporate scene for decades and has won numerous business honors. He sits on the Prime Minister's Council on Trade & Industry and chairs the Mahindra Foundation.

46. Senapathy ("Kris") GOPALAKRISHNAN, India

Estimated net worth: US$930 million.
Position: Co-founder: Infosys Technologies.
Born: April 1955.
Educated: M.Sc. in physics, 1977; M.Tech. in computer science, 1979, Indian Institute of Technology, Madras. Awarded the IIT Madras Distinguished Alumnus Award in 1998.
Marital status: Married to Sudha; daughter Meghana.
Interests: Education.

S. "Kris" Gopalakrishnan took over from Nandan Nilekani as managing director and chief executive officer of Infosys Technologies on June 22, 2007. He had been the company's chief operating officer since April 2002 and its president since July 2006. He also chairs the Infosys subsidiary Infosys Consulting.

After graduating from the Indian Institute of Technology (IIT), Madras (now Chennai), Gopalakrishnan began his working life as a software engineer with Patni Computer Systems in Mumbai in 1979. In 1981, he was one of six Patni staff to join colleague Narayana Murthy in founding Infosys.

From 1987 to 1994 he headed the technical operations of KSA/ Infosys, the joint venture Infosys originally set up in Atlanta, Georgia with management consultants Kurt Salmon Associates. The venture ended in 1989. Gopalakrishnan returned to India in 1994 and was appointed deputy managing director. As chief operating officer, his responsibilities included customer services, technology, investments, and acquisitions. Gopalakrishnan chairs the Indian Institute of Information Technology and Management (IITM) in Kerala and is vice-chairman of Karnataka state's Information Technology Education Standards Board. He is also chairman of the IIT Madras Growth Fund, set up to raise funds for infrastructure, research, scholarships, and special projects.

Gopalakrishnan is passionate about the need to upgrade India's education standards, and says leveraging technology is a must. In a 2006 interview at the hi-tech Amrita Vishwa Vidyapeetham University, on the Kerala–Tamil Nadu border in southern India, Gopalakrishnan told students: "This is one of the most exciting periods to get into the corporate world." He said Indian companies now had "tremendous optimism," and felt they could compete and succeed globally. Gopalakrishnan and his family hold a 3.43% stake in Infosys worth about US$930 million in June 2007. In April 2007, the Infosys board approved the appointment of Gopalakrishnan as CEO.

47. Ashwin C. CHOKSI, India

Estimated net worth: US$930 million (Choksi, Dani, & Vakil families).
Position: Chairman, Asian Paints Ltd.
Born: 1944.
Educated: Ashwin Choksi: M.Com. Ashwin S. Dani: B.Sc., University of Mumbai and M.Sc. in polymer science, University of Akron, Ohio, US. Abhay A. Vakil: B.Sc., B.S.

Executive chairman Ashwin Choksi, vice-chairman/managing director Ashwin Dani, and managing director Abhay Vakil are the three key executives running Asian Paints, and are the second-generation representatives of three of the four families that founded the company in February 1942. Between them, the Choksi, Dani, and Vakil families hold a stake of 47.81% in Asian Paints, which is India's largest paint company (and third-largest in Asia), with a market capitalization in June 2007 of almost US$2 billion. In one of the great corporate sagas of the 1990s, the fourth family, the Chokseys, sold their entire 13.5% during the decade, exiting completely in 1997 after a couple of false starts involving British paint major ICI. Company co-founder Champaklal Choksey, who set up Asian Paints in a Mumbai garage with his three friends Chimanlal N. Choksi, Suryakant C. Dani, and Arvind R. Vakil, began the sale process after a falling out with the other families over a global rights issue in 1990 when he was chairman. He died in July 1997, a few months after telling his son Atul Choksey, then-managing director of Asian Paints, to find a buyer for the family's remaining 9.1% stake. Atul Choksey (B.Sc. in chemical engineering, Illinois Institute of Technology) found ICI, via Kotak Mahindra Capital Co., but after this deal was refused approval, the remaining three families picked up 4.5% and Unit Trust of India bought the rest. Choksey resigned as managing director in August 1997 and now chairs the Apcon group of companies. He is also a member of the Asian executive board of the Wharton School of Business at the University of Pennsylvania.

Ashwin Choksi's brother Mahendra serves on the Asian Paints board, as does Abhay Vakil's brother Amar and Ashwin Dani's son Hasit. Another of Dani's sons, Jalaj, runs the international business unit; and a third, Malav, works in quality support. Vakil's daughter Nehal is a finance executive with the company.

In October 2003, Asian Paints bought a 9% stake in ICI's Indian unit for about US$17 million. It also has a majority stake in Berger International. Today, Asian Paints and its subsidiaries have annual revenues of about US$800 million and operate 29 paint manufacturing plants in 21 countries. Just over 79% of sales are made in India, with overseas markets accounting for 18.2% and chemicals for 2.7%. It is also the second-largest industrial coatings business in India. The Middle East, South Asia, and Southeast Asia are seen as the group's growth areas.

48. Brijmohan Lall MUNJAL, India

Estimated net worth: US$903 million.
Position: Co-founder and chairman, Hero Honda Group.
Born: July 1, 1923 in Kamalia (now part of Pakistan).
Educated: Indian heritage school (*gurukul*), Kamalia.
Marital status: Married to Santosh. Eldest son Raman, first managing director of Hero Honda, is deceased. Second son Pawan Kant Munjal (B.Eng. in mechanical engineering) is Hero Honda CEO, and third son Sunil (B.Com.) is a director of several group companies.
Interests: Flying, philanthropy. Set up Raman Kant Munjal Foundation in memory of his eldest son, to run a high school and hospital at Dharuhera. Supports schemes to provide rural education, vocational training, drinking water, roads, streetlights, and sewerage.

From humble beginnings, working initially with his three brothers as a bicycle component maker in the industrial town of Ludhiana in Punjab, Brijmohan L. Munjal has created the world's largest two-wheeler company, Hero Honda, through a combination of audacity, tenacity, technological awareness, and market savvy. Today, Hero Honda sells more than three million motorcycles a year and has about 47% of the Indian market. In the early 1940s, Brijmohan Munjal and his elder brothers Dayanand and Satyanand, along with his younger brother Om Prakash, moved from Kamalia in Pakistan to Amritsar, then moved again to Ludhiana after Partition in 1947. The brothers gradually expanded their bicycle component distribution network, becoming one of India's largest parts suppliers, and adding manufacturing (handlebars, forks, chains) to their capabilities in the early 1950s. From 1956 onwards, their Hero Cycle brand built a reputation for being reliable and affordable, and Munjal's skill in harnessing a network of distributors, motivated vendors, and satisfied customers enabled him to challenge more established names such as Raleigh, Hind, and Atlas.

Munjal also saw the possibilities in motorcycles as India's living standards rose. In the 1980s, Munjal embraced four-stroke technology for its better fuel economy and lower maintenance costs. He was able to strike a collaborative agreement with Japanese motorcycle maker Honda, and in April 1985, the first Hero Honda motorbike rolled out of the company's Dharuhera plant in Haryana state.

Munjal won Ernst & Young's Entrepreneur of the Year Award in 2001 and was awarded the Padma Bhushan, one of India's highest civilian honors, in the 2005 list. In 2006, Munjal told Hero Honda shareholders that the company had barely scratched the surface of India's market potential, and double-digit growth was achievable even in the medium to long term.

Hero Honda had a market capitalization of about US$3.5 billion in June 2007. Munjal and family hold a stake of 26%. Managing director Pawan Kant Munjal says 100cc bikes remain Hero's mainstay, but scooters and big-engine bikes are in the mix. One drawback: while Honda has extended its agreement with Hero to 2014, Honda has also been selling in India's motorcycle and scooter market under its own name, nibbling at Hero Honda's share.

49. Chinankanna (C.) SIVASANKARAN, Singapore/ India/United States

Estimated net worth: US$900 million.
Position: Founder, Sterling Infotech Group.
Born: 1957 in Mayiladuthurai, Tamil Nadu.
Educated: Harvard Business School.
Marital status: Married.
Interests: His spa and healthfood restaurants, Aiwo, in Chennai and Singapore.

The son of a south Indian schoolteacher, the peripatetic C. Sivasankaran is known as a consummate asset trader, buying and selling businesses from telecoms and IT services to banking, food, and coffee. His latest forays are in the renewable energy sector, where he has set up a fuel ethanol company in the United States, E85 Inc., and Sterling Bio-Diesel in India. He also has a 40% stake in Finnish wind turbine maker WinWinD. Siva, as he is widely known, roams the globe in his Boeing business jet from bases in Singapore, San Francisco, and Chennai in search of investment opportunities. He first came to prominence in 1987 when he launched the Siva PC in India at a then-rock bottom price of 29,000 rupees (about US$650), but it has been his telecommunications ventures that delivered the biggest returns. He was an early acquirer of cellular phone service licenses, and sold Sterling Cellular in Delhi to the Ruia brothers' Essar Group in 1994 for about US$150 million. He bought the RPG Group's Chennai mobile phone service in 2003 for about US$60 million and turned it into part of his biggest play in early 2006, when he sold this and other operations (including Dishnet Wireless) to Maxis of Malaysia and its joint venture partners, the Chennai-based Reddy family's Apollo Hospitals, for just over US$1 billion. In March 2007 he raised more cash when he sold his Barista Coffee and Fresh & Honest Café businesses to Italy's Lavazza coffee company for about US$125 million.

Sivasankaran is using the money to fund his renewable energy plans – wind mills across Tamil Nadu state, and up to 10 ethanol facilities in North America. Sivasankaran, whose first job was at Madras Refineries, bought Sterling Computer from the Amritraj family in 1983 and gradually expanded it into the Sterling Infotech Group. At one point he held a 67% stake in Tamil Nadu Mercantile

Bank, but sold out completely in 2004 for a total of about US$50 million. He also has interests in agribusiness, film entertainment, IT education, real estate, engineering, and construction. Sivasankaran won awards in 1987 and 1988 from the President of India for his entrepreneurial activities, and supports education through government schools in Tamil Nadu.

50. Gautam THAPAR, India

Estimated net worth: US$880 million.
Position: Chairman, Ballarpur Industries Ltd. (BILT), Thapar Group.
Born: December 7, 1960. Son of Brij Mohan Thapar and nephew of Lalit Mohan Thapar.
Educated: Doon School, Dehra Dun, 1979; St. Stephen's College, Delhi; chemical engineering, Pratt Institute, New York.
Marital status: Married; two daughters.
Interests: Golf, horse racing.

Gautam Thapar became chairman of India's largest paper producer, Ballarpur Industries Ltd. (BILT), the flagship of the L.M. Thapar Group in July 2006, taking over from group patriarch and his childless uncle, L.M. Thapar, who would die in January 2007 at the age of 76. Gautam Thapar had been managing director since April 1999 and vice-chairman since April 2001. L.M. Thapar, one of the four sons of group founder Karam Chand Thapar (the others are I.M., B.M., and M.M.), had led the family's entire business before its amicable four-way split in the late 1990s. He stepped back from business in the early 2000s to make way for his energetic nephew, though he remained chairman emeritus until his death. Gautam, who graduated as a chemical engineer in the United States, returned to India and joined the family business in 1998. He is credited with turning around Ballarpur Industries, restructuring it into an integrated paper producer, and divesting non-core businesses. In March 2007, BILT paid US$261 million for Sabah Forest Industries, Malaysia's largest integrated pulp and paper mill.

Gautam Thapar became chairman of his father B.M. Thapar's flagship company, Crompton Greaves Ltd., in July 2004, and is a director of Greaves Cotton, Bata International, and Asahi India Glass. His elder brother Karan is a director of Crompton Greaves and chairman of Greaves Cotton and English Indian Clays. Gautam's older cousin Vikram, son of Inder Mohan Thapar, was once viewed as the most likely of the third generation to head the Thapar Group, but quit BILT in 1998. Vikram is chairman of Waterbase Ltd., and a director of KCT Coal and Cynera Investment & Holdings. Man Mohan Thapar, the youngest of the four sons of the Thapar Group founder, is chairman of JCT Electronics. His sons Samir and Arjun are JCT's chairman and managing director.

The Thapars hold a stake of about 42.3% in BILT, which had a market capitalization in mid-2007 of US$411 million and annual revenues of about US$530 million. Solaris Holdings, controlled by Gautam Thapar, holds just over 39% of Crompton Greaves, which had a market capitalization in mid-2007 of US$2.25 billion.

51. Arnavaz ("Anu") AGA, India

Estimated net worth: US$870 million.

Position: Former chairperson, Thermax Ltd.

Born: August 3, 1942 in Mumbai. Daughter of A.S. Bathena. Lives in Pune.

Educated: B.A. in economics, St. Xavier's College, Mumbai; masters in medical and psychiatric social work, Tata Institute of Social Sciences, Mumbai.

Marital status: Widow of the late Rohinton Aga. Daughter Meher is married to Pheroz Pudumjee. Son Kurush died in a road accident, aged 25, in 1997.

Interests: Social welfare, human rights work. Exercise regime includes yoga and cycling.

Pune-based Anu Aga became chairperson of engineering company Thermax Ltd. after the death of her Harvard-educated husband Rohinton D. Aga in 1996 from a heart attack. She lost her son Kurush in a road accident within a year. The company, founded by Anu Aga's father A.S. Bathena three decades earlier, fell into dire straits, seeing its share price plunge more than 90%, from 400 rupees to a low of 36 rupees, by 2000 before a restructure helped it stabilize and recover. Anu Aga had joined Thermax in 1985 and became head of its human resources in 1991. After she moved into the executive chair's role in

1996 (with company stalwart Abhay Nalwade as CEO), she sought outside advice from the Boston Consulting Group. The resulting restructure brought the company back to profitability. Aga stepped down as executive chairperson in October 2004, but remains a director. Her daughter Meher, a classically trained soprano singer and chemical engineer from the Imperial College of Science and Technology, London, became non-executive chairperson at the same time. Meher's husband Pheroz Pudumjee also works in the company and is on the board.

Aga has been active in the Confederation of Indian Industry. In 2003, the Bombay Management Association gave her its 2002/03 Management Woman Achiever of the Year Award. She spends most of her time involved in social welfare activities, including the Akanksha Foundation (which educates underprivileged children in Pune and Mumbai), the Women's India Trust, and is a member of the Commonwealth Human Rights Commission. She is also a director of the weekly newspaper *Tehelka*, which has made a name for its exposure of corruption.

Thermax, which is active in energy and environment engineering, chemicals, and waste management, had a market capitalization in June 2007 of about US$1.46 billion. Aga, Meher, and family companies hold a stake of about 60%.

52. Habil F. KHORAKIWALA, India

Estimated net worth: US$838 million.
Position: Chairman and CEO, Wockhardt Ltd.
Born: September 22, 1942. Eldest son of Fakhruddin Khorakiwala.
Educated: B.Pharma., L.M. College of Pharmacy, Ahmedabad; M.Sc. in pharmaceutical science, Purdue University, Indiana, US; Advanced Management Program, Harvard Business School.
Marital status: Married to Nafisa; three children, Huzaifa, Murtaza, and Zahabiya.
Interests: Philanthropy, particularly through the Red Cross. Reading, swimming.

Habil Khorakiwala has been practicing the dictum of "hard work" for more than 40 years at the helm of the Mumbai-based pharmaceutical company once known as Worli Chemicals Works. His family bought the business in the early 1960s, and Khorakiwala changed the name to Wockhardt when he began running it in 1966, after finishing his masters in the United States.

Today, Wockhardt Ltd. is India's 10th-largest pharma company by market capitalization (US$1.13 billion in June 2007) and employs 6,000 people in nine plants, including 800 outside India. It makes and sells formulations, bulk drugs, vaccines, and animal health products. It has also moved into recombinant biotechnology, drug discovery, and new drug delivery systems. In 2003 it became the first company outside the US and Europe to make recombinant insulin from the basic stage. The following year, it opened a global-scale bio-pharmaceuticals manufacturing plant, Wockhardt Biotech Park, in Aurangabad.

Khorakiwala bought Irish generic pharma company Pinewood for US$150 million in mid-2006, Wockhardt's largest acquisition to date. Khorakiwala says that Pinewood is a "strategic fit" that expands the company's footprint in Europe. In the United States, Wockhardt entered 2007 with 15 products in its lineup and 29 abbreviated new drug applications (ANDAs) awaiting approval from the US Food and Drug Administration. "We look to the US with great confidence for a significant ramp up of business in the years to come," the company said. But while business in Europe and the United States is growing, Khorakiwala is adamant that there will be no marginalization of Indian operations. He told shareholders in October 2006 that Wockhardt's Indian business was growing at 38%, better than twice the industry average of 17%. Khorakiwala says India's pharmaceutical industry offers "a cost to value proposition" found nowhere else in the world.

Khorakiwala was named president of the Federation of Indian Chambers of Commerce and Industry in January 2007. He and his family hold a stake of 73.7% in Wockhardt, where his two sons, Huzaifa and Murtaza, are executive directors. Daughter Zahabiya works in the company's clinical research center and also runs a Mumbai café. Khorakiwala's father, Fakhruddin, is chancellor of Jamia Millia Islamia (National Islamic University) in New Delhi, chairman of the Akbarallys department store chain in Mumbai, and was awarded the Bombay Management Association's Lifetime Achievement Award in November 2006.

53. Lord Swraj PAUL and family, United Kingdom

Estimated net worth: US$837 million.
Position: Founder, Caparo Group.
Born: February 18, 1931 in Jalandhar, Punjab.
Educated: B.Sc., Punjab University; M.Sc. in mechanical engineering, MIT.
Marital status: Married Aruna Vij in 1956. Three sons: twins Ambar and Akash, and Angad; two daughters. (One, Ambika, died in 1968, aged five.)
Interests: Business strategy, education reform, innovative car technology, cricket.

Industrialist Swraj Paul moved from India to the United Kingdom in 1966 to seek treatment for his daughter Ambika, who suffered from leukaemia. He set up his first UK business, Natural Gas Tubes Ltd., and in 1978 founded his privately held Caparo Group, expanding its operations from specialty steel and engineering into automotive technology and hotels. The UK accounts for about half the group's annual turnover of about US$1.25 billion, followed by the United States with a third, and Europe with about 15%. Paul is looking to expand his Indian business interests, citing the potential of the country's automotive sector.

Steel has long been part of the Caparo story. In December 1994, Paul bought the derelict Sharon Steel business in Farrell, Pennsylvania, out of bankruptcy for about US$26 million and renamed it Caparo Steel. Paul had ambitious expansion plans for the US mill, but funding the modernization program proved burdensome. He turned off the electric furnace in 1997 and stopped production in 1998 as steel prices fell. Paul sold the business to Swiss-based Duferco in 1999.

In 2006, Paul's Caparo Vehicle Technologies unveiled its Caparo T1 prototype, a hi-tech sports car with a staggeringly quick turn of speed: zero to 60 miles (100 kilometers) per hour in 2.5 seconds, and a top speed of 200 miles (320 kilometers) per hour. The ultra lightweight super-car was shown at global motor shows in 2007, with plans for about 25 cars a year to be built.

Paul believes India has nothing to fear from globalization. In a lecture for the Confederation of Indian Industry (CII) in Indore in September 2006, Paul told his audience: "Competition will improve everybody." A few months later he announced plans to invest about US$180 million in Indian acquisitions and greenfield projects by 2010. Meanwhile, back in London, son Ambar is expanding the group's hotels business, established in 2004. Paul was made a UK Labour life peer in 1996, as Lord Paul of Marylebone. He is chancellor of both Wolverhampton University and the University of Westminister, and visiting professor at the University of Surrey. After his daughter Ambika died in 1968, he gave money to London Zoo to keep it open, because it was her favorite place to visit. The zoo was the venue for his youngest son Angad's wedding in October 2004.

54. Gulu LALVANI, United Kingdom

Estimated net worth: US$810 million.
Position: Founder, Binatone (with brother Partap).
Born: September 11, 1933 in Karachi; raised in Mumbai.
Educated: Leeds University, UK.
Marital status: Twice married. Divorced from first wife, yoga guru Vimla, in 1981. Son Dino, daughter Divia.
Interests: Property development in Phuket, Thailand.

In April 2006, Gulu Lalvani staged a huge celebration in the Thai resort of Phuket to mark the marriage of his daughter Divia to chocolate heir Joel Michael Cadbury. More than 500 guests flew in from the UK for the event. It was in the grand tradition of the high-flying Lalvani, who keeps a penthouse in Hong Kong, drives a Bentley Azure convertible, and once escorted the late Princess Diana to a fashionable London nightspot. It's all a far cry from his student days in Leeds in the late 1950s. After university, Lalvani began his Binatone consumer electronics business in 1958, with his brother Partap, importing small transistor radios into the UK market from Hong Kong. They named the company after their sister, Bina. In the 1970s, Binatone was the first company to launch a videogame in the UK. Today, Binatone sells home appliances (including coffee makers, food processors, steam irons, kettles, hairdryers) and a range of digital cordless phones in the UK, Europe, Russia, Africa, the Middle East, Asia, and Australia. It claims to have 25% of the cordless phone market in Britain, and has the manufacture of internet phones for the emerging VOIP (voice over internet protocol) market in its sights. It showed its first iVoice internet phone at the 2007 CeBIT fair in Hannover. Binatone's phones are made in China, with the business headquartered in Hong Kong.

Lalvani says Binatone's mission is to produce high-quality appliances that are easy to use. Lalvani's son Dino is Binatone's chief operating officer and does most of the day-to-day running of the company while his father develops property in Thailand. Since 1989, Gulu Lalvani has controlled Binatone's business in Western Europe and Hong Kong, while Partap Lalvani has the Binatone business in Eastern Europe, Africa, and South Asia. There has been ongoing speculation the Lalvanis will float Binatone, either in the UK or Hong Kong equity markets.

55. Vijay and Bhiku PATEL, United Kingdom

Estimated net worth: US$800 million.
Position: Founders, Waymade Healthcare.
Born: Vijay: November 10, 1949; Bhiku: August 1, 1947, in Kenya.
Educated: Both educated in the UK. Vijay qualified as a pharmacist from the College of Pharmacy in Leicester; Bhiku graduated in architecture.
Marital status: Both married.
Interests: Vijay drives an Aston Martin.

Brothers Vijay and Bhiku Patel arrived in the United Kingdom from the western highlands of Kenya in 1967, part of the great wave of Indians to leave East Africa in the 1960s. Vijay trained as a chemist in the UK and opened his first pharmacy in Essex in 1973. He built that to a chain of 10 shops by 1980, and moved into pharmaceutical wholesaling. Waymade was set up in 1975 and incorporated as a public limited company in 1984. Bhiku is managing director and financial controller.

Waymade has grown from its humble retail beginnings in Essex to become one of the UK's top 10 pharma companies by turnover. It employs about 700 people in a 100,000 square feet facility at Basildon, Essex, from where it supplies and distributes branded and generic pharmaceutical products to customers in the UK and to markets in Europe and the Middle East. Its generics division operates as Sovereign Medical. The brothers' goal is to create a fully fledged pharmaceutical company. In April 2003 they set up a separate company,

Amdipharm, to source low-cost medicines in disease areas under the radar of bigger pharma companies. Amdipharm is now one of the largest producers of injectable and soluble corticosteroids in the UK. The two brothers won the Ernst & Young UK Entrepreneur of the Year Award in 2001; Vijay was a finalist in the 2003 UK National Business Awards for Entrepreneur of the Year. Waymade was named "Best Family Business in the London and South Region" in 2005.

56. Desh Bandhu GUPTA, India

Estimated net worth: US$750 million.
Position: Chairman and CEO, Lupin Ltd.
Born: February 8, 1938. Son of Peareylal Gupta.
Educated: M.Sc. in chemistry; honorary doctorate from Bundelkhand University, Jansi, Uttar Pradesh.
Marital status: Married to Manju D. Gupta (B.A.) who is an executive director at Lupin. Eldest daughter Vinita Gupta Sharma (pharmacy graduate, University of Mumbai; MBA, Kellogg Graduate School of Management, US) is also a director. Second daughter Kavita and son Nilesh (chemical engineering, University of Mumbai; Wharton Business School, US) also work for the company.
Interests: Social welfare, with a focus on education for underprivileged children in Rajasthan.

Gupta started his career teaching chemistry at Birla Institute of Technology and Science in Pilani, Rajasthan, then later joined a British-owned pharmaceutical company in Mumbai. But Gupta was keen to test his entrepreneurial spirit, and in 1968 he bought Lupin, a small drug company that was making vitamin pills. Lupin Ltd. was incorporated in 1983 and went public in the early 1990s, but Gupta suffered a setback when investments in real estate went astray in the mid-1990s. He successfully regrouped, and these days Lupin is India's seventh-largest drug company, with a world-leading tuberculosis treatment – a highly useful product, given the prevalence of TB in India. The world market for anti-TB drugs is about US$600 million. Another big earner for Lupin is a generic version of Ceftriaxone, a drug used to treat pneumonia and ear infections, which came off patent in July 2005. Gupta called it one of the company's major success stories in 2006, as it quickly grabbed a 25% market share. In April 2007, Lupin announced it had won US approval for another of its products, the antibiotic Suprax Cefixime, in oral suspension form for children. In 2005, Gupta had announced his goal was for Lupin to reach annual sales of US$1 billion by 2009. "Based on the year's performance, we are well on track to achieve this goal," he said a year later, when Lupin's sales reached US$372 million. By 2007, the company was selling above US$400 million.

Lupin had a market capitalization in June 2007 of about US$1.43 billion. Gupta's family and associated companies hold a stake of just over 52%.

57. Pankaj Ramanbhai PATEL, India

Estimated net worth: US$733 million.
Position: Chairman, Cadila Healthcare.
Born: 1953 in Ahmedabad. Son of Ramanbhai B. Patel.
Educated: M.Pharma. in pharmaceutical technology.
Marital status: Married to Priti P. Patel, who is a director of Zydus Pharmaceuticals. Son Sharvil graduated in chemical and pharmaceutical science from the University of Sunderland, UK, and is a director of Cadila Healthcare and Zydus Pharmaceuticals.
Interests: Social welfare in education and healthcare, through the Ramanbhai Foundation, named after the company founder.

Ahmedabad-based Pankaj Patel is the son of the late Ramanbhai Patel, co-founder with business partner Indravadan Modi of the original Cadila Laboratories pharmaceutical company in 1952. The Patel and Modi families split the business in 1995, leading to the creation of the Patels' Zydus Group. Its flagship is Cadila Healthcare, which listed in 2000, a year before Ramanbhai Patel's death in September 2001. Ramanhbai was named Gujarat's "Businessman of the Year" in 1999–2000. Pankaj now heads the Zydus Group, which operates generic drug manufacturing and distribution plants and research laboratories in India and other locations, including the United States, Latin America, South Africa, and Europe. It also has a consumer products division that sells sugar-free foods, skincare treatments, and has a stake in top-selling margarine brand Nutralite. Globally, the group employs more than 6,000 people. Pankaj Patel says the goal is to be among the leading pharma companies in Asia by 2010 and a global player by 2020.

After a restructure in 2006, Cadila Healthcare's growth is being driven by good revenues from its export business, particularly in France and the United States. The launch of Cadila's cholesterol-lowering Simvastatin tablets in the US market in December 2006 enhanced its prospects there. In 2007, Cadila firmed up a joint venture with Australia's Mayne Group to make generic injectable anti-cancer medicines, along with active pharmaceutical ingredients (APIs). The two groups will market the products globally in different territories. Cadila Healthcare had a market capitalization of about US$1 billion in June 2007. The Patel family, including sisters Aarti, Gira, and Rita and associated trust companies, hold about 72% of the company.

58. Tom Tar SINGH, United Kingdom

Estimated net worth: US$732 million.
Position: Founder, New Look.
Born: August 29, 1949 in Thakarki, Punjab.
Educated: Wellington School, Somerset; University of Wales, Aberystwyth, 1969.
Marital status: Married.
Interests: Social investment, education in India.

"Gorgeousness at unbelievable prices" is the cheap and cheerful proposition offered by Tom Singh, made an Officer of the Order of the British Empire (OBE) in the 2007 New Year honors list for his services to the British fashion industry. Singh is the son of Indian immigrants who moved to the UK in 1950 and opened a draper's shop in Somerset. He is the brains behind the women's fashion retailer New Look, which has more than 500 shops across the UK and Ireland, another 200-plus in France under the Mim brand, and a recent expansion into Belgium and Dubai. After graduating from the University of Wales (where he studied international politics), Singh opened his first store in 1969 in Taunton, Somerset, using money borrowed from his parents. In 1982, he and his parents joined forces and merged their stores. From his base in southwestern England, it took Singh more than 20 years to get to the level of 70 stores, but by 1994 he had reached the 200 mark. New Look is now the third-largest specialist womenswear retailer in the UK, with annual sales of about US$1.5 billion, an operating profit of about US$270 million, and about 15,000 employees. New Look has signed on to the Ethical Trading Initiative, designed to improve working conditions among companies in its supply chain.

Singh floated the company in 1998, after selling a majority stake to venture capitalists three years earlier for about US$300 million. By 2004, the Weymouth, Dorset-based listed company had a market capitalization of more than US$1.0 billion. But in April of that year, Singh, backed by private equity firms Apax Partners and Permira, took the company private again with a US$1.32 billion buyout. Singh promoted managing director Phil Wrigley to chief executive. Apax and Permira hold about 31% each of New Look, while Singh, his family, and various trusts hold about 23%. In 2007, there was speculation that New Look could be listed again, auctioned off, or that the Dubai-based Landmark Group, headed by Mahesh "Micky" Jagtiani, might buy the company for about US$2 billion. Jagtiani already holds a 3% stake and has a franchise agreement with New Look to open 40 stores in the Middle East. Singh's younger brother Simon Singh is a noted science writer and television producer in the UK.

59. Kiran MAZUMDAR-SHAW, India

Estimated net worth: US$723 million.
Position: Chairman and managing director, Biocon Ltd.
Born: March 23, 1953. Lives in Bangalore.
Educated: B.Sc. in zoology, Bangalore University, 1973; M.Brewing,
   Ballarat College, University of Melbourne, 1975.
Marital status: Married to Scottish businessman John Shaw.
Interests: Art, social work, writing.

Known as India's pioneer "biotech queen," Mazumdar-Shaw became the country's wealthiest woman after the float of Biocon in April 2004. She had set up Biocon India more than two decades earlier, as a joint venture in 1978 with Leslie Auchincloss, owner of the Irish firm Biocon Biochemicals. From that humble beginning, Mazumdar-Shaw has taken the company from a small enzyme maker into a global player in biotech and pharmaceuticals.

She is married to Scottish businessman John Shaw, who controls Glentec International and is Biocon's director of international business. Mazumdar-Shaw holds 39% of Biocon (market capitalization US$1.19 billion in June 2007), while her husband's company Glentec holds 23%, giving the couple a combined stake worth about US$723 million.

Mazumdar-Shaw lives and works in Bangalore, where she is active in seeking to preserve the character of the city. She is also the author of *Ale and Arty: The story of Beer.* This reflects her interest in brewing; her father was chief brewmaster for the Mallya family's brewing group UB, and according to Mazumdar-Shaw, the man who invented UB's top-selling Kingfisher beer. Mazumdar-Shaw graduated with an honours degree in zoology from Bangalore University in 1973, before moving to Australia to continue her studies. She qualified as a master brewer from Ballarat College, Melbourne University in 1975.

From its small start in 1978, Biocon is now a major drug company with annual revenues of about US$130 million. It was named after Mazumdar-Shaw's initial joint venture partner Biocon Biochemicals, whose stake in Biocon India was acquired by Unilever in 1989 and then sold to ICI in 1997. Husband John Shaw bought ICI's Biocon stake to consolidate the pair's ownership of the company. Mazumdar-Shaw says she doesn't think about the money she's made. "What's exciting for me is that I have created intellectual wealth. With frugal resources I have built a company with a market cap of US$1 billion." The money allows her to give back to society. "My focus is on health-care and education. I have developed a low-cost insurance model that for US$3 a year gives free surgical intervention and hospital care. In education, my focus is on improved sanitation, hygiene and nutrition, via food systems in rural areas and slums," she says. "It is a slow process, but I am willing to invest in that."

60. Venu SRINIVASAN, India

Estimated net worth: US$715 million.

Position: Chairman, TVS Motor, Sundram Fasteners.

Born: December 11, 1952. Son of T.S. Srinivasan and grandson of TVS founder T.V. Sundram Iyengar.

Educated: B.Sc., Madras University; M.Sc. in management, Purdue University, 1977; honorary doctorate in science, Warwick University, 2004.

Marital status: Married in 1982 to Mallika (b. November 19, 1959), who has an M.A. in econometrics from Madras University and an MBA from Wharton. Two children, a son and daughter.

Interests: Supporting schools and hospitals.

Venu Srinivasan runs TVS Motor, flagship of the TVS Group, established in Madurai in 1911 by T.V. Sundram Iyengar, initially as a small transport business. The group employs more than 40,000 people across 30 companies, and turns over about US$2.2 billion a year in sectors such as the manufacture of motorcycles and scooters, auto components, computer peripherals, distribution of heavy commercial vehicles and passenger cars, finance, and insurance. Two-wheeler maker TVS Motor, set up in 1979, produced its first two-seater moped, the TVS 50, in 1980 from its factory at Hosur in Tamil Nadu. Today it ranks No. 3 among Indian makers and is among the world's top 10 two-wheeler companies, with annual turnover of about US$650 million and a market capitalization in June 2007 of about US$400 million. TVS Motor and Japanese motorcyle maker Suzuki initially operated a joint venture, TVS Suzuki, that saw the production of popular models Champ and Super Champ. But Srinivasan wanted his own technology and management control; the alliance came to an end from September 2001, when TVS majority shareholder Sundaram Clayton and Suzuki agreed to a phased breakup over two years. TVS went on to create its own range of two-wheelers, including India's 2005 bike of the year, the Apache 150.

Srinivasan, grandson of the TVS founder, first worked for the group as a car mechanic. When he returned from the United States after completing his masters in management at Purdue University in 1977, he resumed duties in the family business, becoming chief executive of Sundaram Clayton in 1979. Later he took over as TVS Motor managing director in 1986, famously shutting down the Hosur plant in the early 1990s after a labor dispute. He became chairman in 2002. In 2004, he received the All India Management Association's JRD Tata Corporate Leadership Award. Srinivasan's pursuit of absolute quality in the workplace has seen Sundaram Clayton and TVS Motor win the global quality benchmark, Japan's Deming Prize, three times. "Persistence and hard work pays off," he told *India Today* in early 2006.

Srinivasan's wife Mallika is the eldest daughter of A. Sivasailam, chairman of the Amalgamations Group. She was named "Businesswoman of the Year" in 2006 by *The Economic Times*, for her role in running the family's Tractors and Farm Equipment (TAFE) Ltd. business.

Srinivasan's brother Gopal (b. August 4, 1958; MBA, University of Michigan) is joint managing director of Sundaram Clayton, which has a market capitalization of about US$440 million. The family, including cousin Suresh Krishna, chairman of Sundram Fasteners and Sundaram Clayton, holds about 41% of Sundaram Clayton, which in turn owns 58.4% of TVS Motor. Krishna, born in Madura in December 1936, graduated from Madras Christian College in 1995, then studied literature at the University of Wisconsin and the University of Munich. He has headed Sundram Fasteners for more than 35 years. The company supplies General Motors with radiator caps and fasteners and was the first Indian engineering business to set up in China, in 2004.

61. Vinod KHOSLA, United States

Estimated net worth: US$700 million.
Position: Founder, Khosla Ventures, California, 2004.
Born: January 28, 1955 in Pune.
Educated: B.Tech. in electrical engineering, Indian Institute of Technology, New Delhi, 1976; M.Sc. in biomedical engineering, Carnegie Mellon University, Pittsburgh, US; MBA, Stanford Graduate School of Business, US, 1979.
Marital status: Married to Neeru; four daughters.
Interests: Hiking, surfing, rafting, other adventure sports. Passionate about alternative energy.

The son of an Indian Army man, Khosla is the pre-eminent Indian-born venture capitalist in the United States and has been instrumental in raising money for a host of technology startups in Silicon Valley. Previously a general partner in US venture capitalist firm Kleiner Perkins Caufield and Byers, Khosla remains an affiliate partner there. In recent years, as founder of Khosla Ventures, his focus has been on helping companies wanting to explore environmentally friendly technologies. Renewable clean energy is a special passion, and Khosla has been vocal about getting the United States and the rest of the world to focus more on biofuels such as ethanol. Microfinance for the poor is another theme of his work; he is a financial supporter of the Grameen Foundation, the international arm of the microfinance provider Grameen Bank, set up by Muhammad Yunus.

Through his interest in The Indus Entrepreneurs (TIE), Khosla has been a huge supporter of India-related ventures. He moved from New Delhi to the United States in 1976 to study in Pittsburgh, and later moved to California, where he founded Daisy Systems. Then in 1982, with student Andreas Bechtolsheim, he co-founded Sun Microsystems, where he pioneered open systems and commercial RISC (reduced instruction set computing) processors for the company that was to become one of the giants of the IT world. He handed over the CEO's role at Sun to Scott McNealy in 1984.

Khosla joined Kleiner Perkins in 1986 and was instrumental in helping form "new economy" companies such as Juniper Networks (now a rival to Cisco Systems), Netscape, Corvis, Excite, and Extreme Networks. He sits on the board of numerous companies, including Quest Communications, Agami, Centrata, eASIC, Infinera, Kovio, Spatial Photonics, Zettacore, and – for a while – Juniper. Khosla is regarded as one of the best strategic thinkers in the industry, and as a man who has turned seed capital investments into assets worth billions of dollars.

In January 2003, Khosla was honored by his alma mater, the Indian Institute of Technology in New Delhi, after he donated US$5 million – the largest gift by an individual – toward a postgraduate school. In 2004 he formed his own company, Khosla Ventures, based in Menlo Park, California. Along with traditional venture capital areas such as the internet, computing, and mobile and silicon technology, Khosla supports breakthrough scientific work in biofuels, and solar and battery power. He is pushing for flexible fuel vehicles (FFVs) that can switch between gasoline and ethanol, and has backed the production of corn ethanol as a step toward cellulosic ethanol or butanol. In early 2007 he invested in Brenco, a new ethanol producer in Brazil.

62. Krishaswamy DINESH and family, India

Estimated net worth: US$700 million.
Position: Co-founder, Infosys Technologies.
Born: June 6, 1954 in Sagar, Karnataka.
Educated: M.Sc. in mathematics, University of Bangalore. Awarded doctorate in literature, Karnataka State Open University, 2006.
Marital status: Married to Asha; children Divya and Deeksha.

K. Dinesh is one of the seven original co-founders of Infosys and its quality guru, with a passion for zero-defect code. He ran the company's software project management operations in the United States from the time of its founding in 1981 until 1988, and from 1991 to 1995 was in charge of worldwide software development activities. Today, he is head of quality, information systems, and the communication design group. He also chairs the Infosys subsidiary in Australia, the former Melbourne-based company known as Expert Information Systems that Infosys bought in 2003 for US$23 million.

Before responding to colleague Narayana Murthy's invitation to help set up Infosys in 1981, Dinesh was working at Patni Computer Systems (PCS). His prior experience was with electrical equipment maker NGEF, the Indian Department of Telecommunications, Bangalore Telecom, and UCO Bank. Dinesh says Murthy's vision of creating a world-class technology company was immediately attractive to him, but the first 10 years of getting a foothold were tough. Phase 2, marked by liberalization of the Indian economy from 1991 onwards, gave Infosys the run-up to what Dinesh calls the phase 3 "big leap" that began in 1999 with globalization, deregulation, industry consolidation, and transformation of financial markets. As head of quality, Dinesh has overseen Infosys's achievement of world-class benchmarks.

K. Dinesh and his family hold a stake of 2.58% in Infosys, worth about US$700 million in June 2007.

63. Baba N. KALYANI, India

Estimated net worth: US$695 million.

Position: Chairman, Bharat Forge Ltd.

Born: January 7, 1949. Eldest son of group founder, Neelkanth A. Kalyani (b. August 20, 1928).

Educated: B.Eng. in mechanical engineering, Birla Institute of Technology & Science, Pilani, Rajasthan; M.Sc. in mechanical engineering, MIT, Boston.

Marital status: Married to Sunita; son Amit (engineering, Bucknell University).

Interests: Philanthropy, including promotion of primary education for disadvantaged children through the Pratham Foundation. Tennis, riding big motorcycles. Has a pilot's license.

Pune-based industrialist Baba Kalyani is a great believer in the benefit of high technology over India's oft-cited competitive advantage of cheap labor. When Kalyani was looking to compete vigorously in the global automotive components business with his Bharat Forge Ltd. (BFL), he refused to accept the perception that India wasn't capable of using high technology in its manufacturing plants. "We changed our entire business model," he told CNN's Andrew Stevens in a 2006 interview. BFL brought in the best technology money could buy to outflank competitors in Japan, Germany, and the US. "The advantage comes out of the capability of Indian engineers, the competitiveness of their capabilities, and the cost at which they can create those capabilities," he said.

BFL is the flagship company of the Kalyani Group, set up by Neelkanth A. Kalyani (Baba's father) in June 1961. Core businesses of the group include automotive components and systems, specialty steels, and specialty manufacturing. The Kalyani family holds 37.25% of BFL, India's largest manufacturer and exporter of automotive components. BFL was floated in 2004, and with a market capitalization of US$1.8 billion, is now the second-largest forgings combine in the world, behind Thyssen Krupp. Kalyani's aim is to make it No. 1 by 2008. Kalyani's son Amit is BFL's executive director of finance and mergers and acquisitions after serving as chief technology officer. Kalyani's younger brother, Gaurishankar, is a director of companies within the group.

BFL began commercial production in 1966, initially with technological collaboration from companies in the US and later with Japan.
Today, it makes complex forgings for the automotive industry such as
machined crankshafts, front axle beams, and steering knuckles. Clients
include GM, Toyota, Ford, DaimlerChrysler, VW, BMW, Renault,
Volvo, and Honda. In 2004, BFL bought the large German forging
firm Carl Dan. Peddinghaus out of insolvency. In the same year,
India's *Business Standard* magazine named Baba Kalyani its "CEO
of the Year" because of his global view and his role in taking Indian
manufacturing to an international level. In August 2006, Kalyani
signed a landmark deal with the government of Maharashtra to jointly
develop a special economic zone (SEZ) near Pune. The partners
expect the SEZ to attract investment of more than US$5 billion and
generate up to 120,000 new jobs.

Other major companies in the Kalyani Group are Kalyani Brakes,
Kalyani Steels, Kalyani Carpenter Special Steels, Kalyani Lemmerz,
Automotive Axles, Kalyani Sharp, Kalyani Thermal Systems, BFL
Utilities, Epicenter, and Synise Technologies.

64. Dr. Kallam Anji REDDY, India

Estimated net worth: US$683 million.
Position: Founder and chairman, Dr. Reddy's Laboratories.
Born: September 17, 1941 in Thadepalli, near Vijayawadah, Andhra
   Pradesh.
Educated: Hindu College and Andhra Christian College, Guntur;
   B.Sc. (Tech) in pharmacology, Bombay University; Ph.D in chem-
   ical engineering, National Chemical Laboratory, Pune.
Marital status: Married to K. Samrajyam. Son Satish is managing
   director and chief operating officer. Son-in-law G.V. Prasad, married
   to Reddy's daughter Anuradha, is vice-chairman and CEO.
Interests: Poverty alleviation through Dr. Reddy's Foundation.

The son of a turmeric farmer in Vijayawadah, Andhra Pradesh, Dr. K.
Anji Reddy is one of the pioneers of India's modern pharmaceutical
industry. After an early stint with public bulk drug maker IDPL and
some entrepreneurial forays in Hyderabad, he set up Dr. Reddy's
Laboratories there in 1984 with about US$40,000 in cash plus a bank
loan. Over the next two decades he gradually built a successful busi-

ness based on producing generic medicines, aided by son-in-law G.V. Prasad, who joined in 1990, and son Satish, who joined in the early 1990s after studying in the United States. Since the mid-1990s, Reddy has been spending significant money on research in the quest for his own original pharma products. Part of the impetus came from India's tightened patent regime, which from January 2005 barred the copying of post-1995 medicines. But Reddy has long been on the lookout for a home-grown blockbuster drug, committing a third of his profits to research. In a 2005 interview, he said that India, along with China, simply had to develop drugs "on their own soil at affordable prices." Otherwise, he said, too many of their people would die. "One hundred percent of our revenue now is generics," he said in 2005. "My ambition is that four years from now we will have our own drugs." By 2007, the timeline had slipped a little to 2011, with the most likely candidate a new treatment for Type-2 diabetes.

Though the pharma business is all about global scale, Reddy believes mergers are unlikely at the top end in India – that is, between Dr. Reddy's and Ranbaxy – so long as generic drugs remain the primary revenue source. In March 2006, he oversaw the purchase of Germany's Betapharm Group for US$570 million, adding its long-term therapy products to the Dr. Reddy's portfolio. The day-to-day running of Dr. Reddy's rests with company vice-chairman and CEO G.V. Prasad, who has a B.Sc. in chemical engineering from the Illinois Institute of Technology, Chicago, and an M.Sc. in industrial administration from Purdue University, also in the US; and with Reddy's son Satish, who has a B.Tech. in chemical engineering from Osmania University, Hyderabad (1988) and an M.Sc. in medicinal chemistry from Purdue University (1990). Satish joined the company in 1993 and became managing director in 1995.

Reddy and his family hold a 25.18% stake in Dr. Reddy's Laboratories, which listed on the New York Stock Exchange in 2001 and had a market capitalization of about US$2.71 billion in June 2007. Separately, Reddy holds a 5.1% stake in Krebs Biochemicals & Industries, a tiny listed company (market capitalization US$13 million) in which arch-rival Ranbaxy Laboratories bought a 15% stake in early 2007. Dr. K. Anji Reddy was awarded the Padmi Shri civilian honor by the Indian government in 2001.

65. Kishore BIYANI and family, India

Estimated net worth: US$670 million.
Position: Founder, Pantaloon Retail.
Born: August 1961.
Educated: B.Com., H.R. College of Commerce & Economics, Mumbai, 1981.
Marital status: Married to Sangita; two daughters.
Interests: Reading, watching Hindi drama and cinema.

Mumbai-based Kishore Biyani, named "International Retailer of the Year" in early 2007 by America's National Retail Federation, has a big vision: deliver everything, everywhere, every time to every Indian consumer in the most profitable manner. Turning that vision into reality – including hitting a turnover target of US$6 billion by 2010 – will take some doing, especially with international competitors hunting in the Indian retail space. Still, Biyani knows his stuff; accepting the award in New York, he said that Pantaloon excelled because of its deep understanding of Indian customers. And those customers are primed to spend: the value of India's total retail market is expected to top US$420 billion by 2010 (including US$60 billion in the modern "organized" retail sector) as middle-class incomes rise in line with economic growth.

Pantaloon Retail (India), valued in June 2007 at about US$1.6 billion, is the listed arm of Biyani's Future Group, which includes retailing, finance, branding, logistics, and media arms. Biyani's family owned a textile trading company, Bansi Silk Mills, in Mumbai and this is where he began his working life after graduating in 1981. By 1987 he was making and distributing menswear under the Manz Wear name, which he changed later to Pantaloon. He followed that with the Bare jeans brand and used the name Pantaloon in 1994 for an exclusive menswear store franchise. But he moved away from franchising, opting in 1997 to venture into modern retailing with the opening of his first Pantaloons family department store in Kolkata. Biyani followed that with a hypermarket chain, Big Bazaar, in 2001, the supermarket chain Food Bazaar, the Central "seamless mall" brand, and a range of specialty formats that include Blue Sky fashion accessories, E-Zone consumer electronics, and Depot books and music. Biyani's brothers Vijay and Anil work in the business, as do cousins Sunil and Rakesh. They and other Biyani family members are

Pantaloon shareholders, holding a total of about 42%. The company now runs more than 140 outlets across 32 cities and has more than 14,000 employees. There are more on the way as Biyani – whose motto is "Rewrite the rules, but retain values" – gears up to meet the challenge of Wal-Mart and other international retailing giants. He aims to have 80 of his Big Bazaars in mid-size Indian cities by 2008, up from 26 in 2006. Biyani is an avid shopper-watcher – it's the way to understand what customers really want, he believes.

66. Ajay G. PIRAMAL, India

Estimated net worth: US$656 million.
Position: Chairman and CEO, Nicholas Piramal India Ltd. Also head of Piramal Enterprises.
Born: December 30, 1955. Son of Gopikisan and Lalita Piramal.
Educated: Masters in management studies (M.M.S.), Jamnalal Bajaj Institute of Management Studies, University of Bombay, 1978; Advanced Management Program, Harvard Business School, 1992.
Marital status: Married to Dr. Swati Piramal; daughter Nandini and son Anand.
Interests: Director of Pratham, an initiative to provide affordable education to underprivileged Indian children.

Ajay Piramal, selected as a "Global Leader of Tomorrow" by the World Economic Forum in 1996, came to head the family business in troubling times. His father died suddenly in New York when Ajay was 29. Ajay's brother Ashok then took over, but five years later he died of cancer.

Ajay Piramal serves on a variety of government advisory bodies, including the Prime Minister's Council for Trade & Industry, and a taskforce on pharmaceutical and knowledge-based industries.

The Piramal family holds just over 50% of Nicholas Piramal India Ltd. (NPIL), which had a market capitalization of about US$1.3 million in June 2007. NPIL is India's fourth-largest pharmaceuticals company, with annual turnover globally of more than US$500 million, plus another US$100 million through joint ventures. Ajay's sister-in-law, Urvi Piramal, Ashok's widow, is vice-chairperson of Piramal Enterprises, which also has interests in textiles, retailing, glass packaging, automotive components, and engineering. The group's listed flagship NPIL began in pharmaceuticals in 1988 with the acquisition of Nicholas Laboratories from Sara Lee and has followed that with the takeover of Indian subsidiaries of multinational corporations such as Hoffam-La Roche, Boehringer Mannheim, Rhone Poulenc, and Hoechst Marrion Roussel.

Getting affordable pharmaceuticals into the hands of India's huge but poor rural market is a big challenge for all of the Indian pharma companies. Ajay Piramal says NPIL is prepared to take calculated risks in developing new drugs, but he wants tax incentives for research because it is such a long process. Meantime, he wants the company to build its brands and develop the culture of fast-moving consumer goods (FMCG) in marketing its medicines.

Piramal's wife, Dr. Swati Piramal, was conferred a Knight of the Order of Merit by the French government in July 2006 for her work in promoting medicine and trade between India and France. Sister-in-law Urvi and her son Nandan Piramal look after the group's Piramyd Retail business, where big expansion plans are in the offing as India's organized retail sector grows.

67. Jasminder SINGH, United Kingdom

Estimated net worth: US$630 million.
Position: Founder, Edwardian Group.
Born: April 2, 1951 in Dar es Salaam, Tanzania.
Educated: East Africa, then qualified as an accountant in London with
    Hacker Young. Oxford Advanced Management Program, 1996.
Marital status: Married to interior designer Amrit; four children.
Interests: Care International. Also sponsors the Hotel Management
    School in India.

Jasminder Singh was born in the East African coastal city of Dar es Salaam in what was then the British trust territory of Tanganyika. He moved to Britain in 1968 as a teenager and studied accountancy, qualifying in 1974. But within a few years he was in the hotel business, initially with his uncle. By the late 1970s he had started the Edwardian Group. His first hotel property was the Edwardian, bought in 1977, and later sold. By the 1990s he was well established in the UK hotel industry and by 1993 had the franchise for the American chain of Radisson hotels. Today, he owns a dozen top hotel properties in

London, Heathrow, and Manchester, including the InterContinental Mayfair Hotel in London, bought in August 2003 for 115 million pounds sterling (US$207 million). It reopened in November 2006 as the Radisson Edwardian May Fair.

Radisson Edwardian Hotels describes itself as London's largest privately owned upscale hotel group. In late 2007 it is to operate a riverside hotel at London's New Providence Wharf, and in 2009 it will open Coventry's first five-star property, in the Belgrade Plaza development.

Singh attended Oxford University's Advanced Management Program in 1996 and said he had a lot of "a-ha" moments. He makes a point of sending his executives to advanced management courses, and says it has helped him abolish the traditional hotel leadership structure, particularly the post of general manager.

Singh is a non-executive director of HSBC, a board member of the Warwick Business School, and a member of the Brunel University's Court. He was awarded the OBE (Order of the British Empire) for services to the hotel industry in the 2007 UK New Year's honors list. His brother Herinder is also a director of Edwardian Group.

68. S.D. SHIBULAL, India/United States

Estimated net worth: US$600 million.
Position: Co-founder, Infosys Technologies.
Born: March 1955 in Cherthala, Kerala.
Educated: M.Sc. in physics, University of Kerala; M.Sc. in computer science, University of Boston.
Marital status: Married to Kumari; two children, Shruti and Shreyas.
Interests: Photography.

S.D. Shibulal (known as "Shibu") is one of the seven co-founders of Infosys and became chief operating officer on June 22, 2007 after being head of the company's worldwide customer sales and delivery. When Infosys started business in 1981, Shibulal set up the North American sales operation and managed customer relationships for the next 10 years. From 1991 to 1996 he was on sabbatical from Infosys, working with Sun Microsystems on the design and rollout of its first e-commerce application, SunPlaza. When he returned to Infosys in 1997, Shibulal set up the internet consultancy practice and also headed manufacturing, distribution, and the Year 2000 unit. He moved to worldwide head of customer delivery in 1999, and in April 2007 was named by the Infosys board as the company's next chief operating officer, filling the seat vacated by new CEO "Kris" Gopalakrishnan.

Shibulal says the most important factor in keeping the Infosys team together has been a set of shared values. He names colleague Narayana Murthy as the man who always inspired him to strive for excellence. Shibulal is chairman of an initiative by Infosys and the Confederation of Indian Industry (CII) to help create the next wave of Indian multinational companies. The CII plan is to share practical experiences of successful Indian multinational corporations and intro-duce global best practices to the next generation of companies.

The Shibulals live in Boston, Massachusetts but are often in Bangalore (headquarters of Infosys), where Kumari Shibulal chairs Akshaya, a charitable trust the family set up to help disadvantaged children in India. S.D. Shibulal and his family hold a 2.26% stake in Infosys, worth about US$600 million in June 2007.

69. Atul C. KIRLOSKAR and family, India

Estimated net worth: US$600 million.
Position: Chairman, Kirloskar Oil Engines.
Born: February 1956. Son of Chandrakant S. Kirloskar.
Educated: B.Eng. in mechanical engineering, Worcester Institute of Technology, Massachusetts, US.
Marital status: Married to Arti, who has a masters in fine arts. Daugh-ters Gauri and Aditi.
Interests: Riding his motorcycle, car rallying. Spent silver wedding anniversary at Aashyana, Candolim Beach in Goa.

Atul Kirloskar and his younger brothers Sanjay and Rahul are the great-grandsons of the Kirloskar group's founder, Laxmanrao Kirlos-kar, and the grandsons of the man who built the multifaceted engi-neering enterprise to national prominence in the 20th century, Shantanurao L. Kirloskar (b. May 1903, d. April 1994). Between them, the three brothers run the Pune-based arm of the group, which includes the flagship companies Kirloskar Brothers and Kirloskar Oil Engines. Their cousin, Vikram, also serves on several key boards.

Following a family split in April 2000, the Kirloskars' nephew Vijay runs the much smaller Bangalore-based faction, which is headed by Kirloskar Electric.

The Kirloskar engineering conglomerate had its beginnings late in the 19th century, when Laxmanrao began tinkering with implements and mechanical devices. In the early 1900s the Kirloskar family, then running a bicycle shop, were forced to move from Belgaum in Karnataka state, and were welcomed into the tiny princely state of Aundh to the north (now part of Maharashtra state). Here, Laxmanrao and his brother Ramuanna created what would become their own industrial township, Kirloskarvadi, setting up Kirloskar Brothers Ltd. to make ploughs, fodder cutters, and other agricultural implements. Later they expanded into fluid handling, making pumps and valves, then added machine tools to the lineup with a new company, Mysore Kirloskar. In 1946, Laxmanrao's elder son Shantanurao (known as SLK) secured land in Pune to establish a diesel engine factory, Kirloskar Oil Engines. Meanwhile, SLK's younger brother Ravi established Kirloskar Electric Co. in Bangalore to make electric motors. SLK led the group's postwar expansion into a range of engineering and manufacturing activities in the 1950s and 1960s, becoming one of the dominant figures of the Indian industrial landscape. The Kirloskars ventured into the hospitality sector from 1964, setting up hotels, catering, and other service companies. But a change of direction after 2000 saw the group decide to refocus on its core engineering businesses in agriculture, water supply, power, and air-conditioning.

Group leader Atul Kirloskar joined the family business in 1978, first with Kirloskar Cummins Ltd., then moved on to become a director of Kirloskar Oil Engines in 1992. He is now chairman and managing director. He also chairs Kirloskar Ferrous Industries and G.G. Dandekar Machine Works. Sanjay (B.Eng. in mechanical engineering, Illinois Institute of Technology, Chicago) is chairman and managing director of Kirloskar Brothers, now the largest maker and exporter of pumps in India, with annual turnover of about US$200 million. Rahul (B.Sc. in mechanical engineering, US) sits on the boards of Kirloskar Brothers, Kirloskar Oil Engines, and Kirloskar Pneumatic. In September 2006, the Kirloskars bought Aban Construction, saying they saw good growth potential in infrastructure companies.

Among the group's listed companies, Kirloskar Brothers had a market capitalization of US$950 million in June 2007 and Kirloskar Oil Engines was about US$650 million. The family controls a stake of about 62% in Kirloskar Brothers. In 1991, the group set up the Kirloskar Institute of Advanced Management Studies at Harihar in Karnataka state to honor S.L. Kirloskar.

70. Karsanbhai Khodidas PATEL, India

Estimated net worth: US$588 million.
Position: Founder and chairman, Nirma Group.
Born: 1944 in Mehsana, Gujarat.
Educated: B.Sc.; honorary doctorate from Florida Atlantic University, US.
Marital status: Married to Shantaben; daughter Nirupama, sons Rakesh and Hiren.
Interests: Social welfare, education. Patel set up his Nirma Education and Research Foundation in 1994 to promote higher education. This has since become Nirma University. Other trusts look after elderly and rural women.

Karsanbhai Patel is the brand king of India's soap and detergents business, through his hugely successful Nirma Ltd. The son of a farmer in the northern part of Gujarat state, Patel graduated in science and first worked as a civil servant, as a laboratory assistant in the state government's geology and mining department. Within a few years he was ready to start his own enterprise, using his scientific knowledge. In 1969 he began mixing chemicals and ingredients in his backyard, then went door-to-door to sell his own washing formulation, a phosphate-free detergent powder that he named Nirma after his daughter Nirupama. The product's low price – about a quarter of what existing producers were charging – brought him ready acceptance in the market. With leadership in the low-price detergent sector, Patel began moving higher up the value chain, into soaps and premium-price washing powders. Today, Nirma has about 38% of the Indian detergent market, the world's second largest for washing products, plus about 20% of the toilet soap market. Nirma has integrated production of raw materials such as soda ash into its business operations. Nirma bought the marketing license for Camay soap from US giant Procter & Gamble and launched the brand in the Indian market in 2003.

Patel was named Gujarat's "Businessman of the Year" in 1998 and has chaired the Indian government's development council for oils, soaps, and detergents. Through his educational foundation, Patel established Nirma University in 2003 in Ahmedabad, Gujarat. It operates various institutes covering management, technology, pharmaceutical sciences, and chemical engineering.

Patel stepped down as Nirma's managing director on March 31, 2006, but remains chairman. His elder son Rakesh (B.Com., MBA, marketing) is vice-chairman. Younger son Hiresh (B.Eng. in chemical engineering, Stevens Institute of Technology, New Jersey; MBA, Drexel University, Pennsylvania) has moved into the managing director's role. Hiresh is also chairman and managing director of the subsidiary, Nirma Consumer Care, while Rakesh runs procurement and logistics, and Patel's son-in-law Kalpesh is executive director and handles human resources. Nirma had a market capitalization of about US$760 million in June 2007, and is held 77.36% by the Patel family and associated companies.

71. Nusli Neville WADIA, India

Estimated net worth: US$575 million.
Position: Chairman, Bombay Dyeing.
Born: 1944. Son of Neville and Dina Wadia; grandson of Pakistan founder Mohammad Ali Jinnah (on mother's side) and Nowrosjee Wadia.
Educated: Rugby School, UK.
Marital status: Married to Maureen, publisher of *Gladrags* fashion magazine. Two sons: Ness (b. May 30, 1970; M.Sc. in engineering business management, Warwick University, UK) and Jehangir (b. 1973; studied at Richmond College; M.Sc., Warwick University, UK; married to Celina).
Interests: Golf, fashion, philanthropy in fields of education, healthcare, and rural welfare.

Bombay Dyeing chairman and major shareholder Nusli Wadia's fighting spirit is legendary in Indian business circles. His battles with the Ambani family during the 1980s, his tussle with the late Rajan Pillai for control of biscuit maker Britannia Industries in the early 1990s, his links to political figures such as L.K. Advani and A.B. Vajpayee, and his clashes with Indian authorities over everything from passport usage to foreign exchange have ensured a constant high profile. In early 2007 he was in the news again for carrying a gun with live bullets on a plane between Mumbai and Dubai.

Wadia, who joined Bombay Dyeing's board in 1968, was made joint managing director in 1970 and has been its chairman since 1977. Born a Parsi Christian, he converted back to Zoroastrianism, and remains one of the most prominent industrialists in the Indian textile industry. At one point, he was offered leadership of the Tata Group by his godfather, J.R.D. Tata. Wadia's Bombay Dyeing, established in 1879, is the textile sector leader, but perhaps more importantly has 2,000 acres (800 hectares) of mill land in Mumbai worth many hundreds of millions of dollars in a city where real estate is becoming ever more valuable.

Wadia is also chairman of Britannia Industries and Bombay Burmah Trading Corp., a director of several Tata Group companies (including Tata Steel and Tata Motors), and a backer of low-cost carrier GoAir, which started flying in 2005. Britannia Industries, in which Wadia and France's Group Danone share a fractious 51% stake, has outstripped Bombay Dyeing as the largest company in the Wadia Group, with a market capitalization of about US$675 million, compared to Bombay Dyeing's US$470 million. Britannia is India's market leader in bakery products, and has big expansion plans for the Middle East. Wadia's elder son Ness is joint managing director of Bombay Dyeing and heir apparent. Younger son Jehangir (Jeh) runs GoAir, and is deputy managing director of Bombay Burmah, heading the group's plantation, chemicals, entertainment, information technology, and other business activities.

72. Vikrant BHARGAVA, Gibraltar

Estimated net worth: US$550 million.
Position: Co-founder, PartyGaming, UK
Born: December 14, 1972 in Jaipur, Rajasthan. Lives in Gibraltar.
Educated: B.Tech. in electrical engineering, Indian Institute of Technology, New Delhi, 1994; postgraduate diploma in management, Indian Institute of Management, Kolkata, 1996.
Marital status: Married; two children.
Interests: Watching poker tournaments.

Bhargava and his Indian Institute of Technology classmate Anurag Dikshit were an integral part of the fabulous PartyGaming story of the mid-2000s. They became instant paper billionaires when the online casino company floated on the London Stock Exchange in June 2005, but the shutdown of its US customer operations in October 2006 after the US Congress passed the *Unlawful Internet Gambling Enforcement Act* brought the dream run to an end. PartyGaming lost its biggest market, its stock tumbled more than 60%, and the company was forced to spend US$250 million in restructuring costs, including the layoff of 40% of its workforce.

It was, the company said, "a bitter blow." Still, it was able to report total revenue of just over US$1.1 billion for 2006 and strong growth of markets in Europe and the Middle East. PartyGaming, which claims to be the world's largest online gaming company, said the rapid reorganization of its business was seeing solid progress. It bought out two smaller online businesses, Empire Online and Intercontinental Gaming, for about US$65 million in late 2006. When PartyGaming began trading on the London Stock Exchange on June 27, 2005, Dikshit and Bhargava between them held stakes worth US$3.51 billion, plus another US$685 million cash from shares sold into the float. Bhargava was PartyGaming's marketing director until May 2006 and retains a stake of about 1%, down from 11.9% pre-float. He sold shares worth about US$220 million into the 2005 float and another US$140 million in June 2006. Bhargava worked as a credit officer for Bank of America and as a business analyst at British Gas before joining, in 2000, Dikshit and the other PartyGaming founders, Californian adult entertainment industry figure Ruth Parasol and her husband Russ DeLeon, who had set up the company in 1997.

According to Bhargava, online poker provides "clean and inexpensive entertainment." When he and Dikshit announced their decisions to leave the PartyGaming board in May 2006, they said: "Deciding when to reduce the level of executive responsibility is one of the most difficult decisions that entrepreneurs have to make."

73. Narendra PATNI, United States/India

Estimated net worth: US$545 million.
Position: Chairman and CEO, Patni Computer Systems.
Born: 1942.
Educated: B.Eng. in electrical engineering, Indian Institute of Technology, Roorkee; M.Eng. in electrical engineering, MIT; M.Sc. in management, Sloan School of Management, MIT, 1969.
Marital status: Married to Poonam; son Anirudh.

Narendra Patni, his wife Poonam, son Anirudh, and two brothers Gajendra and Ashok between them hold about 44% of Patni Computer Systems (PCS), a consulting and IT services provider that the Patnis founded in 1978. A sale of much of that stake is mooted in late 2007. PCS is now India's sixth-largest software company, with 22 international offices and six offshore development centers. It employs more than 12,000 people, has annual revenue of about US$600 million, and has had a long-standing relationship with General Electric. Patni's top 10 clients account for more than half its revenue. The Patnis took PCS public in India in February 2004 and listed it on the New York Stock Exchange in December 2005. Its market capitalization is about US$1.8 billion (June 2007).

Narendra Patni went to the United States in 1964 to study at MIT. PCS grew out of an experiment the Patnis began in 1972, sending data processing work from the United States to India in what was an early example of the offshore business process model.

Before founding PCS, Patni was president and director of Forrester Consulting Group. He also acted as a consultant to US Trust Co. of New York and Arthur D. Little Inc. In the mid-1970s he left Forrester Consulting Group to set up Data Conversion. Wife Poonam returned to India and established Data Conversion in Pune. The company later became Patni Computer Systems. Narendra's elder brother Gajendra and younger brother Ashok are also promoters of PCS and help manage the company, but were said in mid-2007 to be considering an exit.

Patni spends most of his time in the United States and runs the company from offices in Boston's Kendell Square. PCS opened a new "knowledge park" in Navi Mumbai in late 2006 to meet its long-term needs for software development space serving its global clients in insurance, financial services, and manufacturing. In late

2004, PCS bought California-based Cymbal Corporation, a telecommunications software company, for US$68 million. Patni says long-term customer relationships have been the foundation of the company's success. N.R. Narayana Murthy, doyen of the Indian IT industry and co-founder of Infosys Technologies, once worked for Patni and described the experience as "definitely some of the best times of my life."

74. Amin Mohamed LALJI and family, Canada

Estimated net worth: US$520 million.
Position: Chairman, Larco Group. Lives in West Vancouver, Canada.
Marital status: Married to Nazmeen.
Interests: Philanthropy, education.

The Lalji brothers – Amin, Mansoor, and Shiraz – are known as one of Vancouver's wealthiest families. Since fleeing Idi Amin's Uganda in the early 1970s for Canada, the Laljis have built their Larco Group into a major real estate investor, with interests in US and Canadian hotels, motels, office blocks, condominiums, and the prestigious Park Royal shopping mall in Vancouver, bought in 1990 for about US$400 million, and commercial property in the ski resort town of Whistler. They have also been involved in the gaming industry, at one stage taking a 50% profit share from the Rampart Casino in Las Vegas, Nevada via the Hilfreich Stiftung Foundation based in Zurich, Switzerland. London-based Shiraz Lalji, who runs Precis Properties (owner of the London Premier Hotels group) in the UK, is an advisory board member of the foundation and was approved by the Nevada Gaming Commission in November 2004. Larco's US subsidiary began providing management consulting and advisory services in December 2001 to Hotspur Nevada Resorts, which a month earlier bought the 541-room J.W. Marriott Resort, adjoining the Rampart Casino at Summerlin in Las Vegas. Hotspur is owned ultimately by the Hilfreich Stiftung Foundation.

Larco is regarded as a highly efficient hotel owner in Canada. Its Larco Hospitality Management, headed by Amin Lalji, owns and operates four Marriott hotels and the Renaissance Toronto Skydome hotel. There were reports in 2007 that the family planned to sell the hotels for about US$400 million. Larco undertook a US$30 million expansion of its Vancouver Park Royal "lifestyle center" from 2004, though the development caused some community angst. The center is on land owned by the Squamish Nation, which approved it. At New Westminster, 13 miles (20 kilometers) southeast of Vancouver, the Laljis own a large block of waterfront land on which they propose to develop residential apartment towers ahead of the 2010 Vancouver Winter Olympics. The Laljis are prominent members of the city's Ismaili Muslim community. In December 2006 they gave US$1 million to help fund a new Centre for Comparative Study of Muslim Societies and Cultures at Vancouver's Simon Fraser University. Amin Lalji said at the time: "We need to promote in the Western world a better understanding of the people of the Muslim communities."

In August 2007 Larco successfully bid US$1.5 billion for nine Canadian government buildings.

75. Shyam S. and Hari S. BHARTIA, India

Estimated net worth: US$508 million.
Position: Founders and co-chairmen, Jubilant Organosys.
Born: Shyam: November 9, 1952; Hari: 1956 in New Delhi. Sons of M.L. Bhartia.
Educated: Shyam: B.Com.; Institute of Costs and Works Accountants (ICWA), India. Hari: B.Eng. in chemical engineering, Indian Institute of Technology, New Delhi.
Marital status: Shyam is married to Shobhana (b. January 4, 1957), editorial director of the *Hindustan Times*. They have two sons, Priyavrat and Shamit, both of whom studied in the United States and are directors of listed HT Media. Hari is married to fashion designer Kavita. They have a daughter Aashti and son Arjun.
Hobbies: Music, golf.

The Bhartia brothers hold almost 52% of Jubilant Organosys, the integrated pharmaceuticals and life sciences company they founded in 1979 as Vam Organic Chemicals. The company had a market capitalization of about US$980 million in June 2007. Shyam is Jubilant's chairman and managing director, while Hari is co-chairman. Shyam's experience extends to chemicals, food, infrastructure, oil and gas, and information technology. Hari is a specialist in chemicals, biotechnology, food, and information technology. Jubilant is a chemicals manufacturer, but has also become a major outsourcing partner for global pharmaceuticals and agrochemical companies. The company says it is one of the largest custom research and manufacturing services companies in India. Jubilant has set up subsidiaries in the United States, Belgium, and China, and opened its own drug discovery facility in Bangalore in November 2006. In 2005, Jubilant bought US generic pharmaceutical maker Trinity Laboratories and US clinical research organization Target Research Associates (renamed Clinsys).

Annual revenues are about US$400 million a year for Jubilant Organosys. The family's Jubilant Corporation has interests in life sciences, specialty chemicals, oil and gas, foods, retailing, aerospace, and infrastructure. The Bhartia brothers hold the Domino's Pizza master franchise for India, Sri Lanka, Bangladesh, and Nepal. Shyam's younger son Shamit runs the family's retail venture in south India, a chain of superstores called Monday to Sunday. Shyam's wife Shobhana is the high-profile editorial director of HT Media, India's second-largest print company, and the daughter of industrialist K.K. Birla. In 2005, she was awarded the Padma Shri, one of India's highest civilian honors, for services to media. Hari also has a media connection, and sits on the board of Global Broadcast News, which runs the English-language 24-hour TV news channel CNN-IBN.

76. Analjit SINGH, India

Estimated net worth: US$500 million.
Position: Co-founder, Max India.
Born: January 1954. Third son of Bhai and Avtar Mohan Singh.
Educated: Doon School (class of 1971); B.Sc. in business administration, 1977; MBA, Boston University, 1979.
Marital status: Married to Neelu; children Veer, Tara, and Piya.
Interests: Music, education. Serves on board of Welham Girls School, Dehradun; Indian School of Business; Harvard Medical School's microbiology advisory council; Delhi Chinmaya Mission Seva Trust.

Analjit "Mannu" Singh holds a stake of 8.75% in the former Hutchison Essar, the Indian telecommunications company bought by UK giant Vodafone in early 2007 in a deal that valued it at US$18.8 billion.

Singh, Hutchison, and Vodafone have agreed to value his stake at a minimum of US$240 million.

Singh's father was Bhai Mohan Singh (b. 1917; d. March 27, 2006), the man who took pharmaceuticals company Ranbaxy Laboratories to prominence from 1966 onwards. Singh senior split his assets among his three sons in 1989, giving eldest son Dr. Parvinder Singh (who died in 1999) control of Ranbaxy, while middle son Manjit got Montari Industries and youngest son Analjit got Max India, the company that he and his father had founded in 1984. Analjit has since built Max into a business with interests in life insurance, healthcare, information technology, bulk pharmaceuticals, plastics, chemicals, and electronic components.

While Max India operates across a range of businesses, Singh's real financial masterstroke has been his telecommunications dealings, dating back to 1992 when he helped found the Mumbai cellphone business Hutchison Essar (then known as Hutchison Max Telecom) with Hong Kong-based Hutchison Whampoa, the flagship of billion-aire tycoon Li Ka-shing. Singh first began his selldown in 1998, when he offloaded a 41% stake back to Hutchison Whampoa for 5.61 billion rupees (then about US$140 million). He sold another 3% in November 2005 for 6.57 billion rupees (then about US$150 million). But he was back in buying mode a few months later, when (with Hutchison Essar managing director Asim Ghosn) he purchased the stake in Hutchison Essar that Uday Kotak's group sold in early 2006. Singh paid 7.92 billion rupees (then about US$175 million) for a 7.59% stake. It is the value of this share that has propelled him into the higher ranks of India's global wealth club.

Disputes have dogged the Singh family for more than 15 years, after Bhai Mohan Singh's asset disposition was deemed to favor eldest son Parvinder over Manjit and Analjit. Fresh tension came in the early 1990s when Parvinder fell out with his father over the running of Ranbaxy, leading to Bhai Mohan Singh stepping down as chairman in 1999. Analjit Singh also had a strained relationship with his sister-in-law, Parvinder's wife Nimmi, culminating in her lodging a criminal complaint – later withdrawn – following an incident at the Singh family compound on Aurangzeb Road, New Delhi in July 2006. But Singh's nephews – Parvinder's two sons Malvinder (who became CEO of Ranbaxy in 2006) and Shivinder (CEO of Fortis Healthcare) – have kept things on an even keel and there has been a settlement of sorts over the asset disputes. Middle brother Manjit, however, is not part of the settlement.

Singh is also on the board of Hero Honda Motors.

77. Chandru L. RAHEJA, India

Estimated net worth: US$500 million.
Position: Chairman, K. Raheja Corp.
Born: 1941. Son of the late Lachmandas S. Raheja.
Educated: LL.B.
Marital status: Married to Jyoti C. Raheja (B.Com.). Sons Ravi
  (B.Com., MBA, London Business School) and Neel (M.Com., LL.
  B.) hold executive positions in the group's companies.
Interests: Philanthropic work in education, hospitals, and social
  welfare.

Raheja heads the K. Raheja Corporation, established in 1956 by his
father Lachmandas Raheja. Chandru and his brothers Suresh and
Gopal (G.L.) split up the family business in 1996, though some disputes over the asset division still linger. Elder brother G.L. Raheja
runs K. Raheja Constructions and K. Raheja Hospitality, while Suresh
runs Raheja Design & Contract. Chandru's K. Raheja Corp. is now a
diversified conglomerate with interests in property development,
hotels, and, since 1991, retailing, when it launched its Shoppers
Stop chain of department stores. Chandru Raheja has spent more
than 40 years in real estate. The company's flagship developments
include the Mindspace integrated township at Malad, a suburb of
Mumbai, and another in Pune. It also has projects under way in
other parts of Mumbai, including Worli, Bandra-Kurla, Vashi, and
Airoli, and is developing a US$90 million information technology
park in Hyderabad.
    K. Raheja entered the hospitality sector in 1981. The group owns
and manages properties that include St. Mark's Hotel, Bangalore;
Renaissance Hotel at Powai, Mumbai; the Lakeside Chalet Marriott
apartments, also at Powai, Mumbai; and The Resort, Mumbai. K.
Raheja Corp. holds a stake of 66.7% in Shoppers Stop, India's largest
department store chain in the organized retail sector. Chandru Raheja
took the company public in mid-2005 despite an attempted block of
the initial public offer by a G.L. Raheja court action; Shoppers Stop
had a market capitalization of about US$515 million in June 2007.
The group also owns the book retailer Crossword. As an extension
of its property and retailing activities, the group set up InOrbit Malls
to build what it calls family entertainment centers, covering shopping,
leisure, food, and entertainment under one roof. The first such mall,
at Malad, was named India's "Mall of the Year" in 2004/05.

Raheja is a supporter of numerous educational bodies, including the Priyadarshni Academy set up in 1985 by businessman Nanik Rupani to help the artistic development of needy children. Chandru Raheja's cousin, Rajan Raheja, runs the Exide Group and also has property and retailing interests (see profile No. 33).

78. Purnendu C. CHATTERJEE, United States

Estimated net worth: US$500 million.
Position: Founder and executive chairman, The Chatterjee Group (TCG).
Born: 1954 in Kolkata.
Educated: B.Tech., Indian Institute of Technology, Kharagpur, 1971. M.Sc. and Ph.D in operations research, University of California, Berkeley, 1974. Research associate at Stanford Research Institute, 1974–76.
Marital status: Married to Amita, daughter of industrialist and West Bengal governor Viren J. Shah.
Interests: Trustee of the Asia Society; member of the US Council on Foreign Relations. Wife Amita is an art collector.

Chatterjee is a New York-based investor with interests in information technology, biotech, telecommunications, petrochemicals, the aviation industry, and infrastructure. His private equity fund TCG has invested about US$2 billion in India and claims to have assets of US$2.5 billion. Chatterjee is the majority shareholder in the contentious US$1.5 billion Haldia Petrochemicals complex in West Bengal, where the state government and Indian Oil Corp. are his partners.

In May 2005, Chatterjee attempted to organize the buyout of Dutch petroleum company Basell – a leader in global polypropylene production – in a deal worth 4.4 billion euros (US$5.7 billion). His partner was New York-based Access Industries, owned by the Russian oligarch Leonard Blavatnik, a friend of many years. Basell sellers Royal Dutch/Shell and BASF chose Chatterjee and Blavatnik over the National Petroleum Company of Iran. While the deal initially was regarded as one of the Indian business coups of 2005, it fell through for Chatterjee, leaving Blavatnik to go ahead alone.

The Chatterjee empire's eclectic mix of business interests includes stakes in a nightclub and bowling alley in Mumbai; property holdings in Kolkata and in IT and biotech developments in Pune; software development in Mumbai, Bangalore, and Kolkata; and advanced chemical and biological companies in New Delhi, Mumbai, Kolkata, and Pune.

Chatterjee joined McKinsey & Company in 1976 and became a principal there in 1983. He left McKinsey in 1986 to work with George Soros as an advisor to the Quantum Group of funds managed by Soros Fund Management, before setting up The Chatterjee Group as his own private equity fund. Along with Haldia Petrochemicals, he is on the board of Call Sciences, Indigo N.V., GIC Asset Management Company, Global Power Investments, Pench Power Ltd., and R&B Falcon Corporation. He lives at Central Park in New York but has an office in Mumbai. Friends include leading venture capitalist Kanwal Rekhi, a founder of The Indus Entreprenuers (TIE) networking group in the United States, and Rajat Gupta, the former worldwide managing director of McKinsey.

79. Rakesh R. JHUNJHUNWALA, India

Estimated net worth: US$470 million.
Position: Founder, Rare Enterprises.
Born: 1960. Son of tax commissioner Radheshyam Ramkumar Jhunjhunwala.
Educated: B.Com., Associate Chartered Accountant.
Marital status: Married to Rekha; daughter Nishtha (b. June 2004).
Interests: Spending weekends with family and friends at his bungalow at Lonavala, a hill station about 60 miles (100 kilometers) southeast of Mumbai.

Stockbroker and share market guru Rakesh Jhunjhunwala's advice to investors in Indian stocks is to "be greedy, but be long-term greedy." He also cautions them to expect realistic returns and to remember that the market isn't a casino. Jhunjhunwala, known in the financial media as India's Warren Buffett – a sobriquet he dislikes – studied as a chartered accountant but decided it wasn't the life for him. In the mid-1980s he began to play the stock market with an initial investment of about US$100. He found success with an early stock pick, Tata Tea, then did well from iron-ore exporter Sesa Goa. He goes mainly for small and medium-cap stocks. He is chairman of the Mumbai-based

IT education and training company Aptech, in which he holds a stake of 25.4% through his Marganta Textiles.

Apart from buying land at Secunderabad for a possible mall development, Jhunjhunwala has invested all the money he has made back into the market and into some private equity plays.

Jhunjhunwala believes that India's bull market is alive and kicking. "Although factors known or unknown may slow it, it will really need God's wrath for it to be reversed prematurely," he says.

When he's not playing the market, he is playing with daughter Nishtha at his swanky Malabar Hill apartment in Mumbai or entertaining friends in the karaoke studio he has had installed at his weekender at Lonavala.

Jhunjhunwala's listed investment portfolio was valued at about US$400 million in mid-2007. He has another US$70 million in about 15 private equity investments. One Jhunjhunwala resolution since the birth of his daughter: Cut back on the smoking and drinking so that he can live longer.

80. Hari N. HARILELA and family, Hong Kong

Estimated net worth: US$450 million.

Position: Chairman, Harilela Group.

Born: August 1922. Son of Naroomal and Devibai ("Ami") Mirchandani. Father later changed his name to Harilela. Hari's elder brother George and younger brothers Bob and Gary run different aspects of the family business, as did youngest brother Mohan (Mike), who died suddenly in February 2007, aged 64. Another brother, Peter, died in 1999; his interest is represented by his widow Jyoti. A sister, Rani, died in 1992; the remaining sister, Sandee, publishes a magazine for overseas Indians, *BR International*.

Educated: Honorary doctorate of law, Pepperdine University, California.

Marital status: Married to Padma ("Mimi"), who has an honorary doctorate from St. John's University, New York. Son Aron (Ph.D, University of Hull, UK) is a director of Harilela Hotels and a member of the group's board.

Interests: Rotary Club, tennis, philanthropy in the education field.

Hong Kong-based Hari Harilela presides over a vast extended family business that runs hotels, restaurants, a real estate arm, travel agencies, banking, event management, and trading. About 80–90% of the business is in the hotel and real estate sphere. Among the group's nine hotel properties are the Holiday Inn Golden Mile in Hong Kong; other Holiday Inns in Singapore, Bangkok, and Penang; and the Sheraton Belgravia in London. It sold its five-star boutique hotel, the W, in Sydney to the Taj Group for about US$30 million in early 2006.

The family, now one of the wealthiest in Hong Kong, came from poor circumstances. Father Naroomal Harilela moved from Hyderabad, Sindh (now part of Pakistan) to be a small trader in Guangzhou and Hong Kong in the early 1920s, surviving the vicissitudes of the 1930s Depression and then World War II and the Japanese occupation. Postwar, the brothers started tailoring, getting a boost from making clothing and uniforms for the Korean War and, later, the Vietnam War. They diversified, buying their first Hong Kong hotel, the Imperial, in 1960, and completing their landmark property, the Holiday Inn Golden Mile, in 1975. They also have extensive real estate interests.

The sumptuous and expansive Harilela mansion in Hong Kong's Kowloon Tong area is home to about 70 family members, covering four generations. About 35 staff help run it like a boutique hotel. The brothers and sister, their spouses, children and grandchildren share space in a three-story main house that has 40 bedrooms, and an annex at the rear with another 30 bedrooms. Aside from the main Mughal entertaining/dining room, there is a massive home theater, gym, pool, sauna, and multiple entertaining areas, plus space for about 50 cars. So far, the Harilelas have maintained an unlisted family business remarkably free of friction; the challenge ahead will be the smooth transfer of power to their children. Dr. Hari Harilela was awarded Britain's OBE in 1969, Hong Kong's Gold Bauhinia Star in 2000, and India's Pravasi Bharatiya Samman Award in 2003 for services to Indians abroad.

81. Prithvi Raj Singh OBEROI, India

Estimated net worth: US$445 million.
Position: Chairman, Oberoi Group.
Born: February 3, 1929 in New Delhi. Son of Oberoi founder M.S.
   Oberoi (d. 2002) and Ishran Devi (d. 1988).
Educated: Degree in hotel management, Lausanne, Switzerland.
Marital status: Married to Goodie. Son Vikram (B.Sc.) is deputy man-
   aging director. Daughter Natatha is a winemaker in Australia.
Interests: Breeding polo ponies, wildlife and environmental
   preservation.

P.R.S. "Biki" Oberoi chairs EIH, the Mumbai-based flagship that
controls the Oberoi chain of luxury hotels and spas. His Punjabi-born
father, Mohan Singh (M.S.) Oberoi, who died in May 2002 at the age
of 102, was the pivotal figure of India's top-end hotel market for much
of the 20th century. M.S. began his working life as a hotel porter at
the Cecil Hotel in the hill-resort town of Shimla, then spent time in
Delhi working with the Cecil's former manager, Ernest Clarke. He
returned to Shimla with Clarke, was made a partner, and by August
1934 was able to make his first acquisition, buying the Hotel Clarke's.
He took over the lease of the Grand Hotel in Kolkata in 1938, and in
1943 won a controlling interest in Associated Hotels of India (AHI),
which owned leading hotels in Shimla, Delhi, Lahore, Rawalpindi,
Murree, and Peshawar. In 1965, M.S. Oberoi opened India's first
modern five-star hotel, the Oberoi Intercontinental in Delhi, followed
by the Oberoi Sheraton in Mumbai.

   The Oberoi Group has been through many combinations and
permutations since. Today, its flagship company, EIH (founded in
1949), and its associated ventures own and/or manage 23 hotels, with
about 3,200 rooms, plus a luxury cruiser in Kerala. Along with its
Indian operations, it has properties in Mauritius, Egypt, and Indonesia. It runs car rentals, executive air charter, inflight catering, and
airport lounges and restaurants. Its top hotels, notably the Oberoi
Udaivilas and Oberoi Rajvilas, have been ranked among the world's
best. It has an international marketing alliance with Hilton for its
Trident brand.

   P.R.S. Oberoi says the business is now too big to be family run.
But his son Vikram is deputy managing director of operations, and
nephew Arjun Oberoi is deputy managing director of development.

Vikram recalls that his first job with the Oberoi Group was preparing vegetables in one of the hotel kitchens. The Oberoi family holds a stake of 46.3% in EIH, which had a market capitalization of US$960 million in June 2007.

82. Rana KAPOOR, India

Estimated net worth: US$434 million (shared with Ashok Kapur).
Position: Founder and CEO, YES Bank.
Born: September 9, 1957 in New Delhi.
Educated: Frank Anthony Public School in New Delhi; B.Ec., University of Delhi; MBA, Rutgers University, New Jersey.
Marital status: Married to Bindhu; three daughters: Radha (studying fine arts in New York), Raakhe (talented pianist, student at Wharton School, University of Pennsylvania), and Roshini, a student in Mumbai.
Interests: Kapoor says YES Bank is his focus and passion for now. He likes spending time with his family, reading, and playing golf when he gets the chance.

With decades of experience, banking is well and truly in Rana Kapoor's blood. Before setting up YES Bank with his business partner Ashok Kapur in 2004, he was CEO of Rabo India Finance (RIF) from 1998 to 2003, which is now a 100% subsidiary of the Netherlands' Rabobank. He ran the ANZ Grindlays Investment Bank from 1996 to 1998, and before that headed wholesale banking at Bank of America's Indian operations, from 1980 to 1995. Ashok Kapur's own extensive banking experience includes stints with Grindlays and Rabo. Kapoor, named Ernst & Young's "2005 Start-up Entrepreneur of the Year," isn't afraid to borrow. To make YES Bank as innovative and efficient as possible, he sourced smart practices from a variety of models, including banks in Italy, Spain, South Korea, and the United States. For example: "Commerce Bank [in the US] was an attractive model for our branch network. It has excellent touchpoints with customers, and good queues and customer engagement." Kapoor says.

Kapoor and Kapur convinced the Reserve Bank of India that they had the skills, the integrity, and the business plan to run a new bank. When the RBI finally gave the nod, it was the only license awarded to a greenfields banking venture in India in the last decade. Now

Kapoor's goal is to make YES Bank "the best-quality bank in India." "New entities like us have no legacy issues," he says. Kapoor and Kapur hold a combined 37% stake in YES Bank, which had a market capitalization in mid-2007 of about US$1.2 billion. Other key stakeholders are Rabobank International, Citicorp, AIF Capital, Swiss Re, ChrysCapital, and the Malaysian government's investment arm Khazanah Nasional. Kapoor says that while setting up RIF in the late 1990s, he had already started thinking about an Indian bank that would set new benchmarks for customer service, corporate governance, transparency and professional integrity, and would create "shareholders' wealth at large."

83. Gururaj DESHPANDE, United States/Canada

Estimated net worth: US$420 million.
Position: Co-founder and chairman, Sycamore Networks.
Born: November 30, 1950 in Hubli-Dharwad, Karnataka state.
Educated: B.Sc. in electrical engineering, Indian Institute of Technology, Chennai, 1972; M.Eng. in electrical engineering, University of New Brunswick, Canada; Ph.D in data communications, Queens University, Kingston, Ontario, Canada.
Marital status: Married to Jaishree, a computer science lecturer at Clark University, Boston. Two sons.

"Desh" Deshpande is acknowledged as one of the visionaries of the IT industry, and has backed his software engineering expertise with entrepreneurial drive. He found financial success with his second and third IT ventures, and was able to hang on through the dotcom bust, despite a massive shedding of market value for his Sycamore Networks. "You have to be slightly crazy to be an entrepreneur," he says.

After graduating from the Indian Institute of Technology, Chennai, Deshpande moved to Canada in 1973 for further study in electrical engineering. He taught for a while at Queen's University in Kingston, Ontario – where he got his doctorate in data communications – and then went to work for the Motorola subsidiary Codex Corp. Bitten by the startup bug, Desphande moved to the United States, where he co-founded Coral Network. The venture came to an end in 1990 after he parted ways with his partner, but Desphande did much better with his next effort, Cascade Communications, a maker of internet switching gear. Starting in 1991, within six years it grew from a one-man band to a company with 900 staff and revenue of US$500 million. In June 1997, Ascend Communications bought Cascade for US$3.7 billion in stock.

Desphande's greatest success has been Sycamore Networks, which he co-founded in Boston in early 1998 to speed up the performance and bandwidth potential of optical fiber networks. The company's market value hit US$15 billion on the day it went public on the US Nasdaq exchange in October 1999, and reached US$30 billion at the height of the dotcom boom in early 2000. It tumbled thereafter and has been around US$1 billion since 2002. One blight: Sycamore has been in the Securities and Exchange Commission's (SEC) spotlight in 2006/07 over stock options and accounting practices for the 2003–06 period. Sycamore equipment carries voice and data traffic over the networks of some of the world's largest service providers. Desphande and family hold 23% of Sycamore Networks, which had a market capitalization of just over US$1 billion in June 2007.

84. Sabeer BHATIA, United States/India

Estimated net worth: US$400 million.
Position: Founder, Navin Communications.
Born: December 30, 1968 in Chandigarh; grew up in Bangalore. Father Balev is a Ministry of Defence official, and mother Daman, a state bank official.
Educated: St. Joseph's High School, Bangalore; Birla Institute of Technology and Science, Pilani; B.Sc. (Hons), California Institute of Technology, Pasadena; M.Sc. in electrical engineering, Stanford University, 1992.
Marital status: Single.
Interests: Being an entrepreneur. Indian music, table tennis, golf, fast cars. Funding rural education projects.

Bhatia is the brainy Bangalore boy made good – and then some. A scholarship took him from BITS Pilani to Caltech in Pasadena, in the US, and on to Stanford University for a masters in electrical engineering. From Stanford, Bhatia went to Apple for a year and then to Firepower Systems, where with colleague Jack Smith he got the idea for web-based email. He and Smith left Firepower to develop Hotmail, which they launched in July 1996 with backing from Silicon Valley venture capitalists Draper Fisher Jurvetson. By the next year, with Hotmail's subscriber numbers up to about seven million, Microsoft was interested. Smith and Bhatia, who was then Hotmail's president and CEO, played it cool with their suitors. After several rounds of bluster and tough negotiating, they sold the company to Microsoft on December 30, 1997 for stock worth US$400 million. It was Bhatia's 29th birthday.

Next, Bhatia set up an online portal, Arzoo, in 1999, closed it in June 2001 after the dotcom bust, and then relaunched it in late 2006 as a "one-stop travel shop." He runs US-based Navin Communications, which stands for "New Applications for Voice on the Internet," and is working on TeliXO, a product designed to upgrade mobile phones to PDA capability. Another Bhatia startup is InstaColl, in which Japanese internet investor Softbank has taken a stake. It is designed to speed up collaboration between business partners. Another of his ventures is BlogEverywhere. In November 2006, Bhatia signed an agreement with the Haryana government to set up Nano City, a US$400 million knowledge hub on 11,000 acres (4,500 hectares) of land in Panchkula district, about 28 miles (45 kilometers) from the state capital, Chandigarh. Bhatia said Nano City would be modeled on Silicon Valley in the United States and would host companies and research centers involved in future technologies, such as biosciences, energy, and nanotechnology. He has set up the Sabeer Bhatia Foundation to fund education projects in India and other parts of the developing world.

85. Vikram CHATWAL and family, United States

Estimated net worth: US$400 million.
Position: Vice-president, Hampshire Hotels & Resorts.
Born: November 1, 1971 in Ethiopia. Elder son of hotelier Sant Singh Chatwal and Pardaman Chatwal.
Educated: UN International School, New York; Wharton School of Business, University of Pennsylvania.
Marital status: Married model Priya Sachdev in February 2006.
Interests: Acting (he appeared in the 2004 movie *One Dollar Curry*), music, fast cars.

Former model and onetime New York playboy Vikram Chatwal – dubbed the "Turban Cowboy" by *New York Observer* magazine – is now the serious businessman at the helm of a growing hotel empire created by his father Sant Singh Chatwal in the 1980s. Vikram's younger brother Vivek is the group's financial controller.

Sant Chatwal is the high-profile backer of US presidential hopeful Hillary Clinton. He chairs fundraisers for her, has accompanied the Clintons on trips to India, and serves as a trustee on Bill Clinton's AIDS Foundation. The Clintons also attended the lavish February 2006 receptions held in India to celebrate Vikram's wedding to Priya Sachdev. That three-city extravaganza, lasting a week, included dazzling events in Mumbai, Delhi, and Udaipur. Other guests included spiritual/health guru Deepak Chopra, super-model Naomi Campbell, and steel tycoon Lakshmi Mittal.

Vikram was born in Addis Ababa, where his father had moved from the Punjab in the 1970s to open a couple of restaurants. But after Ethiopia's emperor Haile Selassie was overthrown in 1974, the Chatwal family fled to London, before moving on to Canada. There, Sant Chatwal opened the first of his Bombay Palace restaurants, gradually extending the chain and opening in Manhattan in 1982. He also ventured into hotels, first at the modest end of the market and later adding five-star properties under the Hampshire Hotels & Resorts banner. Chatwal fell into financial troubles in the 1990s, owing as much as US$100 million to various banks, and New York City and US tax authorities. In 1996, during a trip to India, he was arrested and charged by the Central Bureau of Investigation with bank fraud, but was freed. He filed for bankruptcy in the United States in 2000 and was fined US$125,000 by the US government in settlement of charges. That has not stopped him from being one of the most high-profile Sikhs in the United States and a contributor to the Democrats. During trips to India in 2006 and 2007, he spoke of plans to establish boutique hotels in cities such as Mumbai, Delhi, Bangalore, and Jaipur. Vikram has given his father's Hampshire hotel chain a modern aura, first with trendy boutique hotels in New York such as the Time, the Majestic, and in 2004, the Dreams. The Chatwals now have 10 hotels in New York, two in Montreal, and one each in London and Bangkok, with more planned.

86. Gunapati Venkata Krishna REDDY, India

Estimated net worth: US$400 million.
Position: Founder and chairman, GVK Group.
Born: 1938.
Educated: B.A.
Marital status: Married to Indira (B.Sc.). Son Sanjay (B.Eng. in indus-
trial engineering; MBA, US) is married to Aparna, daughter of
Subbarami Reddy, Minister of State for Mines.
Interests: Tennis, Indian art and culture.

US citizen G.V. Krishna Reddy runs his US$1.2 billion (assets) GVK
Group from a base in Hyderabad. Reddy started as a contractor for
government construction jobs in the mid-1950s, then set up Novopan
Industries as a particle board manufacturer in the late 1970s. He followed that with GVK Petrochemicals, to make polymers for the particle board industry. Later, Reddy moved into hospitality, setting up a
group of hotels (in partnership with the Tata Group's Taj hotel brand
since 2000), but it has been his recent forays into large-scale infrastructure projects in roads, mining, and power plants that have brought
the GVK name to the fore. Reddy gained more prominence in early
2006 when GVK led a consortium that successfully bid for the right
to redevelop Mumbai's airport, covering both its Sahar and Santa
Cruz international and domestic terminals. GVK's partners in the
US$1.5 billion venture are Airports Company South Africa, Bidvest,
and the Airports Authority of India. Anil Ambani's Reliance-ADA
Group challenged the decision that awarded the rights to the GVK
consortium, but a Supreme Court ruling in November 2006 cleared
the result.

The Mumbai airport modernization program looks to be GVK's
sternest test. The project, in which the joint venture will pay 39% of
its revenues to the Airports Authority of India, is beset by a multitude
of challenges, particularly over land usage rights. The airport has only
2,000 acres (800 hectares) of available land (compared to Delhi's
5,000 acres, or 2,000 hectares), and much of this is compromised by
80,000 squatters, housing estates run by airport-affiliated businesses,
and other leaseholds. Still, Reddy and his son Sanjay are unfazed.
Their goal is to turn GVK into an infrastructure powerhouse, with
some diversification into biotechnology through GVK Biosciences,
where former Ranbaxy CEO D.S. Brar is chairman. On the power

front, GVK's latest project is the 600 MW Goindwal Sahib plant in Punjab, using coal from its mines in Jharkhand.

In January 2007, Reddy unveiled a consolidation plan under which all GVK's infrastructure assets are folded into the listed entity, GVK Power & Infrastructure. Reddy and his family hold about 65% of GVK Power, which had a market capitalization in June 2007 of about US$615 million. The group's turnover for 2006/07 was around US$380 million.

87. Rama Prasad GOENKA, India

Estimated net worth: US$395 million.
Position: Chairman emeritus, RPG Group.
Born: March 1, 1930 in Kolkata. Son of Keshav Prasad and Rukmani.
Educated: B.A. (Hons), Kolkata; Advanced Management Program, Harvard.
Marital status: Married to Sushila. Two sons: Harsh (b. December 10, 1957, educated at St. Xavier's College, Kolkata; MBA from IMD, Lausanne) and Sanjiv (b. 1960, B.Com., Hons); daughter Yashodara.
Interests: Artworks, cricket, spending time with his grandchildren.

RPG Enterprises was formed in 1979 to hold the myriad business interests of the R.P. Goenka family, who control more than 20 companies across sectors such as retailing, manufacturing, energy, telecommunications, pharmaceuticals, tyres, entertainment, and information technology. Power generation and distribution, plus the Ceat tyre business, are the main revenue earners, though the Goenkas see the future in services. Their Spencer's Retail arm is one of the frontrunners in India's fast-growing organized retail market, with plans to lift store numbers from 125 to 2,000 by 2009. R.P. Goenka is a former president of the Federation of Indian Chambers of Commerce and Industry, and served as a Congress Party member of the Rajya Sabha, India's upper house. His elder son Harsh, based in Mumbai, is chairman of RPG Enterprises, while Kolkata-based Sanjiv is vice-chairman. R.P. Goenka remains a non-executive chairman of Ceat and CESC (Calcutta Electricity Supply Corporation).

The RPG Group's origins go back to 1820 when Ramdutt Goenka, a member of the Marwari community from Rajasthan, established a business in Calcutta to trade with the British East India Co. His brothers Ramkissendas and Ramchandra and their sons expanded and diversified the business in the 20th century into banking, textiles, jute, and tea. One of these, Ramdutt's nephew Sir Badridas Goenka, became chairman of the Imperial Bank of India (now the State Bank of India) in 1933. In turn, Badridas's son, Keshav Prasad Goenka, took over the British trading houses Duncan Brothers and Octavius Steel in the 1960s, and expanded into the automotive tyre industry, electric cables, and cotton textiles. Keshav stepped back from running the businesses in the 1970s in favor of his three sons Rama, Jagdish, and Gouri; and in 1979, the companies formally were shared among them. From this process Rama emerged with the electric cables and carbon black companies, but quickly added a swag of new enterprises. Today, companies in the RPG Group have a turnover of more than US$2.5 billion. The Goenka family and associated companies hold a stake of about 41% in CESC (market capitalization of around US$755 million in June 2007) and 43% in Ceat (market capitalization of around US$200 million).

88. P.V. Ramaprasad REDDY and family, India

Estimated net worth: US$366 million.
Position: Founder and chairman, Aurobindo Pharma.
Born: 1960 in Hyderabad.
Educated: Postgraduate in commerce.
Marital status: Married to Suneela Rani.

P.V. Ramaprasad Reddy and wife Suneela Rani founded Aurobindo Pharma in 1986 with fellow promoter K. Nityananda Reddy and his wife K. Rajeswari. The company began operations in 1988 with a single unit in Pondicherry, Tamil Nadu state, manufacturing semi-synthetic penicillins. It is now the market leader in this field, and among the world's top makers of semi-synthetic penicillins. It shifted operations to Hyderabad in 1990, became a public company in 1992, and has expanded its product range to generic pharmaceuticals and active pharmaceutical ingredients (APIs), with Asia's largest sterile API facility. Its products span six major areas: antibiotics, anti-retrovirals, cardiovasculars, central nervous system (CNS), anti-gastroenteritis, and anti-allergics.

Before setting up Aurobindo, Ramaprasad Reddy held management positions in a number of pharmaceutical companies. He looks after strategic planning and joint ventures, while managing director K. Nityananda Reddy runs manufacturing and the company's overall affairs. Aurobindo has focused heavily on exports in recent years, and markets outside India now account for 58% of total sales. The move into regulated markets such as Europe and the US has seen rapid growth in the formulations business, which constitutes 30% of sales.

Ramaprasad Reddy told shareholders in 2006 that the company expected to hit revenue of US$500 million in 2007/08 and US$1 billion in the 2010 fiscal year. "We at Aurobindo believe that we are not competing against multinationals, innovators, or other competitors," he told them. "My colleagues and I believe our fight is against ailments, disease, and ill health. We work the same market with other players, and together we are challenging the spread of ailments such as HIV; providing support to patients to recover from diabetes, migraine, cardiovascular ailments; and help them with our drugs to control several lifestyle disorders. We have a stake in patients regaining their health."

In June 2007, Aurobindo reported sales for the 12 months to March 31, 2007 of about US$500 million, a growth rate of 36% over the previous period.

Ramaprasad Reddy and his wife Suneela Rani between them hold a stake of 40.66% in Aurobindo Pharma, worth about US$366 million at the company's June 2007 market capitalization of just over US$900 million. K. Nityananda Reddy (7.04%) and K. Rajeswari (4.56%) hold a combined stake of 11.6%, worth about US$105 million.

89. Sudhakar and Sreekanth RAVI, United States

Estimated net worth: US$345 million.
Position: Co-founders, Code Green Networks, SonicWall.
Born: Sudhakar, 1965; Sreekanth: 1966 in Hyderabad.
Educated: Sudhakar: B.Sc. in computer engineering, University of Illinois, 1986, US; M.Sc. in computer science, Stanford University. Sreekanth: B.Sc. in electrical engineering, University of Illinois, 1987.
Marital status: Sudhakar is married to Sumithra. Sreekanth is married to Sharmila.
Interests: Healthcare in India. The brothers support stem cell research at the L.V. Prasad Eye Institute, Hyderabad.

The California-based Ravi brothers are the 2004 founders of Code Green Networks, a provider of data loss protection solutions. But they are best known for SonicWall, the internet security company they co-founded and ran between 1991 and 2001, taking it from startup as a maker of Ethernet cards for Macintosh computers to low-cost firewall protection, through an initial share offer in 1999, to a company with annual sales of more than US$100 million and partnerships with names such as Cisco. Sreekanth stepped down as CEO in 2001, though he remained chairman until early 2003, while elder brother Sudhakar also stayed on as chief technology officer and a director after new management took over the running of the company. They both quit the SonicWall board in early 2004 to concentrate on Code Green Networks. There is a long-running class action against Sonic-Wall and Sreekanth over allegations of false information and market manipulation, relating to SonicWall's initial public offer in November 1999 and a secondary offering in March 2000. Like so many other dotcom shooting stars, SonicWall's stock price soared and then crashed in the early 2000s.

In 1972, the Ravi brothers, then aged six and five and in the care of their grandparents, moved from Hyderabad to Ohio to join their parents. Later the family moved to Illinois, where the brothers studied at the University of Illinois in Champaign-Urbana. Sudhakar moved to California to work for Data General, while Sreekanth started video products company Generation Systems in 1988. In the formative days of SonicWall in the early 1990s, Sudhakar was known as the technology guru, while Sreekanth directed strategy and operations. They did well financially, between them selling SonicWall shares worth about US$255 million from November 1999 to November 2003, and another US$40 million in 2005. According to 2007 SEC filings, they still hold shares worth about US$50 million.

The brothers set up their new venture, Code Green Networks, with backing from Sierra Ventures and Bay Partners, to protect company data "in any format and any language." Sreekanth said in early 2006 that US companies lose as much as US$150 billion a year from unauthorized information leaks.

90. Nadathur Sarangapani RAGHAVAN and family, India

Estimated net wealth: US$320 million.
Position: Co-founder, Infosys Technologies.
Born: 1946 in Mumbai.
Educated: B.Eng. in electrical engineering, Andhra University, Visakhapatnam.
Marital status: Married to Jamuna; sons Sriram and Anand.
Interests: Helping new entrepreneurs, philanthropy (particularly for disadvantaged children), cooking.

N.S. Raghavan was one of the seven co-founders of Infosys, and employee No. 1. He spent 19 years at the company as joint managing director until his retirement in 2000, and remains a trustee of the Infosys charity foundation. His house at Matunga in Mumbai was the first registered office of Infosys. He chairs the advisory board of the N.S. Raghavan Center for Entrepreneurial Learning at the Indian Institute of Management in Bangalore, and is a mentor for aspiring entrepreneurs. In March 2001 he and his wife Jamuna (a professor at the Indian Institute of Management, Bangalore) set up FAME (Foundation for Action, Motivation and Empowerment) India, which aids children with disabilities. Its motto is: "I am only one, but I am still one. I cannot do everything but I can still do something."

Before joining Murthy to set up Infosys, Raghavan served in the Ministry of Defence for nine years, working in the electrical and mechanical engineering corps. He also worked as an engineer in the Andhra Pradesh state electricity board, and as head of the electrical department in Kothari Sugars and Chemicals Ltd. in Trichy,

Tamil Nadu. He chairs the private equity firm Nadathur Holdings & Investments, which is an investor in technology-related companies such as Reach Technologies, which develops software for the global apparel industry. Raghavan is a director of several other companies, including ABB India, Syndicated Research Worldwide, and IDFC Asset Management. He is a former board chairman of the Murugappa Group, a diversified conglomerate based in Chennai. The Raghavan family has gradually sold down its holding in Infosys. Jamuna Raghavan holds 1.18%, worth about US$320 million in June 2007.

91. Pradeep SINDHU, United States

Estimated net worth: US$300 million.
Position: Co-founder, Juniper Networks, US.
Born: September 4, 1952 in Mumbai.
Educated: B.Tech. in electrical engineering, Indian Institute of Technology, Kanpur; M.Sc. in electrical engineering, University of Hawaii; Ph.D in computer science, Carnegie-Mellon University, Pittsburgh, US.
Marital status: Married; two children.
Interests: Running.

Venture capitalist Vinod Khosla regards Pradeep Sindhu as one of the "unsung heroes" of the technology revolution. As a general partner at Kleiner Perkins Caulfield & Byers, it was Khosla who saw the potential in Sindhu's thoughts mid-1995 on where the internet was headed and the key role that networking infrastructure would play. Khosla stumped up the seed money for Sindhu's venture that would become Juniper, the company that today is the fiercest competitor for Cisco Systems in the router market. Until he made the jump with Juniper, Sindhu, originally from Mumbai, had spent 11 years with the famed PARC (Palo Alto Research Center) run by Xerox, including stints as a research officer, then principal scientist, and from February 1994 to February 1996, as distinguished engineer at the computer science lab.

Sindhu was Juniper's chairman and chief executive from its inception in February 1996 until September that year. Since then, he has been vice-chairman and chief technical officer. He holds about 1.8% of the company, a stake worth about US$250 million in June 2007. At one point he held about 4% of the company, but sold about US$55 million worth of stock between 2004 and 2006. Like so many of the dotcom boom companies, Juniper has had its share price ups and downs since it floated in 1999. It has also been brushed by scandal over corporate options. On December 20, 2006, Juniper said it would take an earnings charge of about US$900 million over stock options it granted between June 1999 and December 2003. After a seven-month investigation, Juniper said there were serious concerns about the stock option process followed by unnamed "certain former management." Juniper CEO Scott Kriens, who joined Sindhu at Juniper in early 1997, said: "We should have had better stock option granting processes, controls, and oversight in place, and we did not."

92. Ratan N. TATA and Tata family, India

Estimated net worth: US$295 million (family).

Position: Chairman, Tata Group, director of the Reserve Bank of India.

Born: December 28, 1937 in Mumbai. Son of Sonoo and Naval H. Tata. Raised by his grandmother, Lady Navajbai, after his parents separated.

Educated: B.Sc. in architecture and structural engineering, Cornell University, 1962; Harvard Business School's Advanced Management Program, 1975.

Marital status: Single. Has a brother Jimmy and step-brother Noel, and three step-sisters Shireen, Deanna, and Geeta. His aunt Simone Tata is a former chairman of Trent, the Tata Group's retail arm.

Interests: Piloting his helicopter and executive jet, collecting art, spending time at his beach house.

Ratan Tata became chairman of India's most respected business empire, the Tata Group, in 1991. Under his stewardship, the group has grown to a conglomerate with almost a quarter of a million employees and annual revenue of US$25 billion from 100 companies spread across seven business sectors: information systems and communications, engineering, materials, services, energy, consumer products, and chemicals. In 2007, Ratan Tata successfully engineered the group's acquisition of Europe's largest steelmaker, Corus, in a US$12 billion deal that has been hailed as a turning point for Indian business. The

Corus takeover, the biggest yet by an Indian company, was one more step in a 15-year process that has seen Ratan Tata reorganize and rejuvenate a group widely viewed as too unwieldy, lethargic, and underperforming. Along the way, Ratan Tata has made other key acquisitions, including Tetley Tea in 2000 and a 45% stake in telecommunications company VSNL in 2002. And Tata's pet project – the world's most affordable small car – is slated to begin production in 2008, though local unrest at the plant site may yet delay it. Perhaps his biggest success has been the listing of Tata Consultancy Services (TCS), a company so loved by the market that it has grown from an initial listing value of US$10 billion in August 2004 to more than US$29 billion at June 2007. All told, the listed Tata companies have a market capitalization of more than US$60 billion. TCS accounts for almost half that, followed by Tata Steel (about US$9.5 billion) and Tata Motors (about US$7 billion).

The Tata saga began in 1868 when Jamsetji Tata, a Parsi (a follower of the Zoroastrian religion which entered India from Persia), set up a trading company in Mumbai that became Tata Sons, the group's chief holding company today. Ratan Tata inherited the leadership of Tata from his uncle, J.R.D. Tata (d. November 1993, aged 89), who built Tata Sons into India's leading corporate empire and ran it for more than 50 years until stepping down in 1991. In the mid-1990s, Ratan Tata began the process of rationalization, quitting some industries such as cement and textiles, and consolidating the control held by Tata Sons and Tata Industries over key companies in the group. Today, Tata Sons holds almost 80% of TCS, 22% of Tata Motors, and 27% of Tata Steel. The Tatas also hold a stake of 46% in VSNL.

Though he chairs the key philanthropic trusts that control 65.8% of Tata Sons, the unmarried Ratan Tata has relatively minor shareholdings in TCS, Tata Motors, Tata Steel, and Tata Power, worth less than US$25 million in total. Other Tata family members are believed to hold about 1% of Tata Sons, a stake worth about US$270 million.

In a 2004 television interview with CNN's Satinder Bindra, Ratan Tata offered these thoughts on his legacy at the Tata helm: "I would like to be remembered as someone who succeeded, in an environment of change, to uphold the value systems and the ethical standards that our group was built on."

93. Manilal ("Manu") Premchand CHANDARIA, Kenya/United Kingdom

Estimated net worth: US$280 million.
Position: Chairman, Comcraft Group. Cousin Anil (B.Sc., MBA) heads Comcraft's UK arm.
Born: 1929 in Nairobi, Kenya. Son of Premchand Popat Chandaria.
Educated: University of Nairobi; postgraduate degree in engineering, US.
Marital status: Married to Aruna.
Interests: Animal welfare, philanthropy, and education. Founding chairman of the Chandaria Foundation. Sponsors graduate studies at University of Nairobi. Chairs Asian Foundation in Kenya.

Dr. Manu Chandaria heads the Kenya-based Comcraft Group, a loose conglomerate that links about 70 family members operating 40 businesses in Africa, the Middle East, Europe, South Asia, and North America, with total annual turnover of about US$2 billion. Elder brother Ratilal is a director of companies in the United Kingdom and India, another brother Keshav is active in Canada, while their cousin Anil runs the UK/Europe business, aided by his brother Kapoor. The group employs about 6,000 people in Kenya alone, and has interests in industrial manufacturing, steel, aluminum, chemicals, plastics, wholesale and retail trading, information technology, computer hardware and software, and service industries. Key companies include Kaluworks and Mabati Rolling Mills in Kenya, Aluminium Africa Ltd. in Tanzania, and Baati Ltd. in Uganda. In India, the group's listed company is Aegis Logistics Ltd.

Chandaria grew up in Nairobi, where his father (who arrived from India in 1916) had set up a general store in the city's Ngara area, catering mainly to Asian customers. The business expanded to other cities such as Mombasa and Dar es Salaam, and later Chandaria and his brothers and cousins helped move the family's activities into new sectors such as manufacturing.

Chandaria is a believer in professional management. Though the international family members get together at least once a year to discuss potential business directions and to look at entrepren-eurial options brought forward by individual members, Chandaria leaves the running of the various businesses to independent professionals.

In October 2006, he presided over the launch of the SAFAL steel product group's Horn of Africa regional cluster of companies, which includes Mabati and Baati. Chandaria is a former chairman of the Kenya Association of Manufacturers and has been named the "Most Respected CEO in East Africa" by the *East African Standard* newspaper. He was awarded the Order of the British Empire (OBE) in January 2003 and the Indian government's Pravasi Bharatiya Samman Award in the same year. His UK-based industrialist brother Ratilal P. Chandaria spent 20 years devising his Gujarati digital dictionary, launched in 2006.

94. Rajendra Singh PAWAR, India

Estimated net worth: US$250 million.
Position: Co-founder and chairman, NIIT.
Born: March 19, 1951.
Educated: Scindia School, Gwalior, Madhya Pradesh; B.Tech., Indian Institute of Technology, Delhi, 1972; Distinguished Alumnus Award, 1995, Indian Institute of Technology.
Marital status: Married to Neeti; children Urvasi, Unnati, and Udai.
Interests: Computer education for Indian slum children. Reading, writing, music, playing chess.

Pawar co-founded IT training company NIIT in 1981 with his university batchmate Vijay K. Thadani (now CEO), actively supported by their colleague at HCL, Shiv Nadar. P. Rajendran, two years their junior at the Indian Institute of Technology, Delhi, joined them a few months later and remains NIIT's chief operating officer. Working with Nadar and Thadani at HCL, Pawar saw the computer revolution coming, but also realized that people would need training to get the most from the new technology. The lack of computer skills among HCL's potential customers was curbing sales, so Pawar and Thadani turned that problem into an opportunity and brought computer training to the masses. NIIT pioneered the field of IT education in India, is among the top IT training companies in the world, and is rated among India's "super-brands." It operates in 30 countries, and has 500,000 students around the world and an alumni of 3.5 million. Pawar says NIIT aims to be the world's largest IT education and training organization, driven by innovation and brand leadership. In August

2006 he also identified new business areas: IT training for the banking, financial services, and insurance industry; advanced training in executive management and technology education; and assessment and testing services for recruitment, initially focused on IT and business process outsourcing.

Pawar, named India's "Master Entrepreneur of the Year" in 1999 by Ernst & Young, is known as a visionary who wants to develop human resources to their full potential. He looks for intelligence and compassion when he goes hiring, declaring that "a person without compassion has an incomplete brain. He must have what we call emotional intelligence." One of Pawar's great goals has been to bring computer knowledge to schoolchildren across India. In 2000, he linked with the World Bank in creating the "Hole in the Wall" program, designed to expose poor children in rural and urban India to the capabilities of an internet kiosk. He was named by Singapore in 2005 as one of Asia's "visionaries and leaders." Pawar is on the management board of the world's largest distance learning university, the Indira Gandhi National Open University.

Thadani is chief executive of NIIT and its worldwide subsidiaries, and chairman of NIIT USA, being based in Atlanta from 1993 to 2003. He led NIIT's IPO in 1993. The world's largest city, Chongqing in China, has appointed Thadani its economic advisor to help it become the hub of a knowledge-based economy. Pawar, Thadani, their associated companies, and the other promoters of NIIT hold a stake of 34.15% in the company, which had a market capitalization in mid-2007 of about US$340 million. NIIT Technologies was valued at just over US$400 million.

95. Sanjiv SIDHU, United States

Estimated net worth: US$200 million.
Position: Co-founder and chairman: i2 Technologies, US.
Born: June 1957 in Hyderabad. Son of a chemist overseeing India's national laboratories.
Educated: B. Eng. in chemical engineering, Osmania University, Hyderabad, 1980; M.Sc. in chemical engineering, Oklahoma State University, 1982; postgraduate study in systems and control engineering, Case Western University, Cleveland, US.
Marital status: Married to Lekha Singh; two children.
Interests: Sailing, surfing, snowboarding, Indian folk music.

Sidhu started as a software developer with Texas Instruments (TI) in Dallas, working on how to better manage production processes. He quit TI to make his own way, and founded i2 Technologies in 1988 with an Indian friend, Ken (Kanna) Sharma, who died in 1999. i2 was one of the high flyers of the internet boom, looking to ride the wave of enthusiasm for business-to-business (B2B) e-commerce. The i2 stock price hit a historic high of US$111.75 in March 2000, which gave it a stupendous market capitalization of US$26 billion, but the bursting of the internet bubble the following month saw it collapse to an eventual low of 41 cents by October 2002. It was delisted between 2003 and 2005, and in 2004 the company was fined for mis-stating revenue. A 1–25 reverse share split took place in February 2005, and Sidhu now holds just over 5.5 million shares for a stake of 26.6%, worth about US$110 million in June 2007.

Despite its rocky ride, i2 has remained one of the leading US providers of supply chain management solutions, working with customers such as Woolworths, Del Monte, and Dole in the food sector, and with Mitsubishi, Hitachi, and NEC in the technology sector. Its software set the standard for production planning, allowing companies to test "what if" variables related to inventory, plant capacity, and materials supply.

Sidhu told a Dallas business magazine in 2003: "We've been around 15 years, employ 2,600 people worldwide and are still the largest pure-play supply chain management software company in the world."

Sidhu stepped aside from his CEO role in early 2005, and key investor Geoff Raynor brought in Michael McGrath as the new chief executive. Sidhu remains chairman and is still a familiar face at i2's presentations on supply chain management, such as i2 Planet 2007. A new range of software may see i2 grow again, though the dotcom boom times of early 2000 are unlikely to be replicated.

96. Mukesh CHATTER, United States

Estimated net worth: US$200 million.
Position: Chief executive, NeoSaej.
Born: 1960. Lives in Concord, Massachusetts.
Educated: Birla Institute of Technology & Science, Pilani; M.Sc. in computer and systems engineering, Rensselaer Polytechnic Institute, Troy, New York State, 1982.
Marital status: Married to Priti (B.Sc. in biology, Kolkata University; M.A. in administration, Boston College). Daughters Sonal and Saejal.
Interests: Science education for children in India.

Chatter came to the United States as a computer engineering student, getting his masters at Rensselaer Polytechnic Institute in 1982, which named him its "Entrepreneur of the Year" in 2001. Chatter looked at startups, worked for a while as a consultant, and developed an interest and expertise in internet switching technology. He teamed up with Ray Stata, a venture capitalist who had helped found chipmaker Analog Devices in 1965 and was its CEO from 1973 to 1996. In late 1996, Chatter and Stata set up Nexabit Networks, a Marlborough, Massachusetts-based developer of high-speed internet switches and routers that they later sold to Lucent Technologies for US$900 million worth of stock in June 1999. Chatter stayed with Lucent for a while, then left in mid-2000 so that he and Stata could put together their next business, Axiowave Networks. Initially, they planned for Axiowave to develop technology for use in optical networking. But a change of mood in the market saw them switch over to the development of a core/metro router. Axiowave raised almost US$100 million in several rounds of financing, and launched its first product, a convergence router, in June 2004. But things turned sour later in the year, with the company laying off most of its workers in November 2004; by January 2005, Axiowave had closed its doors. Chatter, again aided by Stata, resurfaced in August 2006 as CEO of Burlington, Massachusetts-based NeoSaej. The company, which describes itself as a "red-hot startup in stealth mode," is backed by private equity investment firm NeoNet (where Chatter and wife Priti are general partners) and Stata Venture Partners. It says its mission is to be a leader in the e-commerce software space.

97. Asim GHOSH, India

Estimated net worth: US$200 million.
Position: Managing director, Vodafone Essar (formerly Hutchison Essar).
Born: 1947 in New Delhi.
Educated: St. Columbus, New Delhi; B.Tech. in electrical engineering, Indian Institute of Technology, Delhi, 1969; MBA, Wharton School of Business, University of Pennsylvania, 1970.
Marital status: Married to former banker Sanjukta; two sons.
Interests: Golf, photography, antique furniture.

Ghosh is one of the shrewdest and most experienced business executives in India, with a career that began in the early 1970s with fast-moving consumer goods (FMCG) major Procter & Gamble (P&G) in Cincinnati and later Canada. After a decade with P&G, he moved in 1980 to Rothmans International's beverage business in the North American market, before returning to India in 1989 to be co-head of PepsiCo's food operations. In 1991, he joined Hong Kong-based Hutchison Whampoa's FMCG business. He came back to India in 1998 when he switched to telecoms and took on the role of managing director of Hutchison Whampoa's Indian mobile phone joint venture, Hutchison Essar Ltd. (HEL).

Ghosh found himself in the eye of a financial storm in early 2007 as UK-based phone giant Vodafone sought to win foreign direct investment approval for its takeover bid of the Indian mobile phone company. With Hong Kong tycoon Li Ka-shing's Hutchison Whampoa Group keen to cash out of HEL, Vodafone had seen off rivals such as the Reliance and Hinduja groups in the tussle for India's fourth-largest cellphone operator. But the deal raised all sorts of ownership questions. One issue was the 4.68% economic stake Ghosh had in HEL through his 23.97% holding in Telecom Investments India (TII). His partners in TII were Max India chairman Analjit Singh with 38.78%, and Hutchison Telecommunications International Ltd. itself, with 37.25%. TII held 19.54% of Hutch Essar, which Vodafone's bid valued at about US$18.8 billion. Responding to suggestions that he was holding the shares as a front for another party, Ghosh told a February 2007 media briefing: "The shares I own are mine and mine alone." In April, Ghosh, Hutchison, and Vodafone worked out a minimum valuation of US$175 million for his holding.

98. Vidya M. CHHABRIA and family, Dubai

Estimated net worth: US$200 million.
Position: Chair, Jumbo Group.
Born: 1948 in Mumbai.
Marital status: Widow of the late Manohar Rajaram Chhabria (b. March 1, 1946; d. April 6, 2002). Daughters Bhavika Godhwani, Komal Vazir, and Kiran Chhabria.
Interests: Indian cuisine and music; supporting Manu Chhabria Arts Centre at Dubai's Community Theatre and Arts venue.

When Dubai-based Jumbo Group founder and Harvard attender Manohar ("Manu") Rajaram Chabbria died in a Mumbai hospital of a heart ailment in April 2002 at the age of 56, there was no clear succession plan in place among his three daughters, Bhavika, Komal, and Kiran. Komal was thought to be the most business-savvy. Instead, his wife Vidya – who not long before had given Manu a card that read, "To the king of my castle . . . from the power behind the throne" – stepped forward and was soon confirmed in the role of chairman.

She has since overseen the growth of Jumbo – started by Manu in 1974 – to the point where it is now the largest distributor in the world of Sony products and has annual sales of around US$2 billion. Along with its consumer electronics and home appliances sales, the Jumbo Group is also active in information technology, telecommunications, office automation, manufacturing of freezers, and a heating, ventilation, and air-conditioning business. Jumbo operates in 50 countries and employs 20,000 people. In 2005, Jumbo Electronics opened a 27,000 square feet anchor store at the Mall of the Emirates in Dubai, making it the largest retail electronics development in the United Arab Emirates.

Early in 2005, Vidya Chhabria resolved a long-running dispute with Vijay Mallya's UB Group over ownership of liquormaker Shaw Wallace, selling a 55% stake to UB for about US$300 million. Manu Chhabria had acquired Shaw Wallace in 1987 after a protracted takeover battle. Manu later became embroiled in a bitter dispute with his brother Kishore Chhabria over control of Shaw Wallace, which saw Kishore quit the company in 1992. But the brothers reunited to resist Mallya's advances.

Manu, a onetime radio parts seller from Mumbai who moved to Dubai in 1974, was a controversial tycoon – always in the news for his spats with executives, competitors, and the authorities alike. He was forced to stay away from India for five years between 1996 and 2001 because of tax disputes and the attentions of the Enforcement Directorate over foreign exchange transactions.

Things have been much quieter under Vidya's watch, though Bhavika is said to be unhappy with her role, and Vidya's mother-in-law, Ranibhai Chhabria, claimed in early 2006 that her son's will had been fabricated – an allegation Vidya rejected. Ranibhai's claim for a stake of Manu's estate was thrown out in March 2006.

Within India, Vidya is on the board of Gordon Woodroffe, Narmada Gelatines, and Harshit Finlease & Investments. She resigned as chairperson of MPIL Corp. in mid-2007. Bhavika sits on the board of Hindustan Dorr Oliver, the group's Mumbai-based engineering unit, while Komal and Boston-educated Kiran are directors of Jumbo Electronics in Dubai. The family has begun to sell off some of the businesses (but not the flagship Jumbo Electronics) to make a cash division from Manu's estate to Vidya and her daughters.

99. Gautam Hari SINGHANIA, India

Estimated net worth: US$160 billion.
Position: Chairman, Raymond Ltd.
Born: September 9, 1965. Son of Vijaypat and Ashabai Singhania.
Educated: Cathedral School, Mumbai.
Marital status: Married to Nawaz Modi; one daughter (b. December 2005).
Interests: Family, fast cars, boats, planes, nightclubs.

Apparel tycoon Gautam Singhania is the son of adventurous industrialist and aviator Vijaypat Singhania, who at the age of 67 set a world record height for flying a hot air balloon, taking it to an altitude of 69,852 feet above India on November 26, 2005. Singhania junior, who took over as chairman of the family's Raymond business in September 2000, noted at the time: "My father has proved himself as the 'brave son of India'." Gautam shares his father's love of action and adventure: he has tried his hand at the wheel of a Formula 1 car in France, piloted a Ferrari 360 Modena in a road and track rally across Europe, and took a Lamborghini Gallardo in Europe's CannonBall Run. He is also passionate about boating, running a triple-deck yacht, *Ashena*, built of teak, and a traditional Arabian sailing dhow, *Shazma*. When time is of the essence, he runs a Challenger 504 business jet, and a helicopter to help him commute from downtown Mumbai to the airport. In 2005, he opened a nightclub named "Poison" in the Mumbai suburb of Bandra, with DJ Aqeel.

But business (and family) comes first for Gautam Singhania. He joined the family's JK group of companies in 1986, became a director of Raymond in 1990 and its managing director in July 1999. He moved into the chairman's role a year later, though his father Vijaypat (chairman and managing director since 1980) has taken the title "chairman emeritus." Gautam has restructured the group, dropping the synthetics, steel, and cement businesses to concentrate on fabrics, apparel brands, prophylactics (KamaSutra condoms), men's toiletries, and a file and tool business. Raymond is India's largest exporter of worsted fabrics and readymade wear under brands such as Manzoni, Parx, Park Avenue, and ColorPlus.

The JK Group business began as a manufacturing enterprise in Kanpur under Lala Juggilal Singhania and his son Lala Kamlapat Singhania (the "J" and "K" of the group) in the late 19th century, and extended to Mumbai when the Raymond Woollen Mills on Thane Creek – then owned by the Sassoon family – became available. The group later diversified into a range of businesses, including polyester, rayon, paper, chemicals, tyres, cement, textiles, and pharmaceuticals. Gautam's focus on apparel under the "Raymond" name has seen him line up international partnerships, including a denim joint venture with UCO of Belgium and a cotton shirting joint venture with Italy's Gruppo Zambaiti. He says he wants Raymond to be among the world's best apparel brands. "Our vision is to be at the top end of the global and textiles apparel chain."

100. Karan BILIMORIA, United Kingdom

Estimated net worth: US$150 million.
Position: Founder, Cobra Beer.
Born: November 26, 1961 in Hyderabad.
Educated: B.Com., Osmania University, Hyderabad, 1981. Law gradu-
  ate, Sidney Sussex College, Cambridge University. Fellow of the
  Institute of Chartered Accountants in England and Wales.
Marital status: Married to Heather; two sons, two daughters.
Interests: Tennis, polo, filmmaking, public speaking, business courses.
  Supports Chelsea Football Club, and has a farm in South Africa,
  where his wife was born.

Bilimoria began his working life in 1982 as an accountant at Ernst &
Young. By 1988 he was a consulting accountant at Cresvale Ltd. The
following year, he became sales and marketing director of *European
Accounting Focus* magazine. Despite having no brewing experience,
he started Cobra Beer in 1989, because he loved beer but hated the
gassy lagers that prevailed in the market. With a loan of 20,000 pounds
sterling (at the time about US$34,000), he set up his company, doing
the rounds of Indian restaurants across the United Kingdom as he
sought to convince them that diners would respond well to a less gassy
lager. Today, more than 6,000 restaurants stock Cobra beer and the
brand is exported to 40 countries. For those who want something
stronger, Bilimoria has introduced a King Cobra beer in India with
an alcoholic content of just under 7%. Both beers are brewed under
license in India by the Mount Shivalik Group. Bilimoria also launched
the General Bilimoria wine brand (named after his late father, a lieu-
tenant general in the Indian army) in 1999 to cater to non-beer drink-
ers in Indian restaurants.
    Bilimoria, a Zoroastrian Parsi, was appointed to the House of
Lords in 2006 as a non-party political peer. He made his maiden
speech in November that year on the importance of strengthening
trade relations between India and Britain. As UK chairman of the
Indo-British Partnership, he led a trade delegation to India in January
2007. Bilimoria's goal with Cobra Beer is to have a brand worth US$1
billion by 2012, up from an estimated US$200 million in 2007. Bili-
moria holds 72% of the company, which he may float in 2009.

Some Others Not on the List

There are many more candidates for inclusion on the list of India's global wealth club members. Within India, some of the most obvious examples are Indu Jain, and her sons Samir and Vineet Jain, who own the unlisted media company Bennett, Coleman & Co., publisher of *The Times of India* and *The Economic Times*. Another is Subrata Roy Sahara, who, like Jain, is pained by his inclusion on lists of the rich and powerful. The worth of his Sahara Group is hard to discern; certainly his building and real estate holdings are enormous, and his para-banking activities stretch across the country. But ventures such as Air Sahara (now sold to Jet) have proved costly. His Sahara Media holds his TV, newspaper, and entertainment interests, while tourism and services are on the Sahara growth agenda.

The boom in real estate has created scores of paper fortunes among landowners and developers. Oman-based interior decorator and property developer P.N.C. Menon, who is active in India, is a good example. His company Sobha Developers, which listed in India in December 2006 and has a market capitalization of about US$1.4 billion, is building a massive shopping mall in Bangalore, due for completion in 2009. Menon and wife Sobha hold about 87% of the shares, worth more than US$1.1 billion on paper, but 23% of this stake is locked in until the end of 2009. The remainder can be traded from end-2007. The same applies to Mumbai developer Rakesh Wadhawan. He, his family, and related companies hold a stake in Housing Development and Infrastructure Ltd. (HDIL) that is worth US$1.6 billion on paper, follwing its July 2007 initial public offer. But much of that is locked in for one to three years.

Others on the India wealth list could include Kolkata-based jute trader Arun Bajoria; and the descendants of Murugappa Group founder A.M. Murugappa Chettiar, led by M.V. Subbiah and M.A. Alagappan. Narottam Sekhsaria and brother-in-law Suresh Neotia are out of the limelight after selling their stakes in Gujarat Ambuja Cements to Swiss cement major Holcim in 2006, but remain among India's richest businessmen. Basant Kumar Birla of Century Textiles and elder brother Krishna Kumar Birla of HT Media also are among India's wealthiest industrialists, though not at the same giddy heights as their younger relative Kumar Mangalam Birla. In the pharmaceutical field, the share price surge for bulk drugs maker Divis Labs has delivered a paper fortune to Dr. Murali K. Divi and his family; another contender in this sector is Sudhir Mehta of Torrent Pharma.

As consumer incomes rise, a host of entrepreneurs are expanding their media empires and may well be poised for wealth club membership. They include T. Venkattram Reddy of the *Deccan Chronicle*; Mahendra Mohan Gupta and his son Sanjay Gupta, publishers of India's most-read newspaper, *Dainik Jagran*; the Chennai-based Kasturi family, publisher of *The Hindu*; and Bhopal-based Ramesh C. Agarwal and sons Sudhir, Girish, and Pawan, whose Bhaskar Group publishes the Hindi newspaper *Dainik Bhaska*. Tea magnate Brij Mohan Khaitan of Eveready Industries, Mumbai builder Niranjan Hiranandani, R.S. Agarwal of Enami, the multitudinous Modi brothers (K.K., V.K., S.K., B.K., and U.K.), Rajan Nanda of Escort, oil rig operator Reji Abraham of Aban Offshore, Vikas Kasliwal of the S. Kumars Group, O.P. Lohia of Indo Rama Synthetics, and Nand Khemka and his sons Shiv and Uday of the Russia and India-based SUN Group are all worthy contenders.

Outside India, there are a host of names in the United States: venture capitalist Kanwal Rekhi, founder of TiE (The Indus Entrepreneurs) and mentor to many Indian-led Silicon Valley startups; Vinod Dham, known as the father of Intel's Pentium chip; Arjun Maholtra, a co-founder of HCL who left in 1999 to be part of ventures such as TechSpan and Headstrong; Romesh Wadhwani, a key player in i2 Technologies with Sanjiv Sidhu; Jagdeep Singh of Infinera; K.B. Chandrasekhar of Exodus and Jamcracker fame; and a host of other dotcom boomers such as Rakesh Mathur of Junglee and Stratify, Rajendra and Neera Singh of Teligent, Navdeep Sooch of Silicon Labs, and Naveen Jain, ex-InfoSpace. Some of their companies have faded into the ether, but the fortunes remain. Aside from the information technology sector, there are names such as Uganda-born hotelier

Mike Patel, whose Diplomat hotel chain is one of the largest in the United States; and Darshan Dhaliwal, founder of Wisconsin-based Bulk Petroleum Corp.

In the United Kingdom, some of the top achievers and global wealth club candidates are nursing home operators Ramesh and Pratibha Sachdev; hotelier Surinder Arora; Africa-focused trader Manubhai Madhvani – once imprisoned in Uganda and then expelled by Idi Amin simply for being Asian; pharmaceutical owners Bharat and Ketan Mehta; retailer, property, and IT investor Reuben Singh; Patak's sauce founder Kirit Pathak; and Dinesh Dhamija – who sold his 41%-owned eBookers online travel agency to Cendant for almost US$380 million in 2005. Sweden-based hotelier Bicky Chakraborty, Dubai-based trader and realtor Ram Buxani, Mike and Renuka Jagtiani of the Landmark Group (also based in Dubai), property developer Kartar Singh Thakral (whose Thakral Holdings has extensive interests in Singapore and Australia), and Singapore-based Vikas Goel, whose eSys company has attracted India's Teledata Infomatics as a shareholder, are also global contenders.

Bibliography

REPORTS

20 20 20; Bigger, Richer, Faster Boomers (Hong Kong: CLSA Asia Pacific Markets, September 2005)

Asia Economics: When the U.S. Economy Catches Cold (Hong Kong: HSBC Global Research, October 2006)

Asia Pacific Executive Brief (Sydney: IMA Asia, May 2007)

Asia Ten Years After (Washington, DC: International Monetary Fund, May 2007)

Bribe Payers Index 2006 (Berlin/Brussels: Transparency International, October 2006)

Doing Business 2007: How to Reform (Washington, DC: World Bank & International Finance Corporation, September 2006)

Dupont, Alan and Pearman, Graeme, *Heating up the Planet: Climate Change and Security* (Sydney: Lowy Institute, June 2006)

Global Outlook (Washington, DC: World Bank, December 2006)

Human Development Report 2006 (New York: United Nations Development Program, November 2006)

Index of Economic Freedom 2007 (Washington, DC: The Heritage Foundation, January 2007)

National Family Heath Survey 2005–06 (New Delhi: Government of India, December 2006)

Osborne, Milton, *The Paramount Power: China and the Countries of Southeast Asia* (Sydney: Lowy Institute, 2006)

Podder, Tushar and Yi, Eva, *India's Rising Growth Potential* (Goldman Sachs Global Economic Paper No. 152, January 22, 2007)

Singhal, Arvind, *Impending Economic Impact of a Resurgent Indian Retail Sector* (Mumbai: September 9, 2006)

Singhal, Arvind, *Indian Retail Vision 2015 and Winning Concepts* (New Delhi: Technopak Advisors, February 23, 2007)

State of the World's Children 2007 (New York: UNICEF, December 2006)

The Anatomy of Asian Earnings (Hong Kong: HSBC Global Research, October 2006)

The Bird of Gold (McKinsey Global Institute, May 2007)

283

The United States and the Rise of China and India (Chicago: The Chicago Council on Global Affairs, September 2006)

Thirwell, Mark, *India: The Next Economic Giant* (Sydney: Lowy Institute, 2004)

Vision Mumbai: Transforming Mumbai into a World-class City (Mumbai: Bombay First-McKinsey, September 2003)

Wilson, Dominic and Purushothaman, Roopa, *Dreaming with BRICs: The Path to 2050* (Goldman Sachs Global Economic Paper No. 99, October 1, 2003)

World Economic Outlook (International Monetary Fund, April 2007)

BOOKS

Backman, Michael, *Asian Eclipse* (Singapore: John Wiley & Sons (Asia), 1999, 412 pp.)

Basrur, Rajesh M., *Minimum Deterrence and India's Nuclear Security* (Stanford: Stanford University Press, 2006, 264 pp.)

Chaze, Aaron, *India: An Investor's Guide to the Next Economic Superpower* (Singapore: John Wiley & Sons (Asia), 2006, 321 pp.)

East Asia Analytical Unit, Australian Department of Foreign Affairs and Trade, *India: New Economy, Old Economy* (Canberra: 172 pp.)

Engardio, Pete (ed.), *Chindia: How China and India are Revolutionizing Global Business* (New York: McGraw-Hill, 384 pp.)

Friedman, Thomas L., *The World is Flat: The Globalized World in the Twenty-First Century* (London: Penguin Books, updated edition 2006, 600 pp.)

Gidoomal, Ram, *The UK Maharajahs* (London: Nicholas Brealey Publishing, 1997, 268 pp.)

Hamm, Steve, *Bangalore Tiger: How Indian Tech Upstart Wipro is Rewriting the Rules of Global Competition* (New Delhi: Tata McGraw-Hill, 2007, 329 pp.)

Hiscock, Geoff, *Asia's New Wealth Club* (London: Nicholas Brealey Publishing, 2000, 348 pp.)

Hiscock, Geoff, *Asia's Wealth Club* (London: Nicholas Brealey Publishing, 1997, 312 pp.)

Jit, Inder (ed.), *India Who's Who, 29th Edition 2006* (New Delhi: INFA Publications, December 2006, 645 pp.)

Kristof, Nicholas D. & WuDunn, Sheryl, *Thunder From the East* (London: Nicholas Brealey Publishing, 2000, 377 pp.)

Lala, L.M., *Beyond The Last Blue Mountain* (New Delhi: Penguin Books, 1993, 400 pp.)

Lamb, Alistair, *Asian Frontiers* (Melbourne: F.W. Cheshire Publishing, 1968, 246 pp.)

McDonald, Hamish, *The Polyester Prince: The Rise of Dhirubhai Ambani* (Sydney: Allen & Unwin, 1998, 273 pp.)

Piramal, Gita, *Business Legends* (New Delhi: Penguin Books, 1998, 654 pp.)

Piramal, Gita, *Business Maharajas* (New Delhi: Viking Penguin Books, 1996, 474 pp.)

Rajadhyaksha, Niranjan, *The Rise of India: Its Transformation from Poverty to Prosperity* (Singapore: John Wiley & Sons (Asia), 2007, 176 pp.)

Rawson, Philip, *The Making of the Past: Indian Asia* (Oxford, UK: Elsevier-Phaidon, 1977, 152 pp.)

Rushdie, Salman, *Midnight's Children* (London: Picador, 1982, 463 pp.)

Seth, Vikram, *A Suitable Boy* (London: Phoenix House, 1993, 1,474 pp.)

Thapar, Romila, *A History of India, Volume One* (New Delhi: Picador, 1966, 381 pp.)

Tharoor, Shashi, *Show Business* (New Delhi: Penguin Books, 1994, 310 pp.)

Index